Developing Inclusive Mobile Apps

Building Accessible Apps for iOS and Android

Second Edition

Rob Whitaker

Apress®

Developing Inclusive Mobile Apps: Building Accessible Apps for iOS and Android, Second Edition

Rob Whitaker
Derby, UK

ISBN-13 (pbk): 979-8-8688-2808-9
ISBN-13 (electronic): 979-8-8688-2809-6
https://doi.org/10.1007/979-8-8688-2809-6

Managing Director, Apress Media LLC: Welmoed Spahr
Acquisitions Editor: Miriam Haidara
Editorial Assistant: Marina Engler

Cover designed by eStudioCalamar

Distributed to the book trade worldwide by Springer Science+Business Media New York, 1 New York Plaza, New York, NY 10004. Phone 1-800-SPRINGER, fax (201) 348-4505, e-mail orders-ny@springer-sbm.com, or visit www.springeronline.com. Apress Media, LLC is a Delaware LLC and the sole member (owner) is Springer Science + Business Media Finance Inc (SSBM Finance Inc). SSBM Finance Inc is a **Delaware** corporation.

For information on translations, please e-mail booktranslations@springernature.com; for reprint, paperback, or audio rights, please e-mail bookpermissions@springernature.com.

Apress titles may be purchased in bulk for academic, corporate, or promotional use. eBook versions and licenses are also available for most titles. For more information, reference our Print and eBook Bulk Sales web page at http://www.apress.com/bulk-sales.

Any source code or other supplementary material referenced by the author in this book is available to readers on GitHub. For more detailed information, please visit https://www.apress.com/gp/services/source-code.

If disposing of this product, please recycle the paper.

Table of Contents

About the Author

Rob Whitaker has spent his career making technology work better for everyone. An iOS software engineer with a passion for accessibility, he has worked across the industry – including with Apple's accessibility team – and brings that hands-on experience to his writing. Rob is an invited expert for the W3C's Mobile Accessibility Task Force, contributing to guidance on applying WCAG to native mobile apps, and continues to observe and champion how we can all make our digital interactions more inclusive.

About the Technical Reviewer

Quintin Balsdon is a technical product manager and accessibility advocate at Evinced, specializing in the intersection of mobile technology and inclusive design. With a career spanning over a decade in mobile engineering, Quintin previously served as a subject matter expert for Android accessibility at Spotify, where he integrated WCAG standards into high-velocity products like Spotify Wrapped and pioneered automated accessibility audit pipelines.

Acknowledgments

Such an enormous number of people have helped me in various ways with the content of this book. It's safe to say if I've ever spoken to you in person or online about digital accessibility or inclusion, you've had an impact on this book for the better.

A special thank you to Daniel Devesa Derksen-Staats and Quintin Balsdon for being constant sounding boards for anything related to accessibility, and doubly so to Quintin for agreeing to be the tech reviewer for the second edition. Thank you to Ahmed Bakir for his work reviewing the first edition.

Thank you to Jonathan Rothwell, Paul Hudson, Jon Gibbins, StuffMC, Daniel Steinberg, and Sommer Panage, all of whom have furnished me with advice and fielded my questions that have shaped the book.

Thank you to Jessica Vakili, Aaron Black, James Markham, Sriram N, Miriam Haidara, and all at Apress who have made the book possible. I hugely appreciate the work you have put in to make this project a reality. I'm grateful to Matt Clark for the illustration he kindly provided.

A big thank you to all my colleagues past and present for humoring my constant accessibility talk and for your encouragement. I especially want to mention Weiran Zhang, Matthew Flint, Bas Broek, and Richard Stelling.

Finally, thanks to my family, especially my wife Claire, for having infinite patience and for the support. Thanks also to my dogs Bella and Lyra, who have been excellent at rubber ducking.

Introduction

Accessibility and inclusion are intertwined. Inclusivity is about creating experiences that are welcoming to as many people as possible. Accessibility – the practice of making your app usable by people with diverse needs – is one part of building software that results in an inclusive experience. In Chapter 1, I provide background on accessibility, its history, and why it matters; Chapter 2 extends this into digital inclusion.

The foundation of digital accessibility is the Web Content Accessibility Guidelines (WCAG). These serve as the benchmark by which we judge whether software is accessible. They are built on extensive research and expertise, so to use any other measure is vanity. However, for good reason, they are written in a way that can be impenetrable for anyone who isn't an academic with a deep background in Web accessibility. So in Chapter 3, I aim to present the WCAG requirements in a way that feels more approachable to mobile developers and others working in the mobile space.

This book is intended for anyone involved in creating mobile app experiences who wants to ensure what they are building is accessible and inclusive. I come from a native iOS development background, with occasional work in native Android, and so this book naturally focuses on implementation and how to create accessible apps from a developer's perspective. That said, it is not limited to those who write code. While there are many code samples, they are a means of achieving the concepts discussed in the book – concepts that span visual design, user interface design, system design, and any other decisions that precede writing code.

One of the strengths of software development is that we can build almost anything. However, certain approaches can lead to fragile implementations or poor experiences. The guidelines and discussions in this book should help you identify what makes a robust, accessible experience and guide your decisions. The code examples then demonstrate how to build the most accessible version of the experience you choose to create.

Code is presented in Swift and SwiftUI for iOS and Kotlin and Jetpack Compose for Android. Where these frameworks do not yet support certain features, I may occasionally drop into UIKit or the Android view system where necessary.

This book does not cover mobile web accessibility or any cross-platform frameworks. For mobile web, standard web accessibility techniques should apply. I do not have first-hand experience with cross-platform frameworks, so I have chosen not to cover them. More broadly, my view is that tools aiming to serve both major platforms often struggle to create an experience that feels at home on either, and the accessibility experience magnifies this. This book focuses on the two leading mobile platforms at a code level. However, if you are building apps for alternative operating systems such as KaiOS or Sailfish OS, the principles discussed in the non-code chapters should still apply.

Chapter 4 explores how the accessibility system works on Android with Jetpack Compose, including techniques and knowledge for working with the accessibility tree. Chapter 5 covers feature-specific considerations for assistive technologies and accessibility features on Android.

Chapter 6 examines the accessibility system on iOS, providing the knowledge and tools to allow the system to construct an effective accessibility tree. Chapters 7–10 then cover considerations and implementation details for specific assistive technologies and accessibility features in iOS.

You may notice that Android receives fewer dedicated chapters than iOS. This is not a reflection of one platform being more or less accessible. Rather, it reflects differences in platform design. iOS, being historically design-led, often requires additional considerations to adapt or override default behaviors. Android, due in part to greater device diversity, has evolved differently.

Chapter 11 provides practical guidance for testing accessibility aimed at QA engineers or anyone involved in validating user experiences. It covers both tools and techniques to improve coverage and iteration speed.

Finally, Chapter 12 returns to the topic of inclusivity, exploring how the ideas introduced throughout the book can be applied to create more inclusive experiences for a wide range of users.

CHAPTER 1

Accessibility

My interest in accessibility began back in 2010 when I was managing a small Apple reseller. One of the great privileges of working in technology retail is meeting a wide range of people at various stages in their technology journey. Some customers ask original questions that take a great deal of research to find the right answer. Others have never touched anything you or I might call a "computer" before and are starting at the very beginning.

In June of 2010, Apple released the iPhone 4. After this, I began to notice a significant increase in the number of our customers coming into the store who used British Sign Language (BSL) as their first language. Through interactions with some of these customers, it became clear why this was: with the release of the iPhone 4, Apple had also released a brand-new feature – FaceTime.

FaceTime and other video calling features like it were an incredible improvement in usability for our customers using BSL. FaceTime makes up just one out of a raft of accessibility features that are part of modern smartphones and landline telephones before that.

The Telephone and Accessible Innovation

One aim of inclusive technology is to create a comparable experience for all users, a topic we will revisit in Chapter 2. While Alexander Graham Bell was influenced by his work with the deaf community, he was operating in a time before the formal practice of inclusive design had developed and was unable to benefit from its framing. As a result, accessibility has largely been introduced to the telephone later through retrofitting assistive technologies.

Many technologies have been added, such as the Telecommunications Device for the Deaf (TDD), which we'll cover shortly. Short message service (SMS), voice recognition systems, and video calls have all been accessible advances for the telephone.

R. Whitaker, *Developing Inclusive Mobile Apps*, https://doi.org/10.1007/979-8-8688-2809-6_1

While these assistive technologies have made improvements for people with disabilities, the additions are not seamless. The telephone has a long history associated with making the device more usable for people with specific needs. Today, the most exciting accessible innovation is in the world of augmented reality and AI, but mobile is still where people meet accessibility features most often.

Most of us have been able to use the telephone, as intended, to speak to friends, family, or businesses in the next room, next country, or across the globe since its invention 150 years ago. Consider, if this isn't already the case, that your primary, or perhaps only, form of communication is sign language. This immediately renders the telephone useless. The phone is a ubiquitous invention, but it presents content in a single medium - audio. Innovation has helped make the phone more accessible for those of us who are unable to hear.

Telecommunications Device for the Deaf

The Telecommunications Device for the Deaf is also known as TDD, TTY, textphone, or minicom. It is a QWERTY keyboard with a teleprinter display, invented in the 1960s, that connects to a landline telephone (Figure 1-1). With these additions, the TDD allows people with limited speech or hearing to type their conversation. Conversations can be directed to other TDD users or to an operator relaying the conversation to a non-TDD user.

Figure 1-1. *An example of a Telecommunications Device for the Deaf*

While the TDD is an essential tool for many people, it's not an equivalent to the phone. If you've ever used one of these services, you'll know the interaction is slower and more awkward compared to a voice phone call. In much the same way it might be when having a conversation through an interpreter in a foreign spoken language. The TDD is accessible, but it isn't inclusive.

Video Calling

FaceTime today is a technology we all take for granted. Most of us will use some form of video call system almost daily at work – Microsoft Teams, Google Meet, Zoom, or any number of alternative systems. It's easy to forget that seeing anyone anywhere else in the world instantly in high-quality video and having a conversation with them was groundbreaking technology when new. Yet for our deaf and hard of hearing customers, it was more than ground-breaking. It was transformational to their ability to communicate. The ability to sign conversations finally makes the telephone a comparable experience.

FaceTime didn't become an Apple product because Apple set out to make an excellent accessibility tool for sign language users. Apple set out to create a great product that would work for everyone. By ensuring that it works for everyone and considering accessibility throughout the project, Apple is super-serving one specific audience.

Mobile Innovation

Mobile is packed full of accessibility features like FaceTime. Google Assistant and Siri Shortcuts reduce the requirement for physical interaction. This can help people with learning difficulties. It also reduces the number of touches needed, helping those with motor impairments. Features such as Screen Time, Focus Modes, and Safari Reader help to minimize distractions – ideal for people with attention deficit disorders or those with mental health conditions who can find relief in focus. Dictation, spelling correction, predictive text, voice memos, haptics, third-party keyboards, and external keyboard support are all examples of assistive technologies. There's a good chance you will use these daily, without ever considering them an accessibility feature.

Consider the Telecommunications Device for the Deaf we discussed above. The inventors needed a way to allow digital text to pass over a wire. Their resulting invention was the MODEM. Without the MODEM, much of our modern digital society would simply not be possible. Next time you're at the corner of a street with a roller case or a buggy, notice the dropped curb. It means you won't have to lift your heavy item to the street level, but it was originally designed to help wheelchair users. Great accessibility shouldn't be an obscure feature that only a small number of people use. At its best, accessibility should be a first-class citizen of the product or service you are creating, designed to benefit everyone.

Accessibility is not just something that benefits those who have a disability. It has a much broader reach offering customizability for all users. While disabled users may gain the most, every one of your users stands to benefit from the consideration you give accessibility. At its best, accessibility is inclusion for every one of your customers. We'll cover this more in Chapter 2. For now, let's get a little more context on what we mean by disability, especially disability in a digital context.

What Is Disability?

In January 2019, a photo was shared widely on social media (Figure 1-2). The photo featured an otherwise unremarkable woman going about her business walking along an inner-city street. This lady had two features that led to Facebook users commenting, however. She was using a smartphone, nothing unusual there, but this lady also had a white cane to aid her in navigating the city.

Figure 1-2. *A person using a cane and a smartphone. Posted to Facebook with the caption "If you can see what's wrong say I see it"*[1]

[1] Wendell Hussey, Facebook. January 12, 2019. `https://www.facebook.com/photo.php?fbid=10155762936910826`

The white cane has been used since World War I as a tool to help blind and partially sighted people. Many of whom use it to help them navigate the built environment by feeling the street around them for obstacles and clues such as tactile paving. Its primary purpose, however, may not be immediately apparent to those of us who don't use it; the hint is in the color of the cane. White canes are, indeed, white. Because they are white, they provide a clear indication to those of us who see it that the holder may not see us. It's a clue for us as drivers to take extra caution and as pedestrians to ensure we allow the person room to pass.

Perhaps this was the case with the woman in the photo posted to Facebook. Maybe she had poor eyesight and was using the cane primarily as a hint to fellow pavement users that she may not see them. Possibly she does use her cane to feel for the built environment around her, as she can't see items at a distance but still has vision closer to her eyes and so can continue to use her phone.

I don't presume that anyone reading this book would, as many Facebook users did, question this lady's abilities or perceived lack thereof. Mainly because you likely work in mobile and know there is a raft of display accommodations she could be making to improve her experience and allow her to use her smartphone. Perhaps she has large text or zoom enabled. Maybe she is using inverted colors or increased contrast. Perhaps she isn't looking at the screen at all. She could be using a screen reader with the screen curtain enabled - a feature that disables the screen's visual output - and this is just the natural way to hold a phone while using it. It's impossible to understand someone else's experiences without asking them. If you want to really understand how someone uses your app, this is precisely what I'd recommend - ask them.

All this is to say - disability is not, much like anything in life - merely a binary state. It is not possible to divide the world up into two groups - those who are disabled and those who are able-bodied. Or in our example above, blind and sighted. There is a large section in between. From those of us who need to wear reading glasses for specific tasks. Through to those of us who experience no light perception at all. Via cataracts, color blindness, and others. Visual impairments vary over time, as do all disabilities. As I'm sure we're all aware, not all disabilities are visible.

So, if disability is a broad spectrum, how do we define it? The best way to highlight what I think disability means is to use the World Health Organization's definitions. In 1980, the WHO defined disability in these terms:

> *In the context of health experience, a disability is any restriction or lack of ability (resulting from an impairment) to perform an activity in the manner or within the range considered normal for a human being.*[2]
>
> World Health Organization, 1980

In other words, they defined disability as a feature of that person. Something that makes a disabled person different from the rest of us and unable to do the things we might reasonably expect a "normal" person to be able to. I think we can settle on disability being a "restriction or lack of ability." But a problem arises with the last part – "the range considered normal for a human being." The word "normal" here raises more questions than it answers – what is a normal human being? What would we expect this fictitious normal human being to do? Who decides what is normal? Should I be concerned if I don't match the considered definition of normal? The answer to all these questions is simple – there is no such thing. There is no "normal" for human beings. Without wishing to sound like a preschool kids' TV show – we are all wonderfully different in our own ways.

Visit the WHO's website today, and you'll see an updated definition:

> *Disability is part of being human.*
>
> *Disability results from the interaction between individuals with a health condition... with personal and environmental factors including negative attitudes, inaccessible transportation and public buildings, and limited social support.*
>
> *A person's environment has a huge effect on the experience and extent of disability. Inaccessible environments create barriers that often hinder the full and effective participation of persons with disabilities in society on an equal basis with others.*[3]
>
> World Health Organization

---

[2] "Inclusive," Microsoft Design, 2016. https://download.microsoft.com/download/b/0/d/b0d4bf87-09ce-4417-8f28-d60703d672ed/inclusive_toolkit_manual_final.pdf

[3] "Disabilities," World Health Organization, https://www.who.int/topics/disabilities/en/

This definition considers disability not as a problem with people, but with the society we have built. It recognizes that everyone is different and has different abilities and skills, and that difference is normal. Therefore, when someone struggles with an aspect of our society, such as being unable to use steps to enter a building, this is not an issue with the person but with the culture that has allowed this to happen – the culture that has failed to build a ramp.

Major Minority

People who identify as experiencing disability are a minority. But together they make up one of the largest minority groups across Europe and North America. In the United States, an estimated 13.6% of the civilian, non-institutionalized population have a disability; that's 44.7 million people.[4] More people than the entire population of California. In the UK, 25% of people report having a disability, nearly 17 million individuals.[5] Globally, an estimated 1.3 billion people experience disability, approximately 16% of the global population.[6] There's a good chance your organization's device support policy covers devices with a far smaller market share than your total number of customers with disabilities.

Having read this far, I hope I have convinced you of the importance of considering your users with disabilities. As a result, the quality of your own work will, I'm sure, be much higher. The maximum impact for customers with disabilities, however, comes when your business and colleagues share your conviction for making great accessible experiences. In the next sections, we'll cover ways you can do this.

[4] "Anniversary of Americans With Disabilities Act: July 26, 2025," United States Census Bureau, `https://www.census.gov/newsroom/facts-for-features/2025/disabilities-act.html`

[5] "Family Resources Survey: financial year 2023 to 2024," Department for Work & Pensions, `https://www.gov.uk/government/statistics/family-resources-survey-financial-year-2023-to-2024/family-resources-survey-financial-year-2023-to-2024#disability-1`

[6] "Disability," World Health Organization, `https://www.who.int/health-topics/disability`

The Business Case for Accessibility

Ultimately, the case for accessibility is simple – it is the right thing to do. Prejudicing your customers because of their abilities is wrong. But I realize that if you're making a business case for an increased focus on accessibility, then there are other considerations you need to include.

The American Institutes for Research found that the total disposable income of people with disabilities in the United States is over US$504 billion.[7] In the UK, the spending power of disabled people and their families is referred to as "The Purple Pound." The Purple Pound is recognized as a crucial spending bloc for businesses. Evidence shows that companies that don't consider digital accessibility lose out by causing disabled people to choose alternative services.[8] The UK Purple Pound is worth an estimated £274 billion or US$366 billion.[9]

If an extra US$500 billion in market value is not enough for your business, there is a sizeable legal stick too. One that can result in hefty fines and long-lasting reputational damage.

Accessibility Law

As with any law, national variations on accessibility law are vast.[10] Many countries have no laws governing accessibility at all. Where laws do exist, these will often concern the government or public sector only. Sometimes these are pre-digital laws crudely adjusted through convention to fit digital channels. Many regulations do not explicitly focus on digital accessibility; instead, they are more general non-discrimination laws. You should seek legal advice to find out which rules apply to the markets you operate in and how.

[7] "The Purchasing Power of Working-Age Adults With Disabilities in Boston and Other Top Metropolitan Areas," American Institutes for Research, "https://www.air.org/sites/default/files/Purchasing-Power-of-Working-Age-Adults-Disabilities-Ruderman-July-2020-508.pdf"

[8] "The Click-Away Pound Report 2019," Click-Away Pound, https://www.clickawaypound.com/downloads/cap19final0502.pdf

[9] "Shopping: National Disability Strategy explained," Disability Unit, https://disabilityunit.blog.gov.uk/2021/07/28/shopping-national-disability-strategy-explained/

[10] https://www.w3.org/WAI/policies/

In this section, I cover two of the principal regions with digital accessibility laws that most of us creating mobile apps will have to follow. This section is intended as a high-level overview, not legal advice, so if you think these laws may apply to your business, I'd recommend seeking a professional opinion.

The United States

The United States has one of the world's oldest accessibility laws: the Americans with Disabilities Act, known as the ADA, introduced in 1990.[11]

The ADA covers government requirements for ensuring accessibility from suppliers and within government-supplied services, such as schools. Included in the private sector are "places of public accommodations." While the ADA is not explicit in mentioning digital content, the Department of Justice, which upholds the ADA, maintains that the ADA is broad enough to govern digital experiences too.

In a 2019 landmark case, Domino's Pizza chose to challenge this assertion; the case was taken as far as the Supreme Court. Domino's argued that the ADA didn't apply to their pizza ordering app. The Ninth Circuit Court of Appeals ruled against Dominos, establishing the precedent that the legal requirements of the ADA for mobile accessibility are not a gray area. Other household names like the National Basketball Association, Netflix, and Beyoncé have fallen foul of DOJ court rulings on the ADA.

Europe

The European Accessibility Act (EAA),[12] adopted in 2019 and enforced from 2025, is a more modern piece of legislation. The EAA uses as its reference accessibility legislation from across Europe. It also draws cues from the US ADA. The aim is to set minimum standards for digital accessibility throughout Europe. Unlike the ADA, the EAA explicitly demands that mobile apps be accessible.

The exact implementation of requirements varies from country to country, with some member states choosing to go above EAA's minimum requirements. Enforcement also varies, with most countries imposing dissuasive fines, while Ireland's implementation can result in prison sentences for those who are responsible for inaccessible applications.

---

[11] `https://www.ada.gov`

[12] `https://eur-lex.europa.eu/legal-content/EN/TXT/?uri=COM:2015:0615:FIN`

In addition to varying by country, the act also varies by service type, so it is essential that you seek legal advice to determine the exact obligations for your application in the European markets you serve. But if you follow the guidance in this book, you should have a strong baseline from which to start.

Another important part of the EAA is the requirement to document the accessibility of your product to show conformance. Documentation is also a valuable exercise in ensuring you haven't overlooked any accessibility requirements, revealing any gaps that may have been missed through more informal accessibility development and testing.

Advocating for Accessibility

One of the best ways to increase accessibility in your apps is to advocate for it within your organization. When UX sends you new designs, product asks for a new feature, or your team is refining stories - these are all great times to advocate.

Don't criticize others' work. From my experience, colleagues do care about accessibility and want to do better. Sometimes they lack the knowledge and expertise to do this. Champion work when you can see accessibility has been considered and congratulate when you know something will work well for users with diverse needs. Make small suggestions that will add up to an improved experience. Over time, you'll find your team will take this on board and will begin to think from an accessibility-first perspective.

If your organization has multiple customer-facing software teams, you could start an accessibility advocates network. Encourage someone from each group to get involved. Include UX, product, and management. Share knowledge and questions over a slack channel. In some cases, it may be possible to find a budget for training, providing insight that you can cascade down to your teams. Consider running training sessions for other colleagues from what you have learned.

Summary

- Sometimes, we make technology that excludes people with specific abilities. We can improve this by adding accessibility features. But when added after the fact, these features can feel like add-ons, not seamless parts of the product.

- In the next chapter, we'll discuss digital inclusion. This is the ultimate aim of accessibility – to make technology that feels at home to everyone.
- Disability is not a binary state. We all have abilities and limits to those abilities. Disability happens when we have built something that doesn't work for someone with particular skills.
- There is a strong business case for considering people's different abilities when building your app. A US$500 billion business case – and that's just in the United States. Your business will also be bound by international accessibility legislation. If you aren't following these laws, you stand to receive hefty fines and reputational damage.

We'll continue to look at the background of accessible technology in the next chapter. But we'll move away from considering accessibility as an extra. Instead, we'll consider inclusion and how we can make all our users feel part of our app.

CHAPTER 2

Digital Inclusion

In this chapter, you'll discover a little about the history of inclusive thinking and what this means. We'll cover the fundamental tenets that hold up this thinking and discuss what you should consider when creating software, such as the importance of remembering that your users are real people. We'll cover the single most critical skill any software engineer can have that comes hand-in-hand with taking pride in your work.

The History of Inclusive Thinking

Digital Inclusion has its roots in architecture and product design. In the process of creating mobile apps, good design is essential. But a significant part of an app's accessible experience is created by those of us who aren't designers. Digital Inclusion recognizes that everyone – designers, coders, product owners, testers, and everyone else in the process – has a role to play in encouraging more accessible interactions.

Even if you're not a designer, I think it's worth our time covering some of the background of this school of design. This way, we can understand some of the mistakes that were made and steps taken to fix them. Plus, if you're an engineer, your job is to make designs a reality. So knowledge of the work that has influenced those designs will help you realize them.

Universal Design

Digital Inclusion has its roots in Universal Design, a movement that emerged in the late 1960s and led to many of the commonplace accessibility improvements we see around us today. Architect and designer Ronald Mace coined the phrase Universal Design to describe the concept of designing usable products and the built environment for as many people as possible, while crucially remaining aesthetically pleasing.[1]

[1] The Universal Design Project, "What is Universal Design?", Accessed January 25, 2026, `https://universaldesign.org/definition`

R. Whitaker, *Developing Inclusive Mobile Apps*, https://doi.org/10.1007/979-8-8688-2809-6_2

Fellow architect Selwyn Goldsmith, himself a wheelchair user, progressed the concept of Universal Design by championing the now ubiquitous dropped kerb or curb cut (Figure 2-1).[2] The curb cut allows wheelchair users or those with mobility issues to cross the street more comfortably than with a standard raised curb. The dropped curb is also a prime example of how universal design helps as many people as possible. While initially intended to improve mobility for wheelchair users, it also benefits parents with pushchairs and travelers with rolling cases.

Figure 2-1. *A curb cut providing step-free access to the street*

Universal Design is a series of principles used by architects, product designers, and industrial designers to guide them in achieving Ronald Mace's original aims. In 1997, North Carolina State University gathered some of the leading advocates of Universal Design, including Ronald Mace himself. Together they defined the seven principles of Universal Design[3]:

- Equitable Use
- Flexibility in Use
- Simple and Intuitive Use

[2] Centre for Excellence in Universal Design, "History of Universal Design", Accessed January 25, 2026, `https://universaldesign.ie/about-universal-design/history-of-universal-design`

[3] Centre for Excellence in Universal Design, "The 7 Principles", Accessed January 25, 2026, `https://universaldesign.ie/about-universal-design/the-7-principles`

- Perceptible Information
- Tolerance for Error
- Low Physical Effort
- Size and Space for Approach and Use

I have very briefly summarized what each of these principles covers here. I've also given a quick outline of how each principle might apply to mobile. Some of the concepts here might be new, but we'll cover all of them in later chapters.

Equitable Use

Make the design appealing to all users. The design should be useful and marketable to people with diverse abilities. Avoid segregating or stigmatizing any users. Provide an identical experience for all users wherever possible. If you must provide an alternative experience, make this equivalent. Consider privacy, security, and safety for all your customers.

In a mobile setting, this might mean avoiding using color combinations that don't pass the WCAG 2.2 (Chapter 3) contrast ratio guidelines of 4.5:1.[4] Also, ensure your app works seamlessly with assistive technologies such as TalkBack and VoiceOver.

[4] W3C, "Understanding Success Criterion 1.4.3: Contrast (Minimum) (Level AA)", Accessed January 25, 2026, https://www.w3.org/WAI/WCAG22/Understanding/contrast-minimum.html

Figure 2-2. *VoiceOver navigating iOS' Weather app*

Flexibility in Use

Ensure your design accommodates a wide range of individual preferences and abilities. Provide choices, facilitate the user, and adapt to them.

Examples of this in mobile include supporting varying text sizes and allowing for multiple methods of text input such as on-screen keyboard, dictation (Figure 2-3), or an external keyboard. Both platforms offer your customer various customization settings; respect these as much as you can.

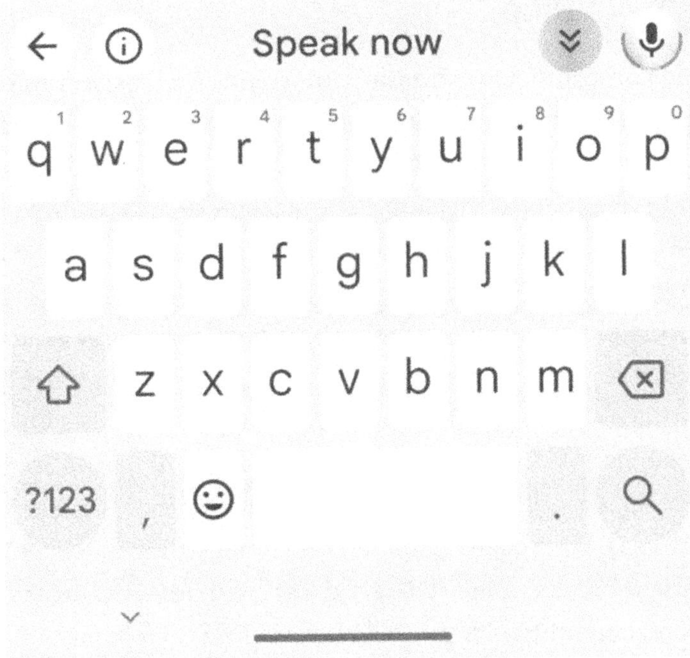

Figure 2-3. *Android's on-screen keyboard allowing text input through dictation*

Simple and Intuitive

Ensure your design is easy to understand, regardless of the user's experience, knowledge, language skills, or current concentration level. Eliminate unnecessary complexity. Be consistent with user expectations and intuition. Accommodate a wide range of literacy and language skills. Arrange information in a manner that is consistent with its importance, keeping the most critical information prominent. Provide effective prompting and feedback during and after task completion.

Stick to a standard design language throughout your app, including using system-provided controls and conventions wherever possible. Summarize information carefully but allow customers to drill down for detail if they would like more information. Keep the language simple and understandable. When your app requires user input, you should be explicit about what information you need and where it is needed. If your customer makes an error, make this clear and allow them to change it quickly.

Perceptible Information

Your design should communicate necessary information effectively to your users, regardless of ambient conditions or the user's sensory abilities. Use different modes (pictorial, verbal, auditory) for redundant presentation of essential information. Provide adequate contrast between the foreground and background - we cover this more in Chapter 3. Provide compatibility with a variety of techniques or devices used by people with sensory limitations.

To meet this principle in mobile, we must ensure all content is accessible to the device's screen reader and any other assistive technologies available on the device. Chapter 4 on the Android accessibility model and Chapter 6 on the iOS accessibility model will give you the tools to do this. Present your content in multiple modes. Use a combination of color, shape, image, text, and layout together to make your content meaningful (Figure 2-4). Your customer's screen reader will turn text content into audio content, but it can at most only make a "best guess" with text you provide as an image. For valuable content, consider offering this in an additional format, such as a video.

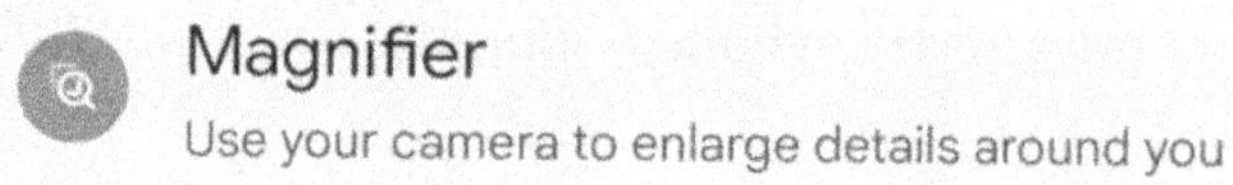

Figure 2-4. *Combining color, shape, text, and an image to convey meaning*

Tolerance for Error

Minimize the hazards and the adverse consequences of accidental or unintended actions. Arrange elements to minimize risks and errors: Make commonly used controls prominent. Provide warnings of dangers and mistakes: Warn your customers in advance if they are about to make a destructive or non-reversible change, such as deleting items or completing a transaction. Allow them to cancel or undo these changes wherever possible. If your customer makes an error, highlight it clearly in position and allow them to change it effortlessly. Before they commit to a destructive or non-reversible action, let your customer review their response and allow them to change or revert it. Provide safety features so destructive effects can't happen by accident.

In mobile apps, this includes using clear and concise information on the consequences of each action when you ask your user to make a decision. Add friction to harmful or destructive actions and provide feedback to your customers on what to expect when they make such a decision.

Low Physical Effort

Ensure customers can use your design efficiently and comfortably and with a minimum of fatigue. Minimize repetitive actions and sustained effort.

All the buttons on your interface should be within easy reach (Figure 2-5), especially on large-screen devices. Provide shortcuts to common areas of your app and support Google Assistant or Siri Shortcuts where possible. Reactions should happen.

***Figure 2-5.** Shortcuts for common features within easy reach at the bottom of the screen*

Size and Space for Approach and Use

The final principle states that you should provide proper size and space for approach, reach, manipulation, and use regardless of the user's body size, posture, or mobility. Make reach to all components comfortable and accommodate variations in hand and grip size.

We can meet this guideline by making our interfaces adaptable to different screen sizes and text sizes. Ensure your app works with Switch Control and Switch Access, as well as allowing keyboard navigation, Voice Control, and Voice Access (Figure 2-6), enabling your customers to control your app with virtually no physical movement whatsoever. Any interactive elements should be at least 44px square so as not to require fine motor control.

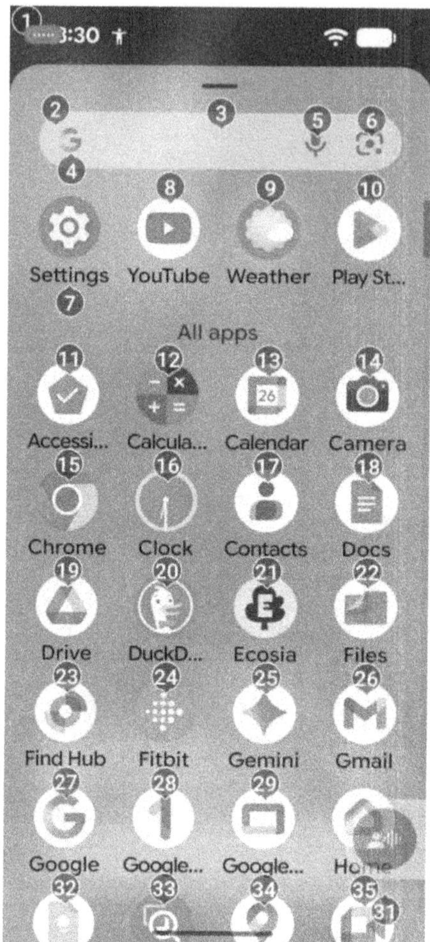

Figure 2-6. *Android's Voice Access feature allowing navigation without touching the screen*

These Universal Design principles have led to the creation of many everyday items, products we may not instantly think of as "accessibility" features. Consider audiobooks, automatic doors, high-contrast signage, and flexible drinking straws. All these products were created following Universal Design guidelines. They serve many people with different abilities but are improvements for everyone else as well. This is what we should strive for in our apps: creating an experience that includes everyone.

Universal Design considers disability and what can be achieved by changing a design to help people who experience that disability, thereby reducing the barriers for the use of the product. Reducing barriers widens the market for potential users. However, as Universal Design was developed before the digital era, the approach was tailored to physical products.

Inclusive Design

Inclusive Design extends the gains made by Universal Design. It is generally more tailored to digital interactions. While Universal Design considers disability, Inclusive Design considers individuals and tends towards a more accessible-first approach. Inclusive Design takes a big step forward in recognizing that disability is not a permanent, binary state, but a spectrum. Inequalities in people's abilities are typical and vary as a function of time or situation. Inclusive Design does this by considering people's needs as permanent, temporary, situational, or changing. By improving the experience for people with specific needs and considering these needs in the first instance, we can extend this benefit to work for a broader population, therefore improving the experience for everyone at some point in their lives.

The seven principles of inclusive design can be found at inclusivedesignprinciples.info. These principles are:

- Provide comparable experience.
- Consider situation.
- Be consistent.
- Give control.
- Offer choice.
- Prioritize content.
- Add value.

I have outlined the principles and how they apply to mobile below.

Provide Comparable Experience

Ensure your interface provides a comparable experience for all. Allow people to carry out tasks in a way that suits their needs without undermining the quality of the content. You can provide audio descriptions or a transcript of a video in your app - these would make your original content accessible, but do these alternatives capture the essence and tone of the original? Mobile interactions have an exceptional ability to surprise and delight their users - you should make sure all your users get such a rich experience, including when using assistive technology.

An example provided by inclusivedesignprinciples.info is that of Android Live regions (Figure 2-7). Live regions are an area of the screen that automatically reports to assistive technologies when the content changes. TalkBack will read this content without the user having to move focus to this content. iOS doesn't have a live region feature, but you can create a similar experience using accessibility notifications. We cover these in Chapter 8.

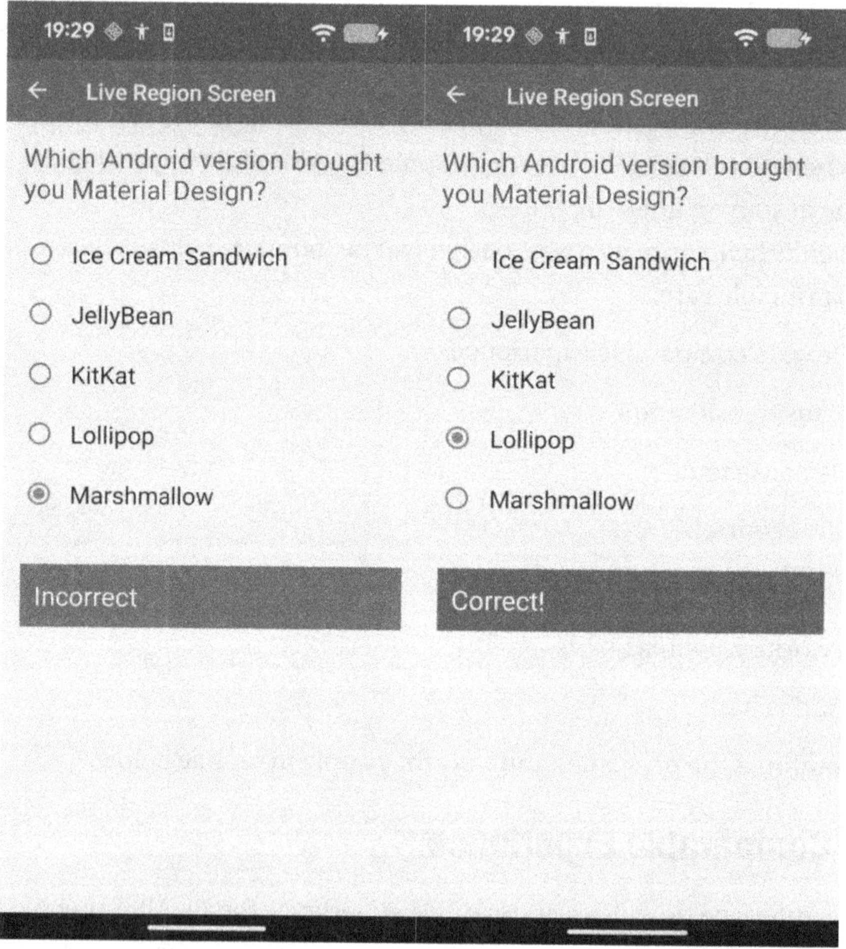

Figure 2-7. *The "correct!" / "incorrect" area of the screen is a live region. TalkBack will automatically announce this content when it changes, without the user losing focus*

Consider Situation

People use your interface in different situations. Make sure your interface delivers a valuable experience to people regardless of their circumstances.

Consider using your phone in bright sunlight; audio and haptic feedback along with high-contrast colors will help in this situation. Providing subtitles or closed captions (Figure 2-8) on video content allows parents to watch videos with the sound down without disturbing sleeping children.

Figure 2-8. *Captions for videos allow people to watch videos without disturbing others, as well as help people with hearing impairments*

Be Consistent

Use familiar conventions and apply them consistently to promote familiarity and understanding. This consistency applies both within your app and against the system you're running on.

Don't reinvent the wheel in your design - stand on the shoulders of giants by using the controls that Android and iOS provide. Feel free to customize the controls to add a feature or appearance as needed, but starting with these as a base will give you so much extra for free. Your user will feel at home because their interactions will feel familiar, and Apple and Google already have you covered for many accessibility features.

Give Control

Ensure that the user is in control. Your customers should be able to access and interact with content in their preferred way. Control interactions and disable features if they wish to. This principle includes obtaining consent from your user when needed and respecting that choice.

Avoid content changes and repeated animation that has not been initiated by your user unless there is an explicit control to stop the movement. Do not suppress the ability to change standard platform settings, such as orientation or font size (Figure 2-9). This might mean you get a pixel-perfect design, but it will significantly affect your user's ability to use your app comfortably.

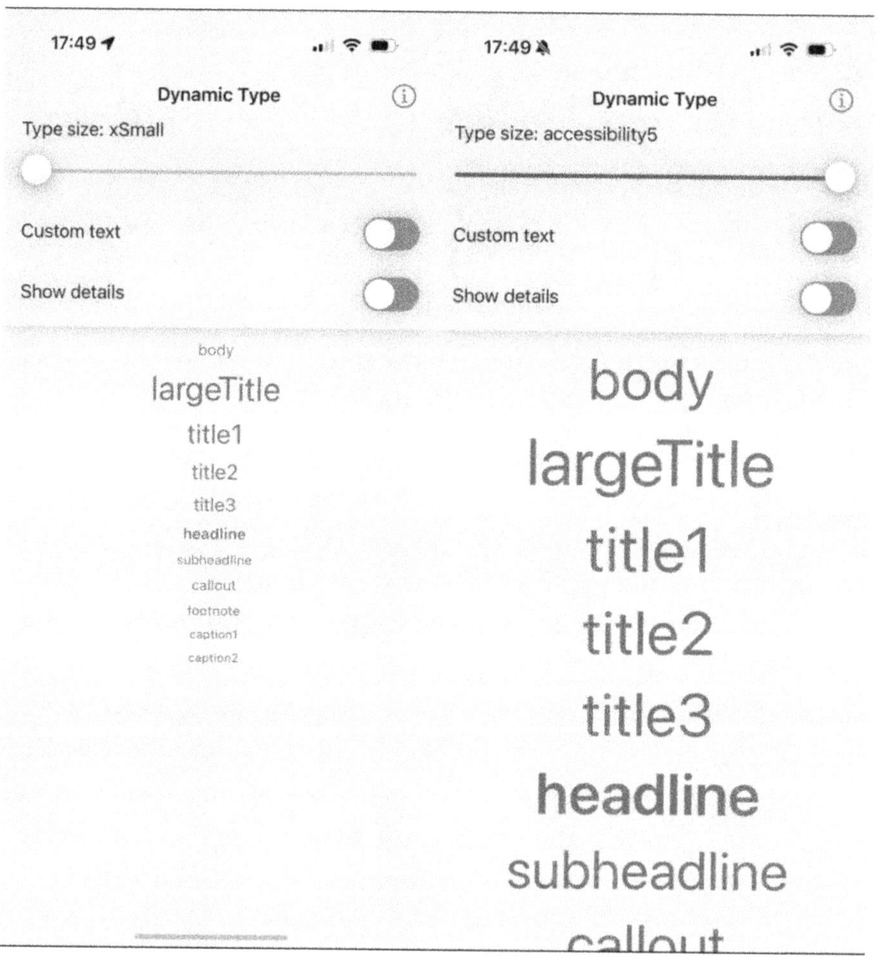

Figure 2-9. *iOS dynamic text styles at their smallest and largest settings. Supporting these is important for your customers and requires a flexible design*

Offer Choice

Consider providing different ways for people to complete tasks, especially tasks that are complex or non-standard. There is often more than one way to complete a task within an application, and you should not assume what someone's preferred method might be. By providing alternatives for layout and task completion, you offer people choices that suit them and their circumstances at the time.

A great example of this is deleting an email in the iOS Mail app. I can do this with a tap (Figure 2-10), a swipe (Figure 2-11), or a long press (Figure 2-12). This lets me, as a user, pick the option that is fastest for how I use the app.

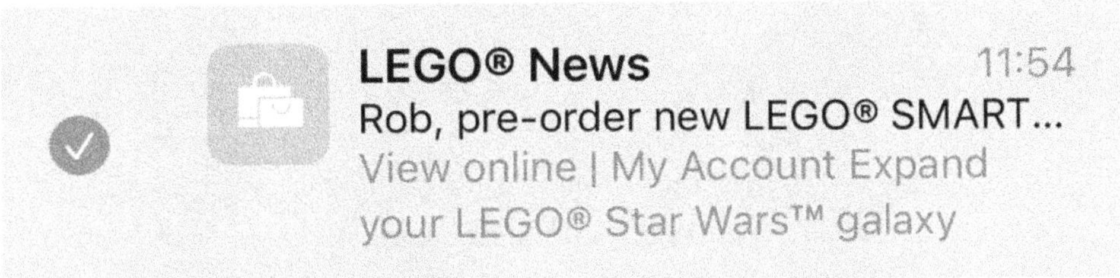

Figure 2-10. *Deleting mail with a tap*

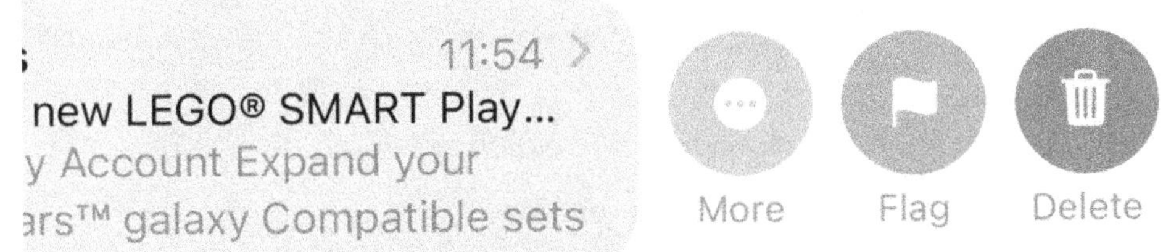

Figure 2-11. *Deleting mail with a swipe*

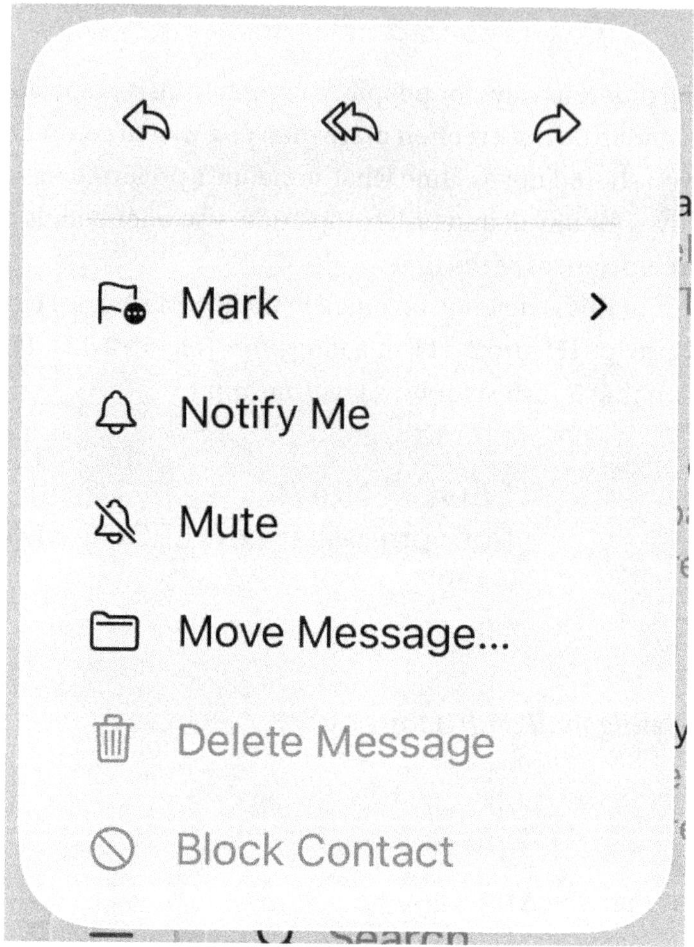

Figure 2-12. *Deleting mail with a long-press*

Prioritize Content

Help users focus on core tasks, features, and information by prioritizing them within the content and layout. Identify the core purpose of the interface and the content and features needed to fulfill that purpose. Interfaces can be challenging to understand when core features are not clearly exposed and prioritized.

Structure your content logically and mark headings with a heading trait or role.

When you launch an email app, you're generally not initially presented with a list of mailboxes and folders to pick from. Instead, you're shown an inbox because this is the most essential feature. Standard features should be simple and always available. More complex actions should be possible but not prominent. Making everything available at once makes for a confusing interface. Consider placing advanced controls behind a secondary gesture such as a long press.

Add Value

Consider the value of features and how they improve the experience for different users. Consider device features such as voice, geolocation, camera, and haptics APIs and how integration with connected devices or a second screen could provide choice.

This is the area of inclusive design where mobile stands far above other platforms. Mobile devices are full of sensors and feedback modes. External devices such as smart homes, screens, or controllers can be connected wirelessly. Picker controls on both platforms use haptics to provide tactile feedback to users when something changes (Figure 2-13). While also being a satisfying experience, this feedback is essential for customers with visual impairments, helping them determine when they have made a change.

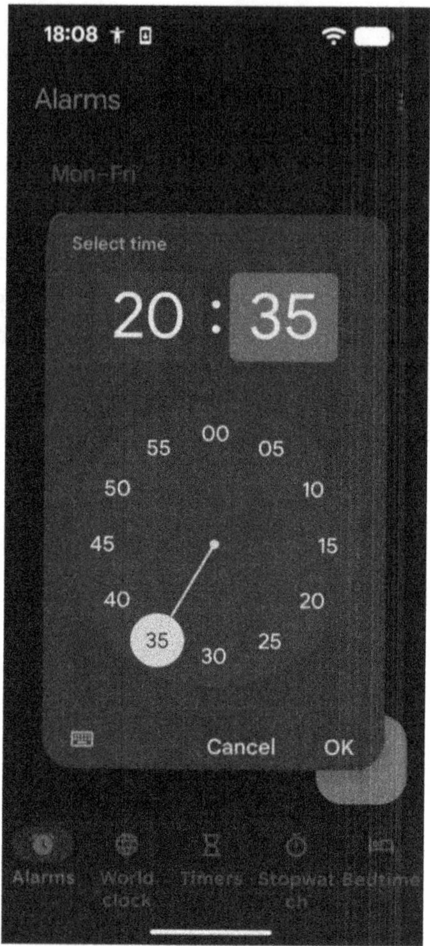

Figure 2-13. *Setting an alarm on Android. Haptic feedback is provided when moving between minute/hour intervals*

Persona Spectrum

One of the greatest proponents of inclusive design in software is Microsoft.[5] Microsoft introduced a tool called the Persona Spectrum (Figure 2-14).[6] The Persona Spectrum helps us to consider what inclusive design means for the people who use our software.

[5] Access more on their Inclusive Design program at `https://www.microsoft.com/design/inclusive/`

[6] Microsoft Design, "Inclusive", 2016. `https://download.microsoft.com/download/b/0/d/b0d4bf87-09ce-4417-8f28-d60703d672ed/inclusive_toolkit_manual_final.pdf`

Consider, as Inclusive Design does, that we classify disability as permanent, temporary, or situational. An example of a permanent disability might be the loss of an upper extremity. Losing an arm would make many everyday interactions difficult, perhaps even impossible. For this person, improving your app might mean ensuring all buttons are within easy reach of the thumb of the hand holding the phone. Or even better, add voice control features. In doing this, you would also help to make your app more usable for people who have recently experienced an arm injury and are using a sling. Arm injuries are a temporary impairment - we would hope, at least. Our customer with a broken arm will regain full use of their limb in a month or so. With this improvement, you would also help new parents. New parents may spend much of their time with the use of one hand while they use the other to hold or feed their infant, control a pushchair, or hold a hand. In this example, our new parent has a situational impairment. The use of their second limb is restored once their child falls asleep or is handed to another family member.

For this example, Microsoft conducted research to highlight how thinking this way can have a great benefit for your customers:

> *In the United States, 26,000 people a year suffer from loss of upper extremities. But when we include people with temporary and situational impairments, the number is greater than 20M.*
>
> Microsoft Inclusive Design Toolkit Manual[7]

[7] Microsoft Design, "Inclusive", Citing research from The United States Census Bureau, Limbs for Life Foundation, Amputee Coalition, MedicineHealth.com, CDC.gov, Disability Statistics Center at the UCSF.

	Permanent	Temporary	Situational
Touch	Loss of Limb	Arm Injury	New Parent
Sight	Blind	Cataract	Distracted Driver
Hearing	Deaf	Ear Infection	Bartender
Speech	Non-verbal	Laryngitis	Heavy Accent

Figure 2-14. *Examples of Persona Spectra*

These examples provided by Microsoft also include visual, auditory, and verbal persona spectra. Designing for visual clarity and testing with screen readers will help ensure your app is usable for people with visual impairments. It can also help someone who has recently had an eye operation, or someone who is currently unable to look at their device screen.

Considering how your app functions for deaf people will help people with an ear infection or those who work in a noisy environment. Similarly, a person who uses nonverbal communication would benefit from the same considerations that help a temporary condition like laryngitis, or a situation like communicating with someone who has a strong accent.

NEW SPECTRA

Can your team create new examples of the persona spectrum?

Consider one of your customers with a permanent disability. What temporary or situational scenarios might you also address if you improved your app for the first group?

Consider the situation of a customer being in the wilderness. What features could you add that would help this user? How would that help people with temporary or permanent impairments? What about a customer who experiences anxiety? What improvements can you make to give this customer a better experience, and how might that benefit others?

Digital Inclusion

Making software in an agile organization consists of more than implementing a "pixel-perfect" screen as a designer has prescribed. There is much we can take from the design approach to inclusion. But not all of it is relevant to those of us who aren't designers, and much doesn't directly apply to the modern digital world.

We need a digital-first approach to inclusion, one that constitutes a more rounded, high-level set of convictions. A strategy that recognizes everyone within the organization has a role to play in ensuring the service created is suitable for the widest possible range of people. Developers, with their advanced platform knowledge, constitute a significant part of this process.

An essential part of digital inclusion is realizing that people with disabilities, while important, are not the only minority who want to use our service. Other factors such as age, gender, education, social grouping, income, and sexual orientation can all influence how we experience technology. Below, I've outlined a framework for thinking about digital inclusion.

Empathetic

Consider others and recognize that everyone is an individual with different knowledge, experience, background, and ability. Acknowledge that this makes people's experiences of your app different. Arguably, this is the key tenet of Digital Inclusion, and we will cover it in its own section below.

Situational

Not all barriers to using your app or service come from people's physical abilities. Inclusion means considering people's situations as a whole. This includes their skills but also other factors: financial circumstances, gender, digital literacy, mental health, and first language, amongst others. Recognize that all these factors affect how someone may use your app.

Institutional

The software your organization creates reflects the organization itself. Consider how the almost libertarian viewpoints of some social media leaders have led to platforms where almost anything goes, including at times racism, election interference, harassment, and worse. Everyone in an organization can play a role in improving the accessibility of an app for its users and arguably has a responsibility to do so. In the following section, we look at what we mean by "users," and who these people are.

Users

In software engineering, we usually create products for our "users." It's sometimes said, in a quote often attributed to data visualization pioneer Edward Tufte, that calling people "users" is a habit we share exclusively with drug dealers. Except that's probably not true either. Drug dealers, I would imagine, still call their customers "customers," because that's what they are. It's only the police and media who use the word "users." I don't intend to police your language, but let's take a moment to consider why we might want to think twice about using the term.

Individuals

I don't believe there is anything inherently wrong in using the word "users"; in fact, I use the term throughout this book. The problem is that this word can often hide who we're really making software for – *individuals*. Each user is an individual with their own wants, needs, abilities, experiences, and requirements for your software.

Employing the word "users" can result in falling into the trap of thinking of users as one group. An amalgamation of people who are somewhere out in the world using your app, a group of people that you'll never meet and never know. This form of "groupthink" leads to creating a "one-size-fits-all" solution that, like everything claiming to be "one-size-fits-all," fits no one.

Remember that time you had a bizarre bug in your app that happened because one person was using your app in a way you could have never envisaged? We've all had that experience. People do unpredictable things precisely because they think and act differently. What may have been an inconceivable combination of actions to you may seem entirely reasonable to someone using your app. Conversely, things that may appear obvious to you are going to be incomprehensible to some of the people using your app.

Vasilis van Gemert, a lecturer at the Communication and Multimedia Design school in Amsterdam, warns us of the danger of thinking we are our own users.

> *In the past 25 years we have been designing [software] mostly for people who design [software].*
>
> Vasilis van Gemert[8]

Your Experiences

Most of us will be able to think of at least one family member who doesn't use the internet. Maybe a family member who has a disability. Or for whom English is not their first language. Your family will make up a much more varied group than your friends and probably even your colleagues.

Considering these three groups and how they differ is probably the best example you can take from your firsthand experiences. But thinking about all these people combined will give you just a few hundred, at most, examples of how people's lives govern their relationship with technology. The world is made up of more than 8 billion people.[9] So to get a representative survey of people's experiences of technology, you need 1,000 examples as a minimum. A sampling method that only chooses people connected to you in some way would not pass scrutiny.

[8] Vasilis van Gemert, "Exclusive Design", Accessed October 19, 2025. `https://exclusive-design.vasilis.nl/`

[9] Worldometer, "Current World Population", Accessed October 19, 2025. `http://www.worldometers.info/world-population/`

> *If we use our own abilities as a baseline, we make things that are easy for some people to use, but difficult for everyone else.*
>
> Microsoft Design[10]

The best way to fix this is to talk to real people. We discuss user testing in Chapter 11. Hopefully, your organization will already be doing some form of user testing. Don't write this off as an activity for design or product. Engineering can learn a lot, too.

YOUR NETWORK

Here's a quick exercise to highlight why the people you know are unlikely to be representative of your customers. Make a list of the top five people you trust the most. These can be colleagues, friends, or family – people you would go to for advice. Do this before reading on. Now add yourself to the list.

Next, list some of their traits. Use the same set of characteristics for each person and fill these out to the best of your knowledge. List their race, sexual orientation, employment status, age, gender, religion, first language, and any disability. There are probably other examples of traits you can think of. It's ok to be honest here and to keep your answers private.

Look at your answers for each person. My guess is that, for most people, these traits will look closely aligned – and that's ok. The purpose of this exercise is not to shame you into expanding your network, but simply to highlight that the people who are close to you are likely closer to you than you may have realized.

PEOPLE PROFILES

A great technique to help your whole team consider customers as individuals is to create profiles.

Have some fun developing a backstory but remember it should be based on reality. A good place to start is by reading customer feedback or observing user research, especially involving assistive technology users.

[10] Microsoft Design, "Inclusive"

Consider what the person wants to do with your app and why. Think of the person's circumstances, experiences, and abilities. Most importantly, give your person a name and refer to them by that name. Use Table 2-1 to guide you in creating a profile.

***Table 2-1.** Profile sections*

Person Name	Have fun choosing a name, but it's essential to refer to this person by name once you've created the profile.
Age	Give an approximate age range.
Gender	Remember that approximately 2% of the US population doesn't identify as either male or female.[11]
Immediate Family	Do they have dependents, either children or adults they care for? Are they married, live with family, or perhaps live alone?
Job & income	Your person could be employed, unemployed, self-employed, underemployed, or hugely successful in their career. Perhaps they are even a lottery winner! The US median household income is $84,000 in 2024.[12]
Disability	Around 16% of people globally experience disability.[13] Aim for a range of profiles that reflect different disabilities – and some with none.
Backstory	Go wild – or not. Remember, this profile is intended to represent a real person, but feel free to have some fun.
Why does this person want to use your app?	What will your app do for your person? Is this a choice, or do they have to use your app for some reason?

[11] Anna Brown "About 5% of young adults in the U.S. say their gender is different from their sex assigned at birth", Pew Research Centre, June 7, 2022, `https://www.pewresearch.org/short-reads/2022/06/07/about-5-of-young-adults-in-the-u-s-say-their-gender-is-different-from-their-sex-assigned-at-birth/`

[12] United States Census Bureau, "Income in the United States: 2024", September 9, 2025, `https://www.census.gov/library/publications/2025/demo/p60-286.html`

[13] World Health Organization, "Disability", Accessed January 25, 2026, `https://www.who.int/health-topics/disability`

Empathy

Software is not made up of cold, unthinking algorithms. Sometimes this claim is used as a weak defense for bad decisions made in software's name. More importantly, it downplays your skills as a developer. It hides the reality that creating software is a craft and that those of us who make it are craftspeople in the truest sense of the word. We build beautiful software by hand and care about what goes into it as much as the end result. We're always sharpening our skills and expanding our personal toolset.

I want to propose that one of the greatest, and most overlooked, tools a software craftsperson can have is empathy: the ability to understand that many other people – people who may be unlike you – will be directly affected by the decisions you make when creating an app. This must be a central tenet of digital inclusion. Empathy is not a skill you can learn by having the highest number of commits to a project or having the most stars on GitHub. It is a tool you can only improve by taking a genuine interest in people and your craft.

Some within the software industry see empathy as a weakness.[14] I argue the opposite; we should emphasize empathy because it helps us recognize and overcome our subconscious bias toward those who are similar to ourselves. It is only possible to practice empathy with emotion and a deep personal understanding of what is right. With the expanded sphere of experience that empathetic feeling gives us, we are better able to reason unemotionally about how to overcome these challenges.

Empathy As a Motivation

So, you're empathetic. You want to make a difference. You want to *fix* things for people with disabilities. This is a well-intentioned aim, but is it helping people with disabilities, or is it making you feel better? By saying you want to *fix* things for someone with a disability, consider what you are implying. Disability is not wrong and doesn't need to be fixed.

There are many horror stories of software made worse in the name of accessibility and disabled users who are expected to be grateful.[15] Be careful to use empathy not as

[14] Cameron Albert-Deitch, "How to Fix the Tech Industry's Empathy Problem", Inc., October 7, 2020, `https://www.inc.com/cameron-albert-deitch/tech-industry-empathy-problem-maelle-gavet.html`

[15] Matt May, "Design Without Empathy", November 7, 2019. `https://vimeo.com/371678402`

a reason to act, but as a reason to investigate and listen. Empathy is not a replacement for genuine experience; someone's lived experience should guide you more than any feeling, guideline, or assumption. The disability community has a common phrase – "Nothing about us without us"[16] – meaning people with disabilities want participation, not simply to be told what is better for them.

People with disabilities want an equivalent experience. They want to be able to use your app just as anyone else does. Accessibility is not a gesture to make you feel better or to gain your brand influence. Accessibility is a tool to achieve inclusion within your software.

Bias

Unconscious bias is something we all have. It is an entirely natural part of being human that we have evolved as a survival mechanism. As such, fighting against unconscious biases is likely unproductive.[17]

The best choice is to acknowledge and accept that we all have biases and use that understanding to help guide you. Ensure your team is as diverse as possible. Diversity of opinion and background will help your team empathize with as many people as possible by using each other's personal knowledge and experience. In this way, you can build a broader base from which to examine the consequences of the decisions made in your software.

Moving Thoughtfully

The old philosophy of "move fast and break things" has, rightly, been consigned to the trash. So instead, let's move thoughtfully. Good engineering isn't about speed at all costs but about considered trade-offs. Accessibility and inclusion are all too often considerations that are skipped. I hope this chapter has shown some of the real-world

---

[16] United Nations, "Nothing about Us, Without Us", Accessed October 19, 2025, `https://www.un.org/esa/socdev/enable/iddp2004.htm`

[17] Paluck, E. L., Porat, R., Clark, C. S., & Green, D. P. "Prejudice Reduction: Progress and Challenges". Annual Review of Psychology, 72, 533–560. 2021. `https://doi.org/10.1146/annurev-psych-071620-030619`

consequences that make skipping these considerations an oversight. In the following chapters, I intend to give you the tools that allow you to integrate accessible and inclusive development into your everyday workflow, so you should no longer have to forego making software for everyone.

Summary

- Inclusive thinking has its roots in industrial design and architecture. But this doesn't mean its guiding principles don't apply to software engineering.
- Accessibility is about inclusion. Make changes that will bring your customer into your app rather than making a separate experience for people with different abilities. Allow your customers to customize their experience to suit them.
- Remember who your users are; they're not always going to be like you, your colleagues, friends, or family. User testing is an essential tool to find out how people experience your app; ensure your participants are varied. Use the persona spectrum and profiles as tools to help you remember our users as real people throughout the development process.
- Empathy is an essential quality of any software engineer. It helps you to remember to treat your users as unique individuals.

We now have some background on what accessibility and inclusion mean and what has driven thinking in these fields. Let's begin to look at practical ways we can help different people who want to use our apps. Before we cover specific technologies, we should look at what our aims are. The Web Content Accessibility Guidelines, or WCAG, form a definitive framework on what improvements we should make to our apps to make them more accessible.

CHAPTER 3

Web Content Accessibility Guidelines for Mobile

With a name like Web Content Accessibility Guidelines, it can be tempting to write these off as not applicable to mobile. The name, however, is a function of the era the standards were originally authored combined with the fact that the initiative comes from the World Wide Web Consortium (W3C). The name is also a mouthful, so we will stick with the common acronym of WCAG.

WCAG has been developed with input from a wide range of accessibility professionals, researchers, and users. Like any set of guidelines, it can feel like conforming to WCAG is a checkbox exercise, but this is necessarily so: accessibility is indeed all about how people experience your app, but unless you have the resources to test and research extensively with large numbers of users of varied assistive technologies, the WCAG guidelines are by far the best guide you will get.

W3C has split the WCAG into four layers. They begin with four overarching *principles* – perceivable, operable, understandable, and robust. These principles each have *guidelines*, followed by *success criteria* and *techniques*. Recommendations were first written expressly for the Web, but most principles and guidelines are generic and do translate to mobile, even if their success criteria and techniques for compliance don't always. The most recent version, WCAG 2.2, was ratified in 2024.

WCAG, an ISO-recognized standard since 2012, forms the basis of many accessibility laws throughout the world. It is often used as the benchmark for courts to decide if a digital experience is accessible or otherwise for the sake of accessibility lawsuits. As such, as far as the law is concerned, WCAG very much applies to mobile.

R. Whitaker, *Developing Inclusive Mobile Apps*, https://doi.org/10.1007/979-8-8688-2809-6_3

In this chapter, I won't cover each guideline in full; for that, I would recommend reading the current WCAG 2.2 specification yourself, available at `www.w3.org/TR/WCAG22`. Instead, I will offer some general advice on how to conform to each guideline on mobile and a high-level introduction to some tools you might use to do this. We cover each of these techniques and tools in more detail later in the book.

For further reading, I would recommend W3C's WCAG2ICT[1] guidance on applying WCAG to non-web technologies. W3C also has a Mobile Accessibility Task Force which, at time of writing, is working to produce native mobile guidance on top of WCAG2ICT.[2] As a rule, when reading WCAG, substitute "web page" for "mobile app screen," and the majority will apply as written.

Perceivable

> *Information and user interface components must be presentable to users in ways they can perceive.*
>
> —WCAG 2.2

The first principle, perceivable, covers the content in your application and the ways in which you make that available to your customer. To summarize this principle in a word, I would use "alternatives."

Recall our discussion of the telephone in Chapter 1; the telephone, as initially designed, uses just one medium: audio. While this covers the majority of use cases, it immediately rules out people who struggle to speak and people who struggle to hear. The invention of the TDD (Telecommunications Device for the Deaf) was a necessary alternative to allow those users to have the same experience.

In the same vein, if you provide content in a visual-only format - such as images, text that is not available to a screen reader, or a captioned video without an audio track - customers with visual impairments will not be able to perceive this content.

[1] `https://www.w3.org/WAI/standards-guidelines/wcag/non-web-ict/`

[2] `https://w3c.github.io/matf/`

Text Alternatives

> *Provide text alternatives for any non-text content so that it can be changed into other forms people need, such as large print, braille, speech, symbols or simpler language.*
>
> —WCAG 2.2

Ensure that all non-text content has an appropriate and equivalent text alternative. Most commonly this applies to meaningful images. The distinction between content and decorative imagery is essential here - providing a descriptive, accessible label to a purely decorative image adds noise and navigation effort.

The ability to add a text alternative to almost any object is built into both platforms. Android's Jetpack Compose uses the `contentDescription` property (Listing 3-1). For SwiftUI on iOS, `accessibilityLabel` will achieve the same (Listing 3-2). Each of these approaches has implementation details; see Chapters 4 and 6 for more.

Listing 3-1. Setting a contentDescription in Jetpack Compose

```
contentDescription = "Submit"
```

Listing 3-2. Setting an accessibilityLabel in SwiftUI

```
.accessibilityLabel("Submit")
```

ALTERNATIVE TEXT FOR IMAGES

When deciding whether to hide an image from assistive technologies or provide a description, the most important question to ask is, "Does this image have a meaning, and if so, what is it?" If you didn't choose the image or icon yourself, ask the person who did. They will know the intention behind the choice.

Images that act as controls, such as an image button, must always have a clear, short but descriptive text label describing the purpose of the action, not describing the image. A single-word verb such as "Close" or "Save" is usually ideal.

Figure 3-1. Image buttons must have an accessible label

Small decorative icons that draw attention to content in a table row should not have alternative text and should be hidden from navigation. Adding a label to these adds unnecessary noise, increases the number of swipes needed to navigate, and confuses the navigation order, resulting in your user losing context.

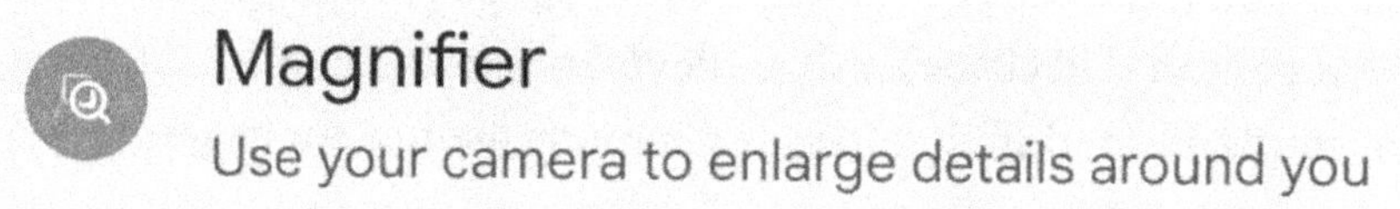

Figure 3-2. The magnifier icon helps draw the eye to this row but has no meaning in addition to the visible text, so it must be hidden from accessibility

If the icon represents status that is not otherwise communicated in text, for example, status icons, then this must have a descriptive label that accurately describes the information the icon represents.

Figure 3-3. The cloud icon represents data that is not presented in text, so it must have an accessible description

If the image contains text that is intended to be read by the user, then this image must have a description that includes the text in the image.

Where images are part of the content – such as a news story, social media post, or image gallery – these images must have a description that adequately describes the content in a way that conveys the meaning behind the image. Context is key here: for example, if you're discussing the artfulness of a photo, you might want to include details of focus depth and colors, but this level of detail is likely unnecessary for most other cases. There is no character limit for an image description, but like any other text content, this should be clear and efficient. With all image descriptions, ensure the most important information is front-loaded.

A common pattern on mobile is the use of large decorative images when presenting full-screen error or "no content" screens. These images generally provide no meaningful information and should be hidden. However, for users with low vision, they may be able to determine that some content is present and try to explore it with their screen reader. On iOS this will result in an annoying "dunk" sound to suggest no content is present. Instead, consider grouping the image with the message title into a single accessible element. We'll cover techniques for "semantic views" such as this in later chapters.

***Figure 3-4.** This 'empty content' screen could have the title and illustration grouped as a single item for accessibility*

Time-Based Media

> *Provide alternatives for time-based media.*
>
> —WCAG 2.2

Most commonly, this means audio and video, but this wording also covers any other media that has a time component, such as animation. Video and audio content should feature captions or a transcript. Preferably, video should include audio description, and ideally both audio and video should incorporate, or have an option for, sign language. More details on captions and alternative tracks for media are available in Chapters 5 and 10.

This guideline excludes video or audio you provide as an alternative to text, for example, a blog article that also provides an audio version. If doing this, I'd recommend making it clear that this is an alternative rather than additional content, so users don't feel excluded.

Adaptable

> *Create content that can be presented in different ways (for example simpler layout) without losing information or structure.*
>
> —WCAG 2.2

The Adaptable guideline moves away from the content itself and covers how you present that content in your user interface (UI).

Present content in a clear, meaningful order. You can achieve this through good interface design built in a robust way. But take care to test with screen readers enabled, as the navigation order derived from your code might not be the logical reading order.

Present information using multiple sensory characteristics. For example, you should not rely on color alone to convey meaning but a combination of attributes such as color, shape, size, location, haptics, or sound. You can use any or all these modes together to convey meaning.

The Adaptable guideline also requires that user interfaces are not restricted to a single orientation. This is possibly the most common accessibility failure amongst mobile applications – fixing orientation means users who have a device mounted in a fixed position or those who do not have the physical dexterity needed to rotate a device may be excluded from using your software altogether.

Distinguishable

> *Make it easier for users to see and hear content including separating foreground from background.*
>
> —WCAG 2.2

The Distinguishable guideline covers how your users tell the difference between elements in your app. This guideline includes essential rules for color contrast, text size and line spacing, background audio, and others. Some disabilities such as color blindness can impede the ability to distinguish between elements. So it's essential to stick to these guidelines and allow customizability where needed. Unless your layout demands it, avoid scrolling in two dimensions, as this can be a trigger for people sensitive to movement and can be challenging to control with some assistive technologies enabled.

This guideline also provides advice on the following elements:

Color

Your use of color in any app is crucial. The right choice of palette can be a significant factor in setting your app apart visually. Well-used color can be a subtle hint at meaning and aid understanding. Remember, however, that not everyone's experience of color is the same; therefore, color should never be the only way to identify elements or convey meaning. Combine coloring with text, shapes, or animation. Road signs are a great example: drivers learn that certain shapes have different meanings - triangles warn, circles prohibit, and rectangles inform. Color reinforces this meaning and aids glanceability, but it's the shape that does the heavy lifting.

The contrast ratio between your text color and the background is a material consideration. Large text - defined as a minimum of 18pt, or 14pt bold - should have a minimum contrast ratio of 3:1. Smaller text should have a contrast ratio of 4.5:1. If possible, your text should have a contrast ratio of 7:1, with large text at 4.5:1. We cover checking your color contrast ratios in Chapter 11.

Some people, such as those experiencing dyslexia, Irlen syndrome, or color blindness, can benefit from being able to customize background colors. This can be a great addition to your app if you're looking to take your accessibility to the next level.

Audio

Any audio in your app, including audio that is part of video, lasting longer than 3 seconds should have controls. These should allow pausing, stopping, and adjusting the volume. The volume control should be independent of the system volume to let your customer maintain their chosen system level.

Speech audio should avoid background sounds. Alternatively, allow the disabling of background sounds or have background sounds at least 20 dB (approximately four times) quieter than the speech audio. Background noise can affect those with attention disorders; it can also make the foreground audio challenging to determine for some people with hearing impairments.

Text

Text should be resizable up to double the default glyph size, without losing content or functionality. Ensuring you support system text sizes on both platforms will fulfill this requirement. Avoid using images of text, as these don't support screen readers or text size adjustments. If you must use an image containing text, ensure you add a screen reader-accessible label including the text to the image. Do this using `contentDescription` on Android or `accessibilityLabel` on iOS.

When formatting text, aim for the following: avoid full justification; keep lines of text to a maximum of 80 characters; and provide paragraph spacing of at least 1.5 times the line spacing. Let your users customize for their needs by offering a mechanism to change text and background colors if possible.

Operable

> *User interface components and navigation must be operable.*
>
> —WCAG 2.2

As the name of this principle suggests, Operable covers how a human can control and interact with your application. This includes working with any assistive technology or other input mechanism a customer may choose.

Keyboard Accessible

> *Make all functionality available from a keyboard.*
>
> —WCAG 2.2

Ensure your app is navigable using an external keyboard. Make sure your app is free of keyboard traps - a control that can be focused by the keyboard but can only lose focus by another means. In the context of a mobile application, a 'keyboard interface' means any assistive technology that can be used to control the application, such as a screen reader, switch control, or voice control, in addition to the keyboard.

Time Limits

> *Provide users enough time to read and use content.*
>
> —WCAG 2.2

Time limits can be desirable for many reasons: to free up products or resources, prevent denial of service attacks, or add security by restricting unauthorized use of authentication tokens. However, time limits can create a barrier for some people. Navigating an app with assistive technology can be time-consuming, especially if the accessible design is not up to standard. Additionally, people with anxiety disorders can find time limits overwhelming.

Avoid time limits where there is no strict requirement for them. If you do include a time limit, consider giving a mechanism for your user to choose the limit or to extend it. Warn users before a limit expires and give them an option to reset or extend it. If reauthentication is needed, allow users to pick up where they left off.

This guideline also provides rules on moving, blinking, scrolling, or auto-updating content. Offer a mechanism to pause, stop, or hide these at the request of the user.

Seizures and Physical Reactions

> *Do not design content in a way that is known to cause seizures or physical reactions.*
>
> —WCAG 2.2

Any flashing or blinking content should not flash more than three times a second, as this is known to cause physical reactions in people with epilepsy. Additionally, you should give an option for users to disable animation unless it is essential to the functionality of your app. Both platforms have multiple system settings for motion that your app should respect if it uses anything more than basic UI animation.

Navigable

> *Provide ways to help users navigate, find content, and determine where they are.*
>
> —WCAG 2.2

Assuming here that you are a sighted user, when greeted with a page of content, your eyes and brain work together subconsciously to build a mental model of what's available to you. This unconscious technique allows you to instantaneously skip between content to find what's most important to you right now. For this reason, digital advertising tries to be as distracting as possible. If the adverts weren't distracting, your brain would likely judge them unimportant and skip past without you even realizing you had done so. If you're not fully sighted, skimming a screen is a tool you're unable to benefit from, and instead you must rely on other clues to orient yourself within the content.

It's crucial to ensure screen readers and other assistive technologies can navigate your app in a logical order, making sure content is separated with meaningful titles. At times, the navigation order for screen readers can differ from the order your eyes may be drawn to. It is possible to achieve correct, semantic screen reader order in many ways: hiding elements from accessibility, adjusting content order or primary focus, or using semantic views. We'll cover each later in the book.

Each screen should have a title accessible to the screen reader, and you should mark any content headings as such. This allows screen reader users to skip through meaningful headings by analogy to the skim reading we discussed above.

You should strive for all your buttons to have unique, meaningful text labels that don't require any visual context to be useful.

Input Modalities

> *Make it easier for users to operate functionality through various inputs beyond keyboard.*
>
> —WCAG 2.2

If your app makes use of the device's built-in accelerometer to determine movement or control features, offer an alternative for people who may struggle with fine motor control.

Tap targets should be a minimum of 44 pixels square. Android's guidelines recommend a minimum of 48dp square.[3] Anything smaller will be challenging to press accurately and will result in accidental input and customer frustration.

This guideline also covers touch gestures that are used to control features in your app. Consider that it may not be possible for all users to perform your prescribed gesture accurately, so offer alternatives. Accessibility actions can be added to any UI element and triggered by users with their chosen assistive technology.

Understandable

> *Information and the operation of user interface must be understandable.*
>
> —WCAG 2.2

WCAG's third principle, Understandable, aims to improve the clarity of your app and its functionality. This principle covers content, design, and the behavior of your app.

Readable

> *Make text content readable and understandable.*
>
> —WCAG 2.2

Avoid idioms, jargon, and abbreviations in your text where possible. For any you do use, offer a mechanism for users to determine their meaning. Ideally, aim for written content to be understandable at a lower secondary education level.[4]

---

[3] Material Design, "Designing," Accessed January 29, 2026, `https://m3.material.io/foundations/designing/structure`

[4] For guidance on tailoring your language, see `https://digital.gov/guides/plain-language` for US English and `https://www.plainenglish.co.uk/free-guides` for UK English.

Predictable

> *Make [mobile apps] appear and operate in predictable ways.*
>
> —WCAG 2.2

Consistency in design and operation is vital for this guideline. No two identical-presenting controls should function differently. The inverse is also true: two controls with the same function should look the same and be presented in the same way to assistive technologies.

Any changes of context - such as moving to a new screen or changing the meaning or behavior of controls or content - should not happen without indication. Such changes should generally occur at the request of the user, for example by pressing a button. Alternatively, you should inform users that a change is pending by using a loading indicator. Failure to prepare a user for a change of context can be a trigger for anxiety. Additionally, visually impaired users may not be aware that context has changed, making the meaning of the new content unclear.

Input Assistance

> *Help users avoid and correct mistakes.*
>
> —WCAG 2.2

When collecting data from your customer through a form, any errors should be highlighted clearly in place. Provide an indication of the cause and how this can be rectified. Each field should provide clear instructions about its purpose and expected input.

Ideally, forms should provide at least one of the following features:

- Reversible

  It is possible to undo the submission of data.

- Checked

  Data entered is validated before submission, and users are provided with an opportunity to correct any errors.

- Confirmed

  Provide your customer with the opportunity to review, confirm, and correct any data entered before finalizing their submission.

Robust

> *Content must be robust enough that it can be interpreted by ...assistive technologies.*
>
> —WCAG 2.2

The final principle has just one guideline. The essential rule is that your app must be compatible with any assistive technology available on your user's chosen platform.

Compatible

> *Maximize compatibility with current and future ...assistive technologies.*
>
> —WCAG 2.2

The purpose of your controls should be determinable by your user's chosen assistive technology. You can achieve this using accessibility traits on iOS or roles on Android. For example, any control that acts as a button should be marked as such. Use standard controls, and this will be provided for you. This allows assistive technologies to determine how to behave for that element.

Summary

- The World Wide Web Consortium's Web Content Accessibility Guidelines set out rules for how you should measure the accessibility of your app. While WCAG is web-focused, it still applies to mobile apps, even if you need to translate some web-specific language.
- It's an international standard and forms the legal framework for deciding whether your app is accessible. If you don't meet the criteria in WCAG, you're at risk of legal disputes. If you're concerned, ask a WCAG expert to review your app and find out which guidelines apply to you and how.

- WCAG is the result of well-resourced research from users and experts, people who really do understand what's best for accessibility. Use the results of their extensive experience to guide you. While it can feel like a checkbox exercise, this is an expertise-backed way to increase inclusion in your app.
- Your app should be Perceivable, Operable, Understandable, and Robust.

We've covered the background to the considerations you should make to improve your app's accessibility and briefly explained why they matter. Let's now move on to the tools each platform provides to help you conform to these guidelines. First, we'll start with Android.

CHAPTER 4

Jetpack Compose Accessibility Model

As is the case with the rest of the platform, Android accessibility is highly customizable. A large part of accessibility is about customizability, so Android has a huge edge here. If Android doesn't have a system setting that suits a specific need, then any developer can create a custom accessibility service to fulfill that need. We'll take an introductory look at this in the upcoming "Viewing the Accessibility Tree" activity. Because of the wide variation in handsets, software versions, and assistive technologies available, it is essential to follow good accessibility practice, rather than coding for any specific technology, such as TalkBack. For clarity, I'm using a Google Pixel 9a device running Android 15 and using Google's provided assistive technologies.

Google's design system, Material Design,[1] runs throughout Android system apps and is the basis for the apps you create. Google developed Material Design with high standards of accessibility in mind and following the best practices of user interface design. Using Android's inbuilt controls[2] and following Material Design principles will mean your app is consistent – not only with the Android system but also within your app. This will help all your users to feel at home when using your app and help you maintain a high level of accessibility.

Material Design's guidelines are a great introduction to using Android's tools to create an accessible experience. Take a read through the guide on Material Design accessibility[3] for best practices. Most of the guidance there is relevant to anyone making Android apps, not only designers.

---

[1] https://material.io

[2] https://material.io/components/

[3] https://m3.material.io/foundations/overview/principles

R. Whitaker, *Developing Inclusive Mobile Apps*, https://doi.org/10.1007/979-8-8688-2809-6_4

Accessibility Tree

Before we cover the accessibility features available on Android, let's cover how the Android accessibility model works for assistive technologies. When using an Android app, you'll be familiar with the controls and views that Android creates from Jetpack Compose, but how are these visual elements translated into a format that assistive technologies can use?

Android creates what is known as an accessibility tree, sometimes called a Semantics Tree in Android documentation, a hierarchical representation of elements that are present on the screen. Assistive services such as Voice Access, Switch Access, TalkBack, and others can use this accessibility tree to determine how to present information. Using your view code, Android makes some reasonable assumptions about your user interface and how to represent it to assistive technology. Most of the time, this will give a functioning, accessible experience, but at times you may need to tweak this tree to present a better experience. This chapter will provide you with the tools and techniques to do this.

Accessibility Nodes

The accessibility tree's leaves are accessibility nodes. These nodes are not actual on-screen elements, but proxy representations. They contain content and metadata useful to assistive technologies about the UI element. This data includes properties such as content description, metadata such as whether an element is scrollable, what actions can be performed, and the element's position on screen. Once the accessibility service receives a node, this node is immutable. Changes to the view are not revealed to the accessibility service until next time the service requests the node.

VIEWING THE SEMANTICS TREE

Android allows any developer to create an accessibility service.[4] This service can be used to present content on the screen, control the screen or device, or perform other tasks you might expect of an assistive technology. We won't cover the ins and outs of making such a service in

[4] https://developer.android.com/reference/android/accessibilityservice/AccessibilityService

this book, although Android does provide a guide on doing so.[5] Instead, we will use this access to the accessibility system to illustrate how the accessibility tree works or, as it is known in Jetpack Compose, the Semantics Tree.

If you haven't already, clone the GitHub repo for this book. Navigate to the folder for Exercise 4-1. Open this example code in Android Studio and click Run.

On your device or emulator, open Settings and find Accessibility. At the top here, you should see your new accessibility service listed under Downloaded apps (Figure 4-1). Open the service and enable it.

***Figure 4-1.** Our new accessibility service in our device's accessibility settings*

The accessibility service will overlay a "Get accessibility tree" button at the top of your screen (Figure 4-2).

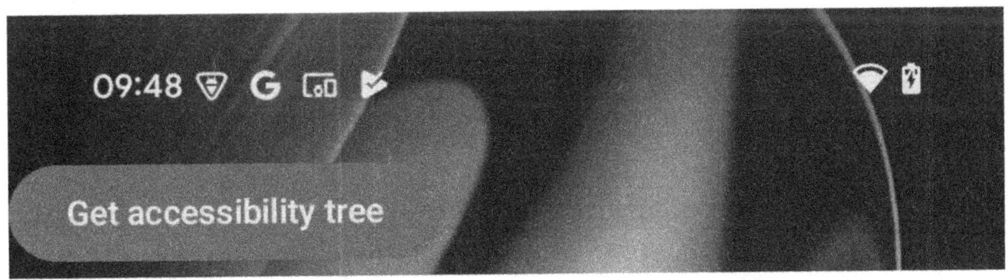

***Figure 4-2.** "Get accessibility tree" button overlaid at the top of our screen*

Open the Logcat tab in Android Studio and tap the new "Get accessibility tree" button. You'll see a bunch of output printed to the console (Figure 4-3). These are the text descriptions and labels of all the current elements on the screen. Try navigating to different screens and click the button again to see what is presented to the accessibility service with different layouts.

[5] `https://developer.android.com/guide/topics/ui/accessibility/service`

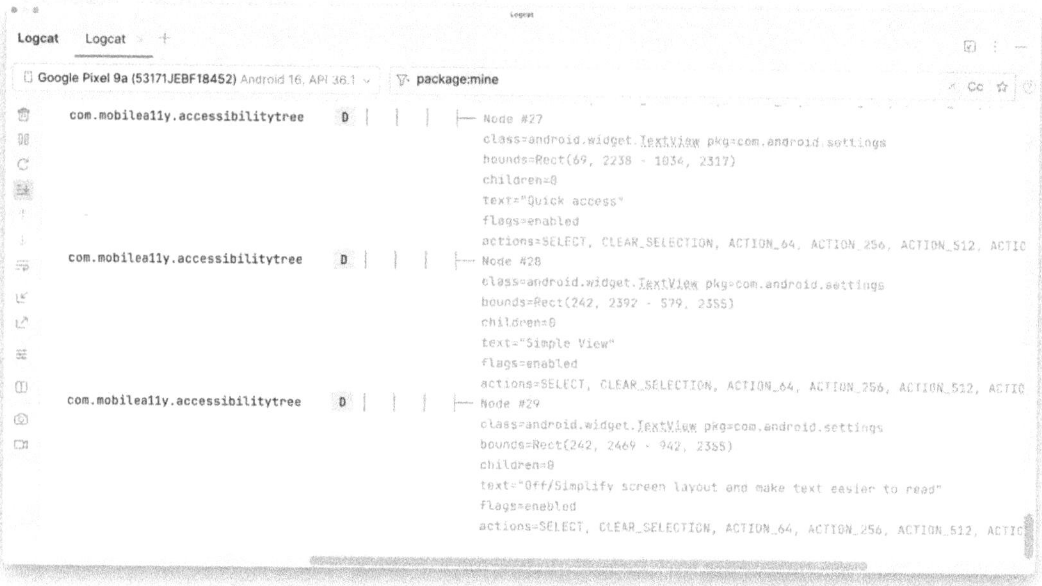

Figure 4-3. Accessibility tree output from the Android app launcher

For the full list of properties available to accessibility services, check out the Android developer documentation[6] and explore ways you can extend your new service to get the most out of the accessibility tree.

Semantics

The Jetpack Compose accessibility tree is built on a system of semantics.[7] Semantics are metadata applied to UI components that are used by the system, including accessibility services, to determine how to present and interact with a UI element. Standard UI elements provided by Material Design and Jetpack Compose provide built-in semantics, so stick with these controls, and you'll have a strong baseline for accessibility. But there will be times you'll need to make tweaks to improve what we present to assistive technology users. This is especially true when you create your own custom controls.

[6] https://developer.android.com/reference/android/view/accessibility/AccessibilityNodeInfo.html

[7] https://developer.android.com/develop/ui/compose/accessibility/semantics

If you change the built-in controls, it's essential to check that you haven't unintentionally removed or overridden any accessibility features. We'll take a look at some of the properties you might need to consider setting below.

Semantics are inherited from descendant elements and can be set explicitly on an element by calling `Modifier.semantics {}` setting semantic values inside the lambda. For example, if we want to set explicit text for accessibility and mark the element as a heading, we would apply semantics as below:

Listing 4-1. Setting semantics

```
Text(
    text = "Hello World! 🌍",
    modifier = Modifier.semantics {
        heading()
        contentDescription = "Hello world!"
    }
)
```

If we want to ignore any semantics inherited from descendants, we instead use `clearAndSetSemantics` (Listing 4-2), again, passing the semantics we want to add to the element. A common usage of this API is to hide an element from assistive technologies by passing an empty lambda – i.e., setting no semantics.

Listing 4-2. Hiding a view from assistive technologies by clearing semantics

```
Text(
        text = "Hello World!",
        modifier = Modifier.clearAndSetSemantics { }
    )
```

Custom Controls

Before we dig into the details, the golden rule is this: When building any UI, start with standard controls and customize as needed. Then test the accessibility and make targeted adjustments only if you don't get the expected behavior for free.

The platform vendors have already done a huge amount of work for you in research, development, and testing to ensure the controls they provide meet a high standard for accessibility. They have resources and experience most teams can't match, so relying on their expertise is the pragmatic approach.

If you want to customize a control, take the existing component that's closest to what you want to achieve and extend it. Sometimes, though, you have little choice but to build a control from the ground up. If you do choose the completely custom option, be prepared to implement and maintain many of the APIs discussed in this and the next chapters, resulting in a much higher support burden. It is essential to thoroughly test your custom control with different accessibility services and settings.

Name, Role, Value

One of the most fundamental Success Criteria (SC) in WCAG (Chapter 3) is SC 4.1.2: Name, Role, Value. It requires that for any given element on screen, assistive technologies must be able to determine its label (name), its role (purpose), and the current state or value of the element.

In Jetpack Compose, Name, Role, and Value map to the properties `contentDescription`, `role`, and `stateDescription`. Understanding the purpose of each and how to apply them correctly is fundamental to creating an accessible experience in your Android application.

Don't mix up the usage of each. A common accessibility mistake is to add the type or state of the control into the Content Description. The Role and State Description properties are separate for a reason. Cramming everything into the Content Description interferes with how assistive technologies interpret elements. It can override user preferences and prevent assistive technologies from functioning correctly.

Content Description

For an assistive technology like TalkBack to present an element to your user, the technology needs a textual representation to present. This is done with the `contentDescription` value. Commonly, this may be known as alternative text or alt text. This is set to your view's text value by default, but for elements with no text value or where the text value is not meaningful when presented by assistive tech, you should set an explicit `contentDescription` value (Listing 4-3).

`contentDescription` should be a concise, descriptive label. Often one word is plenty, for example, "Submit."

Listing 4-3. Setting a contentDescription in code

```
contentDescription = "Submit"
```

As with other semantic properties, this is set in the semantics lambda, with the exception of Image and Icon composables. These take the `contentDescription` value as a parameter. On these, omitting this parameter or explicitly passing null will hide the image from accessibility services, meaning we don't need to call `semantics` or `clearAndSetSemantics` explicitly.

Listing 4-4. Explicitly hiding an image from assistive technologies by setting a null description

```
Image(
    painter = painterResource(id = R.drawable.badge),
    contentDescription = null,
)
```

Role

An element's role defines its purpose. This data is used by the accessibility system to describe the element or to determine how assistive technologies interact with the element. In most cases, the semantics system will resolve a suitable role for you based on the semantics information provided. However, for complex controls or fully custom elements, it may be necessary to set this explicitly.

Listing 4-5. Providing a Button role for an element that would not otherwise automatically resolve one

```
Box(
    modifier = Modifier.semantics {
        role = Role.Button
    }
) {
    Text("Hello World!")
}
```

State Description

`stateDescription` is the "value" part of Name, Role, Value. It, as the property name suggests, describes the current state, or value, if any, of the focused element. For a text field, this would be the current text entered into the field; for a switch, it would be the current on/off state.

As with other semantic values, the semantics system will, in most cases, inherit this for you correctly. But in cases where you have created a custom control, you may find you need to explicitly set a state description. In some cases, adding a custom description can add essential context. For example, with a slider, depending on the use case, 70%, 0.7, 7, Friday, or any other formatting of the current value may be more suitable than a raw numeric value.

Listing 4-6. Providing an explicit state description when a raw numeric value is unclear

```
val months = listOf(
        "January", "February", "March", "April", "May", "June", "July",
        "August", "September", "October", "November", "December"
    )

var monthIndex by remember { mutableIntStateOf(0) }
Slider(
    value = monthIndex.toFloat(),
    onValueChange = { monthIndex = it.toInt() },
    valueRange = 0f..11f,
    steps = 10,
    modifier = Modifier.semantics {
        stateDescription = months[monthIndex]
    }
)
```

Progress

An exception to using the state description is for components that indicate progress. For these, use the `progressBarRangeInfo` semantic (Listing 4-7). For such components, pass the current progress value and the range of valid values.

Listing 4-7. Using progressBarRangeInfo to provide state information on progress

```
CustomProgressBar(
    modifier = Modifier
        .semantics {
            progressBarRangeInfo =
                ProgressBarRangeInfo(
                    current = progress,
                    range = 0F..1F
                )
        }
)
```

This semantic can also be used on a custom slider to indicate the current state.

Selected

One further exception to using a content description is for selected elements, for example, when a user can pick an item or items in a list or collection on which to perform subsequent actions. For this, add the `selected` semantic, setting it to `true` when the element is selected (Listing 4-8). The use case for this is tightly scoped – this is not appropriate when using a checkbox, for example, where adding a suitable state description is more desirable.

Listing 4-8. Adding a selected semantic to a list item

```
CustomListItem("Item one",
                           modifier = Modifier
                               .semantics {
                                   selected = true
                               }
                          )
```

Traversal Order

The accessibility tree is built in natural reading order. This means the order that TalkBack and other assistive technologies will navigate from the top-left-most item to the bottom-right-most item in left-to-right languages. This is generally the correct behavior. But some designs, such as staggered elements or grid designs, can read differently to how a visual user might read them. An example of this can be seen in the Google Play Store, where an app's download numbers are presented directly vertically above the "Downloads" heading.

Figure 4-4. *Vertically stacked labeled data in a Google Play listing*

In this situation, we might want to improve our accessibility tree by telling Android which element should come next or previous when an accessibility service navigates our UI. Android features two mechanisms for specifying traversal order depending on the type of technology your customer is using. If you find the traversal order of your screen as determined by Android is not ideal, then be sure to set both options.

As with most accessibility APIs, your first approach should be to structure your UI so that traversal order is correct by default through proper use of APIs and careful architecture. If that's not possible, you can change the order explicitly. However, doing so requires extra testing and introduces the risk of regressions if the UI changes.

Accessibility Traversal Order

Most assistive technologies follow the `traversalIndex` property set on an element's semantics. This takes a float value indicating the order in which the element should be navigated, in the order of lowest to highest value. The default value is 0, so anything above or below that will override the system-defined traversal order.

Traversal order values are evaluated only among sibling elements within the same container. Indicate to the accessibility subsystem that you have customized traversal order for a container by setting `isTraversalGroup` on the semantics of the parent.

***Figure 4-5.** A data readout stacked above the label for the data. We want the label to be announced first to provide context*

Listing 4-9 demonstrates a layout where the label "Temperature" is stacked visually below the "20°C" content. In this example, we need to ensure TalkBack focuses on the label first before the content. We do this by ensuring that the label has a lower `traversalIndex` value. As the default is 0, we only need to set a single value to guarantee the order.

Listing 4-9. Defining accessibility traversal order

```
Column(
    Modifier.semantics {
        isTraversalGroup = true
    }
) {
    Text("20°C")
    Text("Temperature",
      modifier = Modifier.semantics {
          traversalIndex = -1.0F
      }
  )
}
```

Directional Control

In addition to setting the accessibility traversal order, we need to set the focus order for any interactive components. Focus order is used by Android when users navigate your UI with a directional pad, remote, or keyboard arrow keys. We set these on an element to specify which element should be next focused when a customer presses a key in the specified direction. Assignable directions are `next`, `previous`, `up`, `down`, `left`, `right`, `start`, and `end`.

If your app features a staggered UI (Figure 4-6), you may find that the calculated focus order does not match user expectations. In this example, we may expect a left key press to move focus from button 1 to button 2. However, because the left edge of button 3 sits further to the left than the start of button 1 (as shown by the dashed line), the default behavior would move focus to button 3 instead. We can resolve this by explicitly defining the navigation order from button 1.

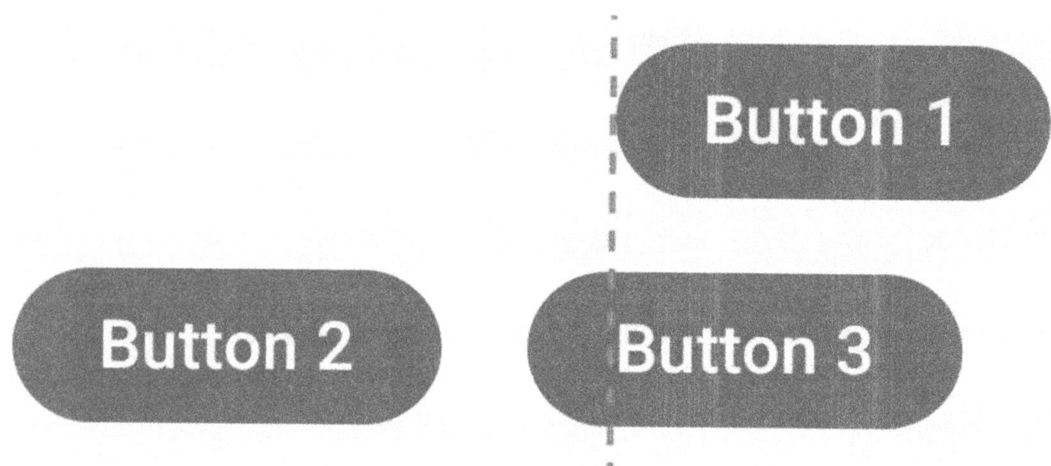

Figure 4-6. *A staggered button layout. The calculated focus order may not match expectations*

First, we need to set up a `FocusRequester` for each button. `FocusRequesters` are unique identities for each focusable element that need to persist across recompositions. We assign these to their corresponding element using the `.focusRequester()` modifier. Then using the `.focusProperties` modifier, we can assign which of our `FocusRequesters` come next, left, first, and so on.

Listing 4-10. Defining directional focus order

```
Column(Modifier.fillMaxSize(), Arrangement.spacedBy(16.dp) ) {
 val (item1, item2, item3) = remember { FocusRequester.createRefs() }
    Row(Modifier.fillMaxWidth()) {
        Spacer(Modifier.weight(1f))
        Button({},
            modifier = Modifier
                .focusRequester(item1)
                .focusProperties {
                    next = item2
                    right = item3
                    left = item2
                    down = item2
                    previous = item3
                }
        ) { Text("Button 1") }
    }

   Row(Modifier.fillMaxWidth(), Arrangement.SpaceEvenly) {
        Button({},
            modifier = Modifier
                .focusRequester(item2)
       ) { Text("Button 2") }
       Button({},
           modifier = Modifier
               .focusRequester(item3)
       ) { Text("Button 3") }
    }
}
```

Ensure you test your focus modifications carefully. It's easy to create an unintended focus trap – a "Hotel California" state where it's possible to move focus to an element or group of elements but never leave. For modal views, it should not be possible to move focus outside of the modal view to the content behind.

If you're creating a control from scratch using an element that is not already a focusable control, you may need to let the system know your element should be focusable by adding the `.focusable()` modifier. Only elements providing interaction should be made focusable in this way. Adding non-interactive elements to the focus engine increases the effort needed when using Voice Access, Switch Access, or a keyboard.

When focusing on controls with the keyboard or other directional device, the standard Android highlight for controls is, unfortunately, not sufficiently high contrast. You should change the appearance of focused controls yourself. This can be done per-control using the `.onFocusChanged` modifier to listen to focus state changes and respond appropriately. Or by creating a custom reusable `Indication` that responds to changes in `FocusInteraction`. Exact code for either choice is out of scope for this book.

Accessibility Actions

The semantics system automatically exposes actions applied to a composable. For example, applying `.clickable` will add "*Double tap to activate*" to an element's TalkBack utterance, and activating with an assistive technology will invoke the same action. However, customizing actions for assistive technologies is a powerful way to add functionality and context and reduce input effort. If you add custom gestures, adding alternatives as a custom action is essential.

Our first option is to add context to existing actions. By adding `onClick` to our item's semantics, we can provide a custom action label. In Listing 4-11, this element will be announced by TalkBack as "*Customize. Double tap to open settings.*" Always return `true` to indicate the action was triggered successfully.

Listing 4-11. Adding a custom action label

```
Button(
    onClick = {},
    modifier = Modifier
        .semantics {
            onClick(label = "open settings") {
                onClickAction()
                true
            }
    }
) { Text("Customize") }
```

Custom Accessibility Actions

If we want to include more functionality, we can do this using custom actions. These actions are presented in an additional menu for assistive technology users. Adding custom actions allows us to present actions that would otherwise be difficult to activate using assistive technologies, for example, actions requiring physical gestures. Alternatively, they can be used to reduce UI complexity or repetitive navigation of common elements; see our semantic views example later in this chapter.

Custom accessibility actions can be accessed from the TalkBack menu (Figure 4-7); this is generally opened using a three-finger tap. With Voice Access you can view the same actions by saying, "Show actions for {number}." With Switch Access, when an element is activated, all available actions are shown in a menu, provided the "Auto-select" setting is disabled.

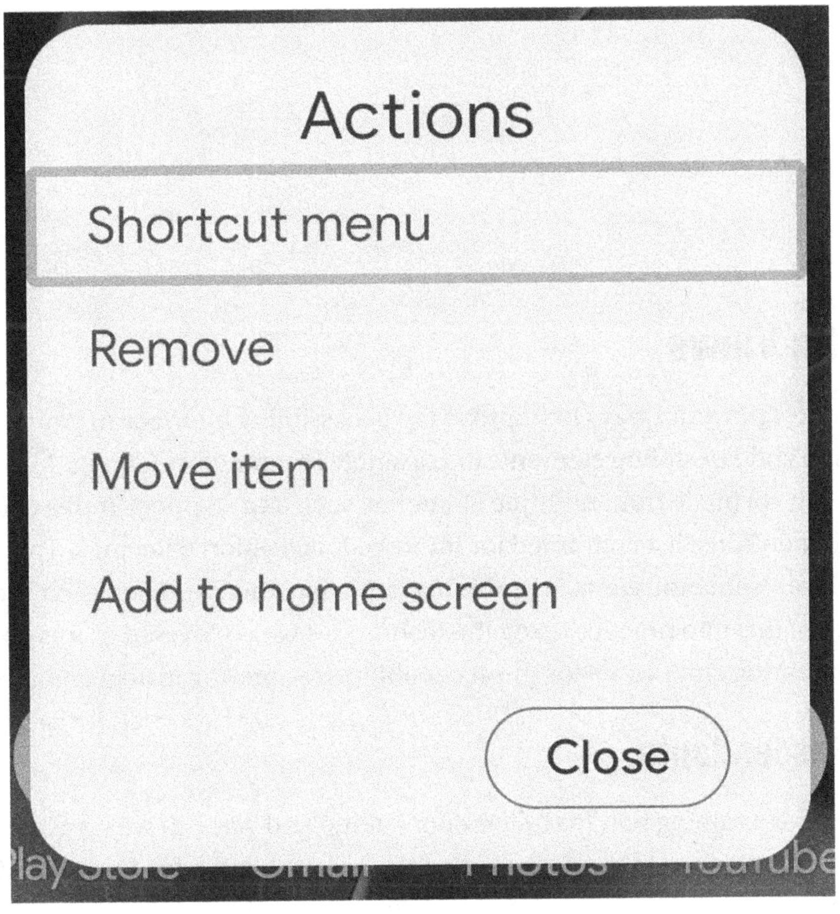

***Figure 4-7.** The TalkBack accessibility actions menu*

These actions must have a label provided, and as before, return `true` to indicate the action was triggered.

Listing 4-12. Adding a custom accessibility action

```
Button(
    onClick = onClickAction,
    modifier = Modifier
        .semantics {
            customActions = listOf(
                CustomAccessibilityAction(
                    label = "Delete message",
                    action = {
                        deleteMessage()
                        true
                    }
                )
            )
        }
)
```

Semantic Views

One of the most powerful ways to improve the accessibility interface of your application is to combine child or sibling elements into a single meaningful element. Maybe this could be a control made from multiple elements, such as a stepper. Or this could be repeated elements in a list combined for improved navigation efficiency. This is a technique I call "semantic views," combining views together based on their meaning. Later, we'll put this into practice using the techniques we've covered in this chapter. The APIs for combining child views for the accessibility tree are key to achieving this.

Merge Descendants

Imagine a row containing two `Text` elements – a title and value. If we have a list of several such rows, that's going to mean a lot of unnecessary navigation for screen reader users. Realistically, the title and value together form one semantic element, so we should group them as one for assistive technologies.

We can do this using the mergeDescendants parameter of the semantics modifier. The default value for this is false, but setting it to true hides any child elements from assistive technologies and merges their semantics into the parent.

In this example (Listing 4-13), our containing element is a Row, so we'll make this our new node in the accessibility tree by setting .semantics(mergeDescendants = true). Now, instead of navigating twice - once to hear "*Downloads*" and again to hear "*100,000*" - TalkBack will focus on the full row and announce "*Downloads. 100,000.*" If we want to replace individual semantics, we do that by setting the properties inside the semantics lambda.

Listing 4-13. Merging semantics into a single accessible object

```
Row(
    modifier = Modifier
        .semantics(mergeDescendants = true) {}
) {
    Column {
        Text("Downloads")
        Text("100,000")
    }
}
```

Clear Semantics

We touched on clearAndSetSemantics earlier as a way to hide an element from assistive technologies by passing an empty lambda. Another common use is to replace inherited semantics with new explicit ones defined on a parent object.

In Listing 4-14, we have a Row containing a button and an icon. Visually, the icon adds no meaning; it is a purely decorative element provided to draw the eye to the row. In our current implementation, TalkBack will first focus on the icon and announce "*Settings, image.*" Then the user would need to navigate again to hear "*Settings*" for a second time, this one for our button. This duplicates information, increases navigation effort, and exposes irrelevant implementation details.

Listing 4-14. Multiple child views with a single meaning

```
Row{
    Image(
        painter = painterResource(id = R.drawable.gear),
        contentDescription = "Settings"
    )
    Button(onClick = onClickAction)
    { Text("Settings") }
}
```

The ideal experience is to focus on the whole row as a single element, announcing "`Settings, Button`" when focused and activating when tapped. This resolves the navigation and verbosity issues but additionally makes it obvious to low-vision users when focused with TalkBack that the elements are considered to have a single meaning.

As there are several changes required, the simplest choice here may be to ignore all the semantics of the child elements and provide whole new semantics for the `Row`. This is where `clearAndSetSemantics` comes in. But where this is different from what we saw at the start of this chapter, this time, we must set some new values in the lambda.

Remembering the Name, Role, Value rule - first, we want a single `contentDescription` for our name: "Settings." The row has no value, so a `stateDescription` is not needed. The last part of this is the Role; for this, we provide `Role.Button`. Remember that we must also provide an `onClick` semantic so that the row responds when activated with assistive technology. Our updated view code looks like Listing 4-15.

Listing 4-15. Creating a new accessibility node with semantics

```
Row(
    modifier = Modifier.clearAndSetSemantics {
        onClick {
            onClickAction()
            true
        }
        role = Role.Button
        contentDescription = "Settings"
    }
```

```
) {
    Image(
        painter = painterResource(id = R.drawable.gear),
        contentDescription = null
    )
    Button(onClick = onClickAction)
    { Text("Settings") }
}
```

Clearing semantics often requires more code and can be more fragile, but for complex views, this effort can really pay off for ensuring you present your UI in the most accessible way possible.

CREATING SEMANTIC VIEWS

Google makes use of semantic views in the Google Play Store. When looking at a listing page for an app or game, we see three boxes just under the app icon (Figure 4-8) – the app's rating, number of downloads, and an age rating. The first item, the app's rating, displays "4.1 ★" then on a new line "2m reviews." Additionally, the rating text and the age rating text are buttons. If you access these elements with TalkBack enabled with no changes to the accessibility tree, TalkBack might behave something like this:

Figure 4-8. *Google Play Store app info*

"Four point one star." Swipe.

"PEGI rating, Image" Swipe.

"500m plus" Swipe.

"2m reviews" Swipe.

"Information. Double tap to activate." Swipe.

"Parental guidance" Swipe.

"Information. Double tap to activate." Swipe.

"Downloads."

That's a lot of swiping. For example, on the final focus we hear only the word "downloads" with no context provided. What does 500m refer to? Fortunately, this isn't how TalkBack actually presents this view. The Google Play Store developers have improved their accessibility tree to provide a better experience. Instead, this is the interaction:

"Average rating four point one stars in two million reviews. Double tap to activate." Swipe.

"Content rating Parental guidance. Double tap to activate" Swipe.

"Downloaded 500 million plus times."

Grouping these elements together has several benefits. Firstly, it reduces the number of swipes needed from five to three. Meaning navigating is faster and simpler. Grouping-related elements like the app review value and the number of reviews provide context to what each value means. The text has also been altered to be more meaningful for TalkBack users by changing "2m" to "2 million." While visually it's clear to see the m means million, we'd rarely say "m" aloud in that context.

In the GitHub repo for this book, open the Exercise 4-2 folder. I've built something that looks similar using Jetpack Compose. Put the techniques we've learned in this chapter to use to make a more accessible experience from these views. I've included my solution too if you want to compare it.

One final note: if you try the real Play Store version with TalkBack, you may notice the button role is omitted. If you do this in your application, it will fail WCAG SC 4.1.2 as discussed earlier and will not function correctly for assistive technology users. Be careful when looking to platform vendors for accessibility best practice. While their approach is generally good, "This is how Google or Apple does it" does not exempt you from following the WCAG requirements.

Summary

- Android's accessibility services use a representation of your view called an accessibility tree to understand and interact with your app's UI. This is built from the semantics system that is part of Jetpack Compose.
- Stick with Jetpack Compose and Material Design's provided views and controls wherever possible and customize them as you need. Accessibility becomes complex when creating custom components, and Android has already done much of the hard work for you.
- You can manipulate the semantics of any view if the defaults don't work in any given context.
- Group connected views together as semantic views. This will make your app faster to use and easier to understand for assistive technology users.

In this chapter, we covered how Android's accessibility system works with Jetpack Compose and how semantics translate your views into representations for assistive technologies. You should now have a clearer idea of how to make an interface that is symbiotic with assistive technology.

In the next chapter, we'll take a closer look at some of the accessibility features Android provides to our customers. We'll also cover some of the semantics and APIs available to developers to best support them.

CHAPTER 5

Android Accessibility Features

In this chapter, we'll look at the accessibility features that are part of Android. This is not an exhaustive guide; we'll focus on the features that may impact you as a developer, either because you need to provide support or make some decisions for the feature to work or because it may change how your app looks or feels in some way. For a more consumer-focused introduction of features available, check Google's support pages.[1]

Android's accessibility features vary between device and vendor, as do many features on the platform. It's also possible to add third-party accessibility tools through the Google Play Store. A major aspect of accessibility is customizability. For users, the ability to pick a device with features that suit them, then add and customize those features as needed, is a boon. But this does mean your development target is a moving one, so manual testing across devices is essential. As a reference device for this chapter, I am using a Google Pixel 9a running Android 16.

Features

Your device's accessibility settings are a top-level option in your system settings app. Android enables most options in this menu instantly when you toggle it. Most provide a short textual description of what the customization does and how it works. Many offer a visual example of the change you're making, and some even offer a tutorial.

None of these settings are destructive, and you can disable them again by toggling them off. So I'd recommend taking a few minutes to familiarize yourself with the content of these settings. Try enabling each one in turn, then navigate your app with the setting

[1] `https://support.google.com/accessibility/android`

R. Whitaker, *Developing Inclusive Mobile Apps*, https://doi.org/10.1007/979-8-8688-2809-6_5

on, and see what differences it has made to your experience. Does your app still work as you would expect? Maybe you will discover some quick wins you can make from using your app with these accessible considerations enabled.

Some of these settings, like TalkBack, change how you interact with your device. So I'd recommend reading this chapter first. But if you want to get stuck in, Android will give you a tutorial and visual demonstration the first time you toggle many features, including TalkBack.

These accessibility settings are all about customizability, so you may find a setting that you want to enable on your own device.

Accessibility Shortcuts

Before starting accessibility testing on Android, the superpower is setting up accessibility shortcuts.[2] These allow you to enable and disable a selected accessibility service quickly, providing frustration-free access to the service wherever you are, without navigating to settings and back.

Most features provide options of an overlay button, a two-finger swipe up gesture, volume keys, or a screen triple tap. Some provide a quick setting when swiping down from the top of the screen. I'd suggest keeping things consistent, so everything is in the same place. The volume keys are an excellent choice for this: long press both the up and down buttons, and you'll get a menu with accessibility services to enable.[3]

Each feature must be enabled separately in its own subsection of the Android accessibility settings, so toggle them as we go through this chapter. To enable the volume key shortcut for each, tap the disclosure indicator, not the toggle, in the shortcut row; otherwise, you'll get the Android-recommended option, which varies by service.

One feature of accessibility shortcuts that developers should be aware of is triple tap activation. Triple-tap activation of the accessibility shortcut will override any triple tap events that your app listens to, meaning if enabled, your app won't receive any triple tap gestures. This is just one reason why you should always provide alternatives to any touch gestures your app uses.

[2] `https://support.google.com/accessibility/android/answer/7650693?hl=en`

[3] This behavior varies by device manufacturer.

TalkBack

When we talk about accessibility for mobile, we often use the word "accessibility" as a proxy for screen reader navigation services like TalkBack. The chances are that if you know one Android accessibility service, it will be TalkBack.

Tip Read the section on Navigating with TalkBack before enabling the service.

TalkBack is Google's built-in screen reader service. Devices from other manufacturers may come with different screen readers installed - such as Amazon VoiceView - or a different fork of TalkBack - e.g., Samsung devices. Some users may also choose to download a third-party screen reader from the Google Play Store.

TalkBack enables blind and low-vision users to hear content available on the screen, but it is more than just a screen reader. By announcing controls and allowing users to interact with them through defined gestures, TalkBack allows your customers to navigate their entire device, without ever having to see the screen (Figure 5-1). Your app is already compatible with TalkBack, without requiring any setup on your part. But how well your app works with TalkBack is a different question. Android's in-built controls are all created with TalkBack in mind, so if you have used these controls as a base, you may find it is already adequate before you make any changes.

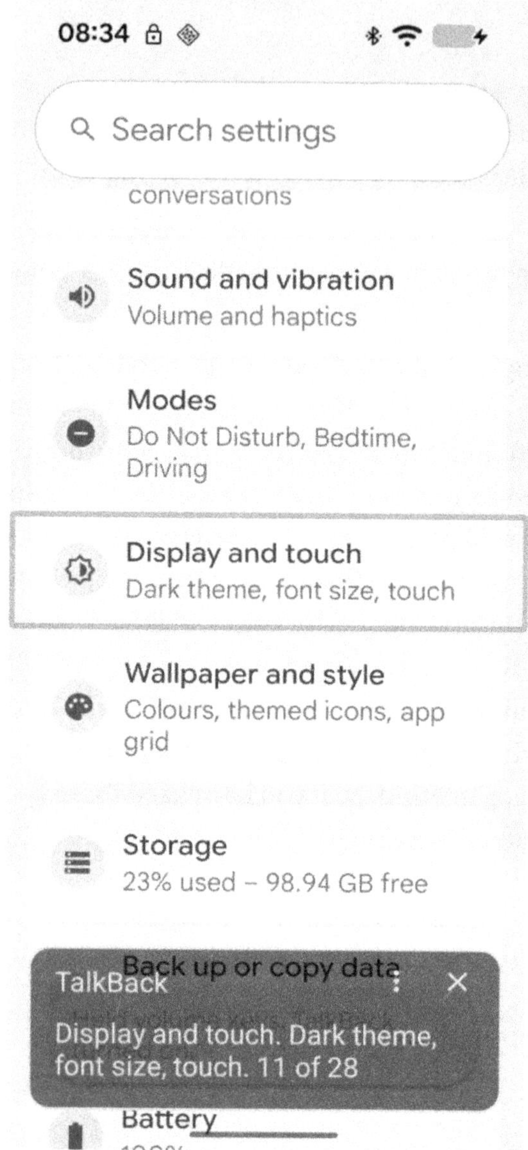

Figure 5-1. *TalkBack highlighting the Display settings and reading the control's content*

TalkBack requires elements to have a textual representation so the element can be announced to your customer. The information TalkBack reads varies by element. By default, TalkBack will read an element's text value if it has one.

If your element's text is short, it may be missing context that visual users would derive from the elements around it. If your element's text is long, it may be too verbose, so setting an explicit content description in the view's semantics might work better.

Before reading the content description, TalkBack will announce a state description, if present, and will end with a role description where applicable - although this all varies by user setting, and vendor. We have covered these in more detail in the previous chapter. While TalkBack is just one accessibility service, it uses the same accessibility tree as any other. Generally, if your app works well with TalkBack, you'll find other accessibility services will work ok too.

For testing and learning, I'd also recommend enabling the Display speech output setting. You can find this in TalkBack settings under Developer settings. This shows a toast with the current utterance on screen as it is spoken. This should help you to understand precisely what you are presenting to your customer.

TalkBack changes how your users interact with your app. Some gestures are not passed through, elements are activated differently, and interactions such as hovering may stop working. It can therefore be useful to know if your customer's device has TalkBack's touch exploration feature enabled, as you may need to adjust how your app handles touch gestures. You can do this by querying the `isTouchExplorationEnabled` property on Android's `android.view.accessibility.AccessibilityManager`[4] (Listing 5-1). That said, changing your app's behavior for assistive technologies often becomes brittle. If you do find your app has interactions that break under TalkBack or other assistive technologies, it's usually better to avoid using these interactions altogether.

Listing 5-1. Determining if explore by touch is enabled

```
val context = LocalContext.current
val accessibilityManager = remember {
    context.getSystemService(Context.ACCESSIBILITY_SERVICE) as
    AccessibilityManager
}
```

[4] https://developer.android.com/reference/android/view/accessibility/AccessibilityManager

```
var touchExplorationEnabled by remember {
    mutableStateOf(accessibilityManager.isEnabled && accessibilityManager.
    isTouchExplorationEnabled)
}
```

For more information on detecting if TalkBack or other accessibility services are enabled, see the section "Detecting Accessibility Services" later in this chapter.

Live Regions

Live regions are parts of the interface where content may change that is away from the user's current TalkBack focus, but where those updates are still important enough to announce.

An example could be a counter showing the number of filtered search results displayed. While typing in a search field, a customer will want to know if the number of results returned has changed, but navigating into and out of a search field each time would be laborious. These updates should be debounced, ideally to a pause in typing, to prevent excessive announcements.

In these instances, you could mark your visual results counter as a live region (Listing 5-2). A live region will announce its content each time it updates without any further interaction from your customer. There are two modes for live regions: `polite` and `assertive`.[5] `polite` will wait for any in-progress utterances to finish. `assertive` will interrupt any existing announcements and should generally be avoided.

Listing 5-2. Creating a live region

```
Text("$results results", modifier = Modifier.semantics { liveRegion =
LiveRegionMode.Polite })
```

Using live regions is a technique that can be powerful but should be used sparingly. If you feel a live region is necessary, consider first if there are changes you can make to your design so TalkBack users will get the context they need without extra announcements, as users relying on magnification may also miss live region updates.

[5] https://developer.android.com/reference/kotlin/androidx/compose/ui/semantics/LiveRegionMode?hl=en

Errors

Live Regions can be a great tool to inform TalkBack users of errors as they appear on screen such as in toasts. But errored components must also have an `error` semantic applied; this allows assistive technologies to present the errors prominently as appropriate. `TextField` components will apply error semantics for you when you add a `supportingText` value and set `isError` true as in Listing 5-3.

Listing 5-3. Providing an error semantic for a text field

```
TextField(
    value = text,
    onValueChange = { newText -> text = newText },
    supportingText = {
        if (text.isEmpty()) {
            Text("Please enter a valid password")
        }
                    },
    isError = text.isEmpty(),
    label = { Text("Password") }
    )
```

For other errored composables, apply the error semantic explicitly, along with a description informing the user that an error exists (Listing 5-4). TalkBack's default behavior is to announce "Error" followed by the contents of the description, before announcing the text content.

Listing 5-4. Providing an error semantic for a custom view.

```
    CustomComponent(
        text = "The password cannot be empty",
        modifier = Modifier
            .semantics {
                if (text.isEmpty()) {
                        error("Invalid password")
                    }
        }
    )
```

In both cases, consider if adding a polite live region is also necessary, but take care not to make the TalkBack utterances too noisy or they may no longer provide value to the user.

NAVIGATING WITH TALKBACK

TalkBack changes the model of interacting with your app.[6] Once you enable this service in your device's accessibility settings, TalkBack is running, so it's important to understand how interaction differs, not least so you can turn the feature off when you're finished!

TalkBack navigates all the readable elements of your screen's UI in natural direction – from top left to bottom right in most languages – highlighting each element with a cursor box as it progresses. You can select an element by tapping it; a single tap no longer activates a control; activation now requires a double tap. Swipe right anywhere on the screen to navigate to the next element or left for the previous.

Fortunately, TalkBack features a fantastic tutorial app that allows you to practice using the screen reader's features. If this is the first time TalkBack has been activated on this device, the tutorial will launch as soon as you toggle the service on (Figure 5-2). If TalkBack has been enabled before, you can manually start this tutorial. Find it in the TalkBack settings near the bottom of the list. To navigate there, remember – tap once to select; double tap to activate. To scroll in the list, swipe right then left in a single motion to page down, or the opposite to scroll up. Complete the tutorial before trying anything else with TalkBack; it will save you a lot of frustration later.

[6] https://support.google.com/accessibility/android/answer/6006598?hl=en-GB

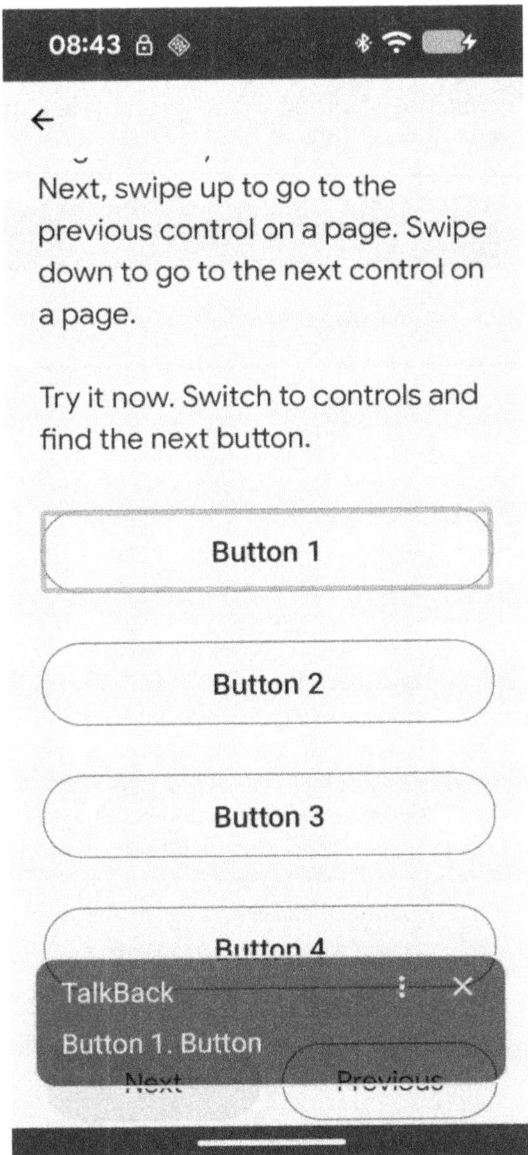

Figure 5-2. *Android's TalkBack tutorial app*

Select to Speak

Select to Speak will read any textual content that appears on the screen under the cursor in the order it appears. Select to Speak doesn't provide any assistance with navigating or interacting with your app. This makes it an ideal tool for people who struggle to read because of low vision, dyslexia, or low literacy, for example.

As such, select to Speak has a few differences when compared to TalkBack about what it reads, how, and when, for example, it does not announce role descriptions. Select to Speak priorities visible text, only falling back to content descriptions if no visible label is available.

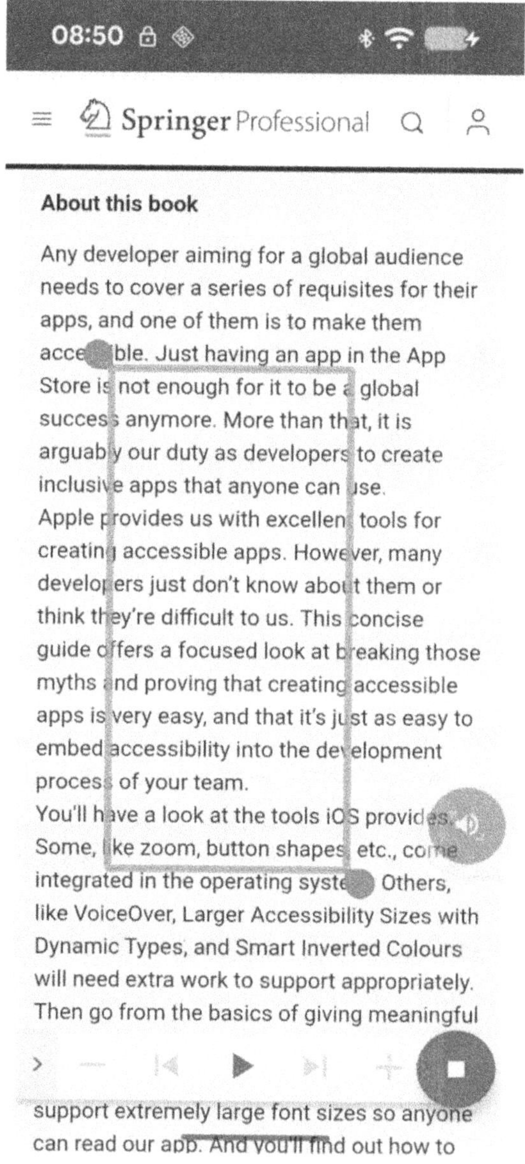

Figure 5-3. *Select to Speak enabled with an area being selected for reading*

Font Size

Android natively supports global scaling font sizes to fit your customer's preference (Figure 5-4). The number of options varies by vendor and operating system version, but Google's Pixel 9a running Android 16 supports seven distinct sizes.

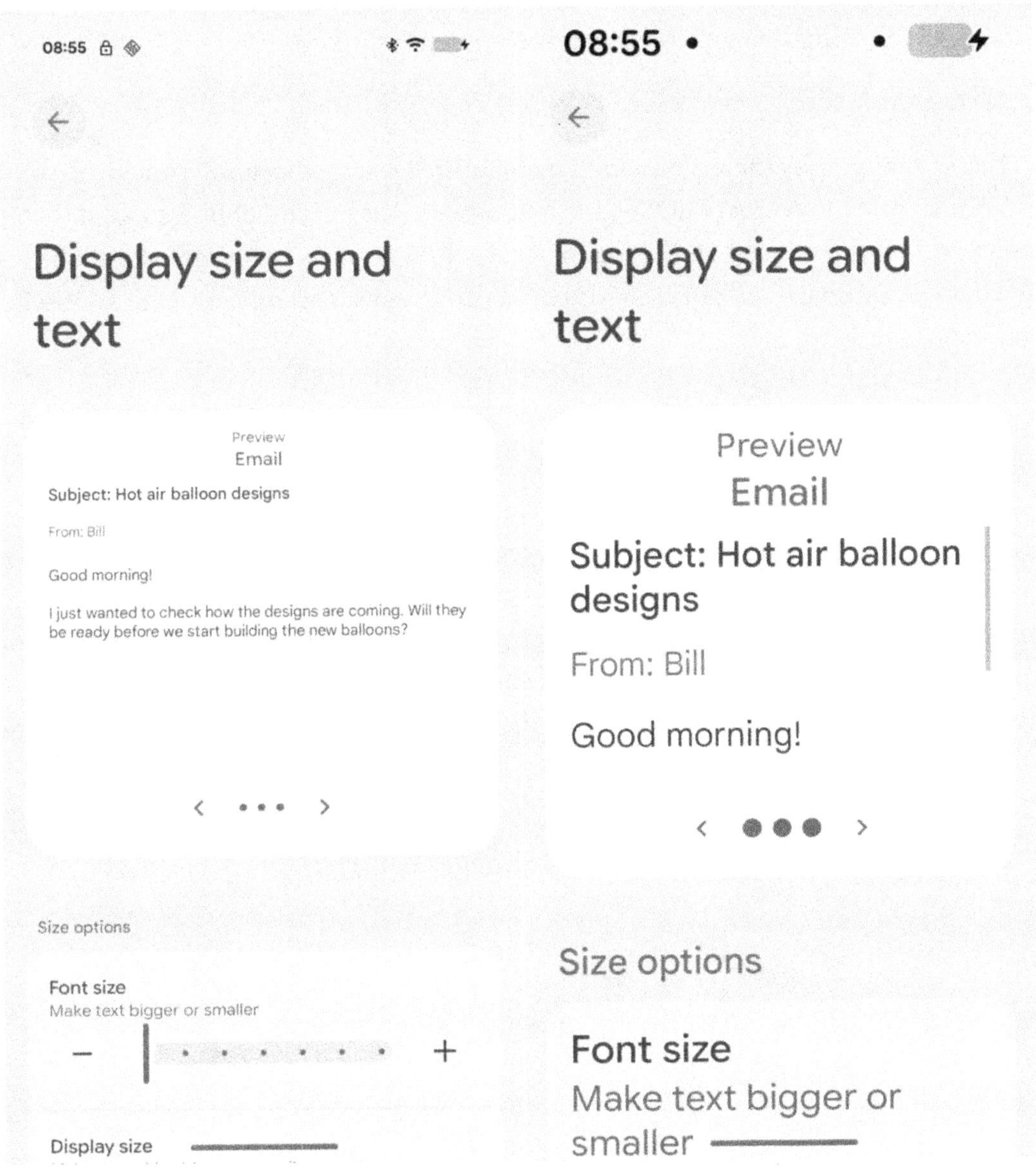

***Figure 5-4.** Android's smallest (left) and largest (right) font sizes. Appearance will vary by device*

You can achieve automatic font scaling in your app using scale-independent pixels; when specifying a `fontSize` in your compose code, ensure you follow the font size with `.sp` (Listing 5-5). This allows designers to specify a font size, say 14px; we can then input `14.sp`. At standard text sizes, this will then appear as the equivalent of 14px but will scale up or down appropriately.

Listing 5-5. Setting text size by scale-independent pixels

```
Text("Scalable text", fontSize = 30.sp)
```

If using typography tokens provided by Material Design, these will provide SP units and will also provide correct line heights and other values. If you define custom tokens, the same rule for specifying SP units over pixel values applies. Extra care should be taken if specifying custom line heights, as this could cause lines to merge into one another at larger scales.

Display Size

Android's ability to support a vast range of screen shapes and sizes lends itself to frictionless support for another accessibility feature: adjustable display size (Figure 5-5). This works seamlessly for your app, provided you avoid fixed pixel values. Jetpack Compose will push you towards using dp units (density-independent pixels) (Listing 5-6) as these will ensure your layout can support various screen sizes and densities, as well as allowing for display size scaling.

Listing 5-6. Adding padding to a composable using dp units

```
Text("Text with padding", Modifier.padding(12.dp))
```

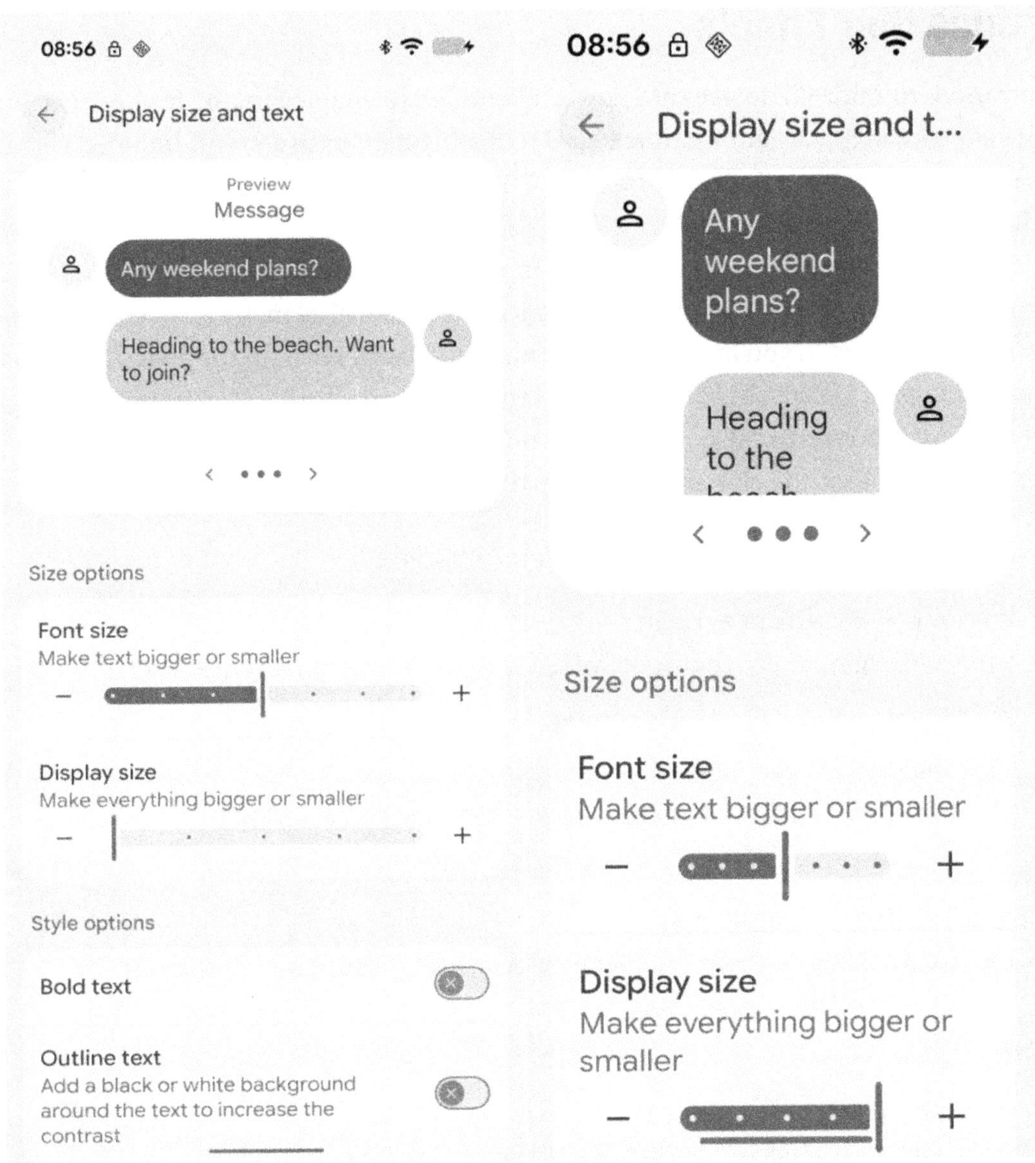

Figure 5-5. *Android's smallest (left) and largest (right) display sizes. Appearance will vary by device*

Reduce Blur Effects

Many modern Android devices are powerful enough to enable striking blur effects, but these effects can make your interface hard to distinguish for users with reduced vision, especially if their vision is already blurred. The "Reduce blur effects" setting allows users to disable these effects if needed.

If supplying a blur effect via a `.blur()` modifier, the modifier will respect this setting by default, and providing a fallback is good practice, as many devices may not support blur effects. If you are adding custom blur effects, listen to the `android.view.WindowManager`'s `isCrossWindowBlurEnabled` property (Listing 5-7), and provide fallback UI if this returns false. While not a one-to-one mapping to the Reduce blur effects setting, this is the closest developer API available to check.

Listing 5-7. Detecting "reduce blur effect" status

```
val context = LocalContext.current
val windowManager = context.getSystemService(Context.WINDOW_SERVICE) as
WindowManager

var blurEnabled by remember {
    mutableStateOf(windowManager.isCrossWindowBlurEnabled)
}

DisposableEffect(windowManager) {
    val listener = java.util.function.Consumer<Boolean> { enabled ->
        blurEnabled = enabled
    }

    windowManager
        .addCrossWindowBlurEnabledListener(listener)
    onDispose {
        windowManager
            .removeCrossWindowBlurEnabledListener(listener)
    }
}
```

```
if (blurEnabled) {
    // UI with blur effect added
} else {
   // UI without blur effect
}
```

Color Contrast

The Android Display & touch settings provide options for customizing color contrast, from Default through Medium to High. This setting governs how the Material 3 dynamic colors are processed, and if using that theming system, color adjustments will be handled for you.

If using custom colors, in places where your interface would benefit from a higher contrast appearance, you can listen to the state of this setting by querying the value of `contrast` on `android.app.UiModeManager`. `contrast` will return `0.0f` for regular contrast, `0.5f` for medium contrast, and `1.0f` for high contrast. You can of course switch on this value, or by using linear interpolation, as in Listing 5-8, you can specify the Default and High contrast values and allow the algorithm to calculate the Medium value.

Listing 5-8. Calculating custom colors based on the users contrast setting

```
val uiModeManager = context.getSystemService(Context.UI_MODE_SERVICE) as
UiModeManager
val textColor = lerp(
    start = Color(0xFF767676), // Default contrast
    stop = Color(0xFF000000),  // High contrast
    fraction = uiModeManager.contrast
)
Text("Hello", color = textColor)
```

Note that you must continue to conform to the WCAG SC 1.4.4 required text contrast ratio of 4.5:1[7] even when this setting is set to Default.

Dark Theme

I know many developers love using interfaces with a dark theme. Because we spend hours looking at screens, it makes a noticeable difference to our eyes if we don't have bright white light shining in them constantly. Plus, it looks cool.

But dark theming is also an important accessibility feature. Large amounts of bright light can be problematic for people with certain vision conditions, such as cataracts, where glare can cause discomfort and wash out the rest of their vision. For some, dark theming can also make it easier to distinguish between elements.

So while it's tempting to think of dark theming as nice to have, for many, it's an essential accessibility feature. But don't assume dark automatically means accessible – for some people light text on a dark background is difficult to read, which is why supporting both light and dark themes is equally important.

Material includes a comprehensive theming system that will switch colors for you depending on the user's system appearance setting. Your responsibility is to define what those colors are. The Material Foundation provides a great tool to help with this at `https://material-foundation.github.io/material-theme-builder/`. Remember to check the contrast, especially between text and background, in both light and dark variants.

Once you've decided on your color variants for both light and dark, create an instance of `lightColorScheme` and one of `darkColorScheme` (Listing 5-9), specifying which color to use for each semantic role.

Listing 5-9. Specifying color use in light and dark themes

```
private val LightColors = lightColorScheme(
    // where my_theme_light_primary is a color definition
    primary = my_theme_light_primary,
    // Specify further color uses
)
```

[7] `https://www.w3.org/WAI/WCAG22/Understanding/contrast-minimum`

```
private val DarkColors = darkColorScheme(
    // where my_theme_dark_primary is a color definition
    primary = my_theme_dark_primary,
    // Specify further color uses
)
```

Now that we've defined our color schemes for each theme, we can let Material switch them automatically (Listing 5-10).

Listing 5-10. Defining a dynamic App Theme

```
@Composable
fun AppTheme(
   useDarkTheme: Boolean = isSystemInDarkTheme(),
   content: @Composable() () -> Unit
) {
   val colors = if (!useDarkTheme) {
       // Our light theme as defined in Listing 5-9
       LightColors
   } else {
      // Our dark theme as defined in Listing 5-9
       DarkColors
   }

   MaterialTheme(
       colorScheme = colors,
       content = content
   )
}
```

Finally, we need to apply the theme to our app. We do this in our `MainActivity`'s `onCreate` by wrapping our composable content inside our new `AppTheme` (Listing 5-11).

Listing 5-11. Adding our theme to our app

```
class MainActivity : ComponentActivity() {
    // ...
    override fun onCreate(savedInstanceState: Bundle?) {
        super.onCreate(savedInstanceState)
        setContent {
            AppTheme {
                MyApp(
                    // Composable app content
                )
            }
        }
    }
}
```

Magnification

Android developers need to be aware of magnification for two reasons, the first of which can affect any app. As text is written left to right (natural alignment – right to left in some languages), any magnification users will usually scan the magnifier down the left of your screen. This means that if you have content that is not naturally aligned, magnification users will often miss this. For example, if you add an icon conveying status next to a row in a table, if your icon is to the right of the text, a magnification user may not notice the status icon (Figure 5-6). Where possible, keep any meaningful content naturally aligned. For the same reason, any UI changes should happen close to the control that triggers the change.

***Figure 5-6.** Navigating accessibility settings with magnification enabled. Any right-aligned content may be missed*

Once activated, magnification works using two finger swipes to move the viewfinder and two finger pinch gestures to zoom in and out. Because of this, your app may not receive two finger swipe or pinch gestures while magnification is active. If your app does make use of two finger gestures, it is essential to test with magnification enabled. As with any complex touch gestures, you must always offer an alternative that allows users to perform the action without requiring the gesture.

Color Inversion

Inverting colors has benefits for several impairments. It reduces glare and increases contrast. This means people with light sensitivity, color deficiencies, or reduced vision can all benefit from this feature. Color inversion inverts all colors on screen, regardless of where or how they are used and how your app is set up. This includes images and videos. Some users will benefit from inverted images, but for many, it will just look weird.

A better experience for most customers, if possible, is to support both dark and light theming. With dark theming, covered earlier, you can choose which colors your app changes for light and dark themes and how, resulting in a solid accessible experience while keeping a good-looking app.

Remove Animations

Animations can trigger vertigo and nausea in people with balance disorders. Animation can also be worrying and distracting for people with certain learning difficulties or disorders such as attention disorders, autism, and anxiety. For these reasons, it's necessary to listen to this setting and use it to determine if you should reduce or remove animation. With this setting enabled, you should look at places in your app where you have custom fast, zooming, or multiple plane animation and auto-playing video. Animations provided by Compose already honor this setting.

Android provides us with a float value to inform us of how fast we should run animations, with 0 meaning animations should be removed.[8] For Compose animations, you can listen to this value using Listing 5-12[9]:

---

[8] https://developer.android.com/reference/kotlin/androidx/compose/ui/MotionDurationScale

[9] https://developer.android.com/reference/kotlin/androidx/compose/ui/MotionDurationScale

Listing 5-12. A composable returning false if the user has requested animations removed

```
@Composable
fun animationsEnabled(): Boolean {
    val motionScale = LocalMotionDurationScale.current
    return motionScale.scaleFactor != 0f
}
```

For any animation created with any other framework read the `ANIMATOR_DURATION_SCALE` setting as in Listing 5-13.

Listing 5-13. Reading the system animation-duration scale for non-Compose animations

```
Settings.Global.getFloat(
  context.contentResolver,
  Settings.Global.ANIMATOR_DURATION_SCALE,
  0f
)
```

Switch Access

Switch access is an accessibility service intended to help people with limited motor abilities by allowing your user to navigate and control your interface using an external hardware device. A switch can be many things, like a regular keyboard. Third-party switches explicitly designed for this purpose are also available to purchase.

Tip Read the section on Navigating with Switch Access before enabling the service.

Switch Access highlights each interactive element in turn with a bounding box. Your user can then press a switch to either skip to the next element or activate the current selected one. Navigating with one button is time-consuming, meaning Switch Access users are often the users most affected by any timeouts in your app. Where possible, consider extending or removing timeouts - see Time to Take Action.

Figure 5-7. *Switch Access highlighting a row of apps*

To achieve this control, the Switch Access accessibility service uses the accessibility tree discussed in chapter 4. This is the same accessibility tree used by other services such as TalkBack. So if your app works well with TalkBack, it will often work well with Switch Access too. However, Switch Access will only focus on interactive elements, so you can't assume that a good TalkBack experience will translate to Switch Access.

For example, creating a "button" by adding a `pointerInput` modifier to an element will mean assistive technologies won't have the correct semantic information to interact with the element. Stick with the provided controls, and semantics will be provided for free.

NAVIGATING WITH SWITCH ACCESS

When enabling Switch Access for the first time, Android will present you with a setup guide (Figure 5-8). This app will take you through getting Switch Access configured, then give you a test area to get used to how Switch Access makes interacting with your device different.

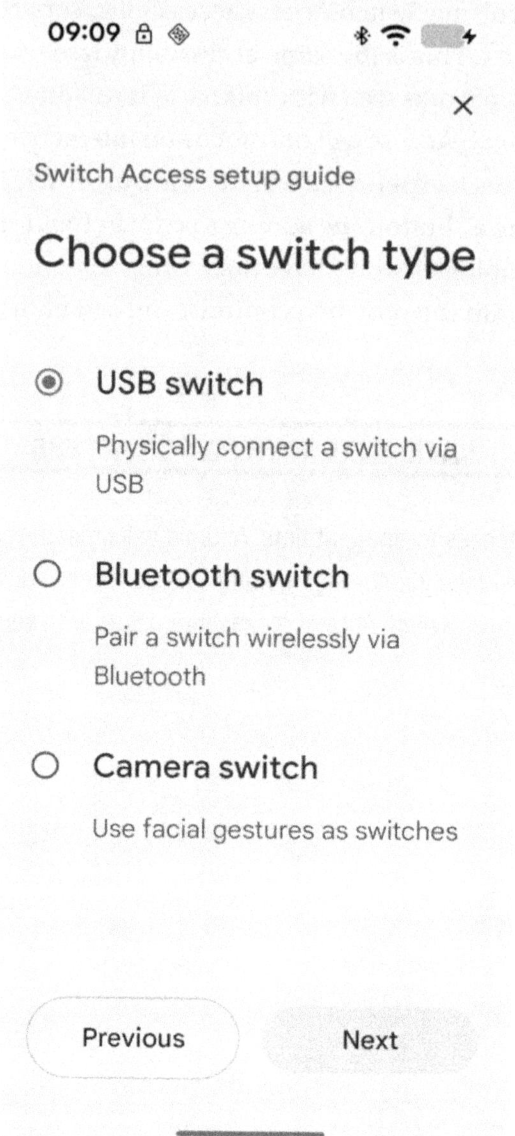

Figure 5-8. *Switch Access setup guide*

To begin, connect a switch. While there are switches available specifically for Switch Access, I'd suggest for testing purposes a keyboard; either USB or Bluetooth is the best way to get started. This way, you can also check your app using Keyboard Navigation. But if you have no keyboard, you can also use your device's volume keys.

Select the control mode based on the number of switches you want to use (Figure 5-9). I'd suggest trying both modes out so you can get an idea of how your Switch Access users will experience your app.

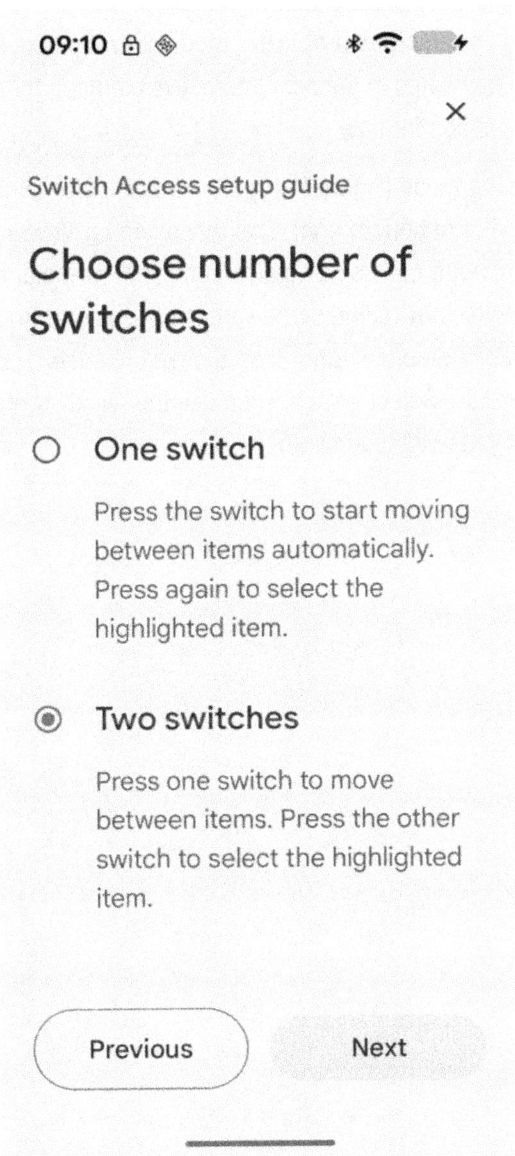

***Figure 5-9.** Selecting the number of switches available to Switch Access*

Choosing One Switch, press your switch once to begin scanning the screen. The bounding box highlight will move automatically between interactive elements. Press the switch on an element to activate it. This form of interaction is prolonged but is essential for people with the most limited movement.

Two Switches is the more straightforward, faster mode of navigation, as it is all done at the user's pace. One switch navigates to the next interactive element; the second switch activates that element. Select this option for now.

Next, choose your scanning mode (Figure 5-10). Linear scanning[10] highlights every interactive element in turn from top left to bottom right. This mode can be slower as we must visit every element on screen, but it makes navigation simpler. Row–column scanning will group elements by row. This makes navigating some screens faster. Pressing the "Next" switch will navigate to the next row of elements, rather than the next element. If you want to activate an element in that row, press the Select switch. Then use the "Next" switch to navigate to the element in that row that you want to activate.

[10] Android does warn that Linear Scanning mode doesn't work with keyboards, although I have never found this to be the case.

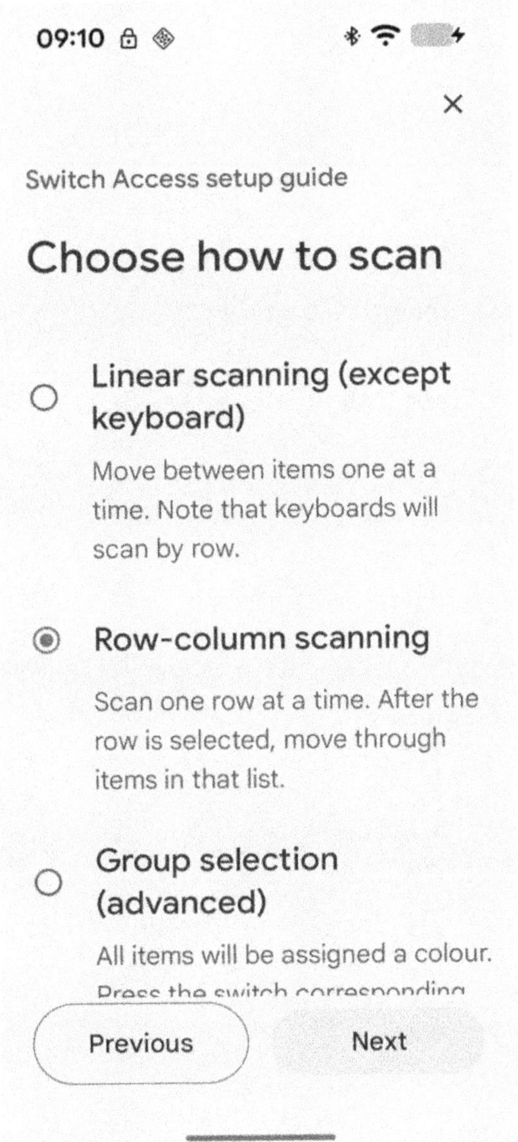

***Figure 5-10.** Choosing a scanning mode in Switch Access Setup*

The next two screens cover choosing your two switches. Pick any two keys on your keyboard, but I'd suggest two that are close to each other.

Finally, we're presented with a game of tic-tac-toe to help us practice (Figure 5-11). Press your assigned "Next" key to begin scanning. If you're stuck with navigating with this setup or want to try something different, press Previous (the screen still works with regular touch input) and reconfigure. Before you disable Switch Access, remember to navigate your app with it too.

Figure 5-11. *Practicing Switch Access with a game of Tic-Tac-Toe*

If you're feeling adventurous, try out some of the other options available in the Switch Access settings. They all make a noticeable difference in how the interface of your app is presented to your user. I'd recommend checking out the following:

- Auto-scan

  When Switch Access is configured with one button, auto-scan will automatically navigate from one element to the next in second intervals.

- Point scan

  A horizontal line scans from the top of the screen to the bottom; press Select to stop (Figure 5-12). A vertical line then moves from left to right. Press Select when the crosshairs are over the element you want to activate.

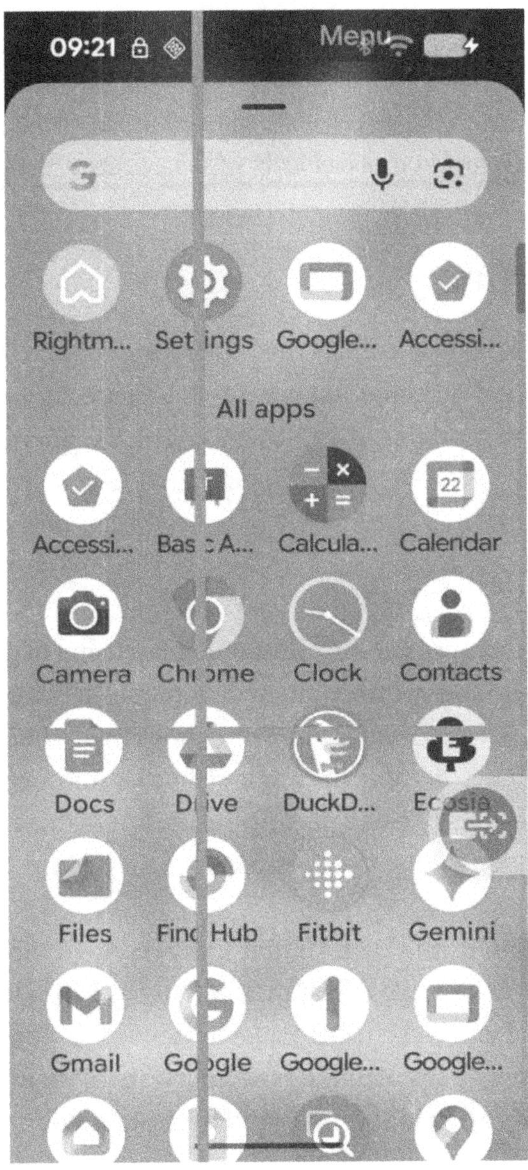

Figure 5-12. *Switch Access in Point Scan mode selecting the Drive app*

- Camera Switch

  Use facial gestures such as eye and mouth movements to control your device. This works best on a fixed device, and for regular testing, it is not the fastest option, but it is fun to try out.

- Speech, sound, and vibration

  Enable spoken feedback from this menu. This mode combines the features of TalkBack with Switch Access by reading all text-representable elements aloud. This means switch control will focus on all elements while navigating, not only interactive ones.

Touch and Hold Delay

The touch and hold delay setting adjusts the time required for a long-press event to be fired. This helps to control for accidental presses. If you are adding a long press action, use a `combinedClickable` modifier to add an `onLongClick`, and this setting will be taken into account for you.

Time to Take Action

Time to Take Action, or the Accessibility Timeout, gives users extra time to see temporary visual elements and act on them if needed. Accessibility users are often slower to navigate apps than non-accessibility users. Sometimes this is because of their abilities; for others, it's a consequence of their chosen assistive technology's interaction modes.

This feature offers various options from 10 seconds to 2 minutes. Any later toasts or snack bars will be displayed for the user's chosen length of time, overriding the value you have set in code.

If you have implemented your own UI that shows content temporarily, firstly, I'd ask you to reconsider this decision. But if this is an integral part of your application, it is essential you call `calculateRecommendedTimeoutMillis` on the `LocalAccessibilityManager` to calculate how long your UI should be present for, see Listing 5-14. This takes into account the desired default timeout and the nature of the UI present.

Listing 5-14. Calculating the minimum time on screen for an element containing icons, text, and controls, with an original timeout of 10 seconds

```
LocalAccessibilityManager.current?
    .calculateRecommendedTimeoutMillis(
      originalTimeoutMillis = 10000,
      containsIcons = true,
      containsText = true,
      containsControls = true,
  )
```

Captions

Android natively supports captions with the `ExoPlayer`. Users can enable these globally in the accessibility settings, as well as choosing options such as size and color (Figure 5-13).

Figure 5-13. *Android's caption preferences*

As a developer, the simplest option is likely to ensure that captions are embedded in video files or streams. But if you need to provide separate subtitle tracks, add these to the media item before passing it to the player (Listing 5-15).[11] Once you have done this, the video player will handle rendering these as per your user's preference.

[11] https://developer.android.com/reference/kotlin/androidx/media3/common/MediaItem.SubtitleConfiguration

Listing 5-15. Loading a subtitles file from a URL and adding those subtitles to a `MediaItem` instance

```
val subtitle =
  MediaItem.SubtitleConfiguration
        .Builder(subtitleUri)
       // Ensure you specify the correct format
      .setMimeType(MimeTypes.TEXT_VTT)
      .setLanguage("en")
      .build()

val mediaItem = MediaItem.Builder()
    .setUri(videoUri)
    .setSubtitleConfigurations(listOf(subtitle))
    .build()
```

If you're displaying video or animation in a custom composable, you are responsible for displaying and rendering the captions yourself. You can retrieve your customer's settings using the `CaptioningManager`[12] class seen in Listing 5-16.

Listing 5-16. Accessing caption settings from the system's captioning manager

```
val captioningManager = LocalContext.current
    .getSystemService(Context.CAPTIONING_SERVICE) as CaptioningManager
val captionsEnabled = captioningManager.isEnabled
val captionStyle = captioningManager.userStyle
val textScale = captioningManager.fontScale
```

The `CaptioningManager` class provides a `userStyle` value returning a `CaptionStyle` class object as seen above. This class provides information such as the font, foreground, and background colors, and more. Check the Android developer documentation for the full range of values.[13] You should follow these preferences as much as possible, as your customer will have chosen this combination of font, size, color, etc. To suit their own requirements.

---

[12] `https://developer.android.com/reference/android/view/accessibility/CaptioningManager`

[13] `https://developer.android.com/reference/kotlin/android/view/accessibility/CaptioningManager.CaptionStyle.html`

Outline Text

Outline text adds either a black or white background to text, depending on the text's original color (Figure 5-14). On older Android versions this setting was called "high contrast text" and added a border around text. This is effect is added by Android's regular text rendering system, so it will be processed automatically in most instances.

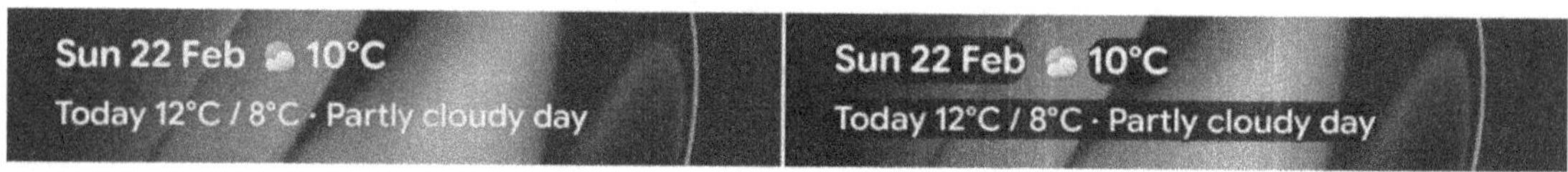

Figure 5-14. *Standard text (left) and outline text (right)*

If you're rendering your own text, `android.view.accessibility.AccessibilityManager` exposes `isHighContrastTextEnabled()` to detect if the user has enabled this feature. If this returns true, ensure your text has a flat black or white background to aid readability.

Voice Access

Voice Access allows completely hands-free access and control of the device. This is a helpful feature if you're unable to look at your screen temporarily, but it's invaluable for people with limited mobility, especially those with the most limited movement but who can speak. Voice Access uses voice alone not to perform tasks such as you might ask of the Google Assistant, but to fully control the device. As well as being a significant accessibility feature, Voice Access is also fun to use, so it's worth checking it out.

You may need to download Voice Access from the Google Play Store. After enabling the feature in your device's Accessibility settings, try saying "Show numbers" and "Tap {number}" to control your device. For more commands, try saying "What can I say." A full list of commands is available from the Android support website: `https://support.google.com/accessibility/android/answer/6151854`

Like other accessibility services on Android, Voice Access uses the accessibility tree we discussed in chapter 4. For simplicity, Voice Access will display numbers next to every interactive element (Figure 5-15), but these can also be triggered by the name displayed on the screen. Whereas TalkBack will read an element's content description over the element's text value, Voice Access will favor the element's text value over the content description.

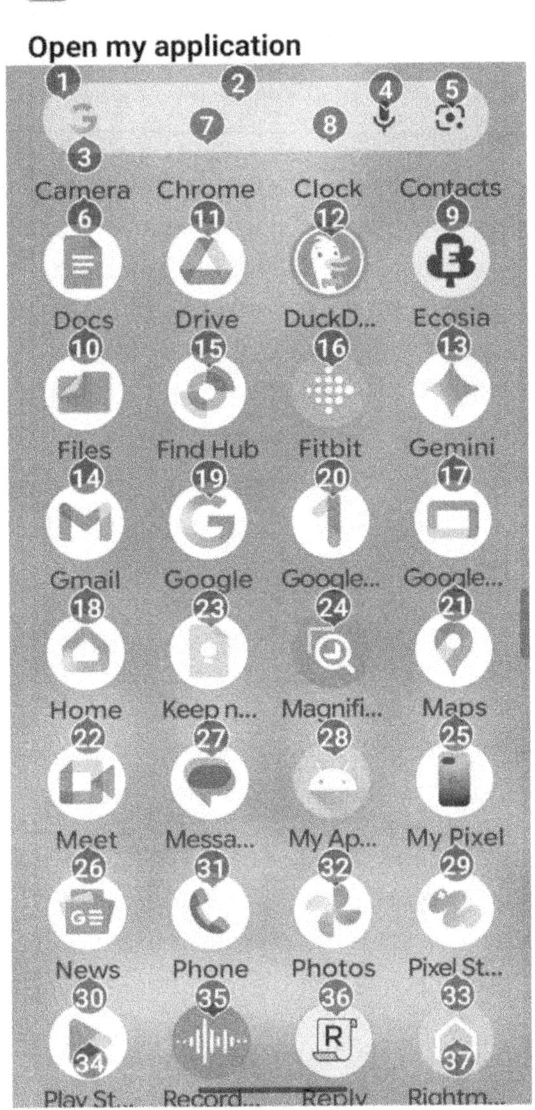

Figure 5-15. *Voice Access enabled. The user has requested "Open my application"*

As with Switch Access, if you add a `pointerInput` modifier to an element that is not usually a control, an image, for example, Voice Access will not recognize this as an element it can interact with. Stick with Android's standard controls whenever possible.

Localization

While your app may only be available in one territory, creating an app ready for localization is good practice regardless. It will save you a lot of effort in the future when you want to change strings or other resources. Plus, the option for localization opens your business up to new markets. Even in a single market, you'll find more people than you might predict who would prefer your app to be available to them in another language. The US Census Bureau found that nearly 22% of Americans, around 70 million people, spoke a language other than English when at home.[14]

When creating a new app, Android Studio will create a strings.xml file for you (Listing 5-17). As a good practice, always add any strings used in your user interface here. Give your string a name value; this is what you will use in code to reference your string, then add your string between the `<string>` tags. While this section deals with localized strings, you can localize any other resource in the same way, including drawables, dimensions, and others.

Listing 5-17. A strings.xml file as generated by Android Studio

```
<resources>
      <string name="app_name">My Application</string>
      <string name="action_settings">Settings</string>
</resources>
```

To use these string resources in your app, refer to them by the name you provided in the string value. Consider our `action_settings` string. We can refer to this in a composable using `stringResource(R.string.action_settings)` (Listing 5-18).

Listing 5-18. Accessing a string resource in compose

```
Text(stringResource(R.string.action_settings))
```

[14] "New American Community Survey Statistics for Income, Poverty and Health Insurance Available for States and Local Areas," United States Census Bureau, September 14, 2017. `https://www.census.gov/newsroom/press-releases/2017/acs-single-year.html`.

Translating Your App

Before we send our app for translation, spend some time annotating the contents of your existing strings.xml file. Add comments above strings explaining where the string is used and what its purpose is. Include any restrictions or requirements you have for that string. This will help your translator, whether human or AI, to pick the most right word or phrase for each usage.

To create a localized version of your strings, choose File ➤ New ➤ Values Resource File. Name the file strings to match the original and select the Locale modifier in the list on the left (Figure 5-16). Press the Add button. A new list appears of Android-supported locales. Select the locale you want to localize for - you can type in this list to filter it - and press OK. You'll see that you now have two strings.xml files in the project navigator, your original and your newly localized one (Figure 5-17).

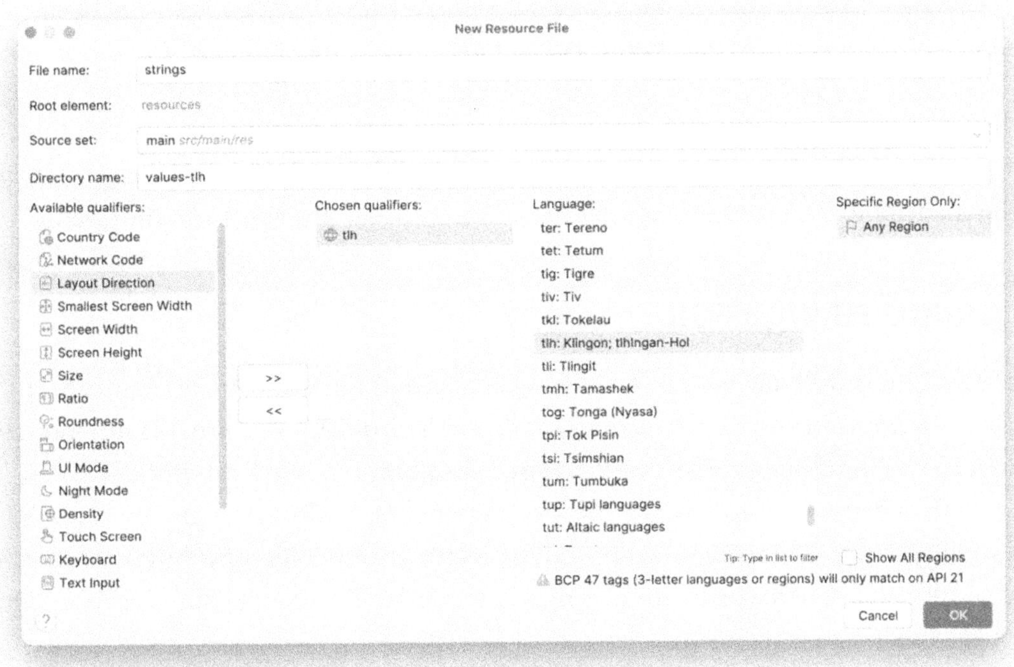

Figure 5-16. *Creating a new localized strings.xml file*

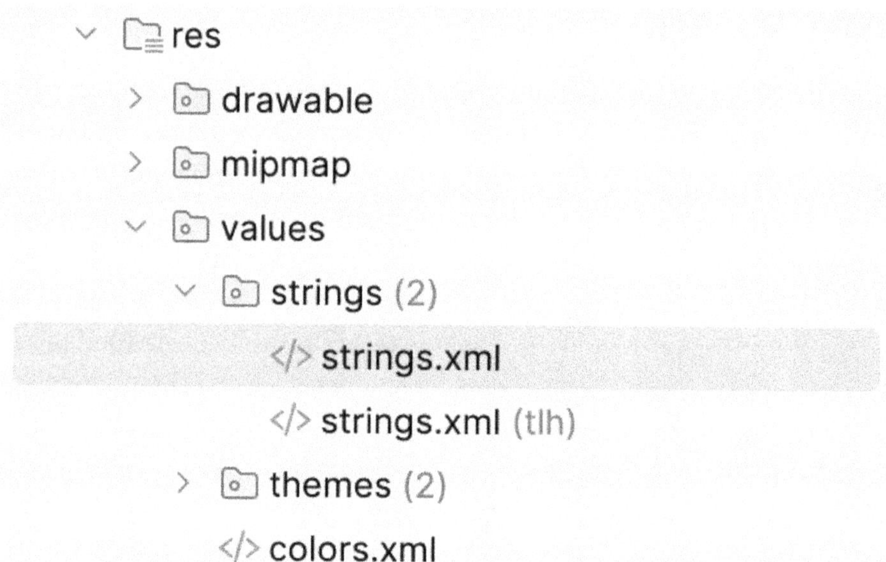

Figure 5-17. *Two-strings files in our project navigator, one as a "tlh" localized variant*

In your new strings file, copy any of the XML string entries that need translating, and change the value between the `<string>` tags to your newly translated value. Any string you choose not to localize here will fall back to your original strings.xml file's value.

Keyboard Navigation

Android supports full navigation through a keyboard or remote control (Figure 5-18). In fact, certain Android apps, such as ones made for Android TV, require this functionality. Connect a USB or Bluetooth keyboard to your phone, and as well as typing, you can use the tab or arrow keys to navigate between elements. Android will use your app's accessibility tree to determine the order in which to present elements but will sometimes need some hints. So it's worth connecting a keyboard to find out if your screen navigates as you'd expect.

Figure 5-18. *Keyboard Navigation with Drive selected*

Detecting Accessibility Services

Android's `android.view.accessibility.AccessibilityManager` (Listing 5-19) service will provide you with a range of information about the accessibility environment for the device on which your app is running.

I include this information here, as on occasion it can be useful to know - perhaps we want to increase the prominence of some information if an assistive technology is enabled. In general, I would recommend against using this information, as it is highly personal and protected. If you find yourself in a situation where this information may be needed, take a step back and reevaluate other options first.

Listing 5-19. Getting the accessibility service

```
val accessibilityManager = LocalContext.current.getSystemService(Context.
ACCESSIBILITY_SERVICE) as AccessibilityManager
```

We can discover more about the accessibility services available, what is currently running, and what these services can provide for our customers by querying this manager. To get a list of all installed accessibility services, we can request `getInstalledAccessibilityServiceList()` (Listing 5-20).

Listing 5-20. Getting a list of all currently installed accessibility services

```
val accessibilityManager = LocalContext.current
    .getSystemService(Context.ACCESSIBILITY_SERVICE) as AccessibilityManager
val installedServices = accessibilityManager.getInstalledAccessibility
ServiceList()
```

Running Services

While the list of installed services will tell us what your customer's device is capable of, it doesn't mean any of these services are in use. The accessibility manager provides a Boolean value telling us if one or more services are currently running (Listing 5-21).

Listing 5-21. Detecting an accessibility service. Returns true if any service is running

```
val accessibilityManager = LocalContext.current.
    getSystemService(Context.ACCESSIBILITY_SERVICE) as AccessibilityManager
val isAccessibilityEnabled = accessibilityManager.isEnabled
```

Now that we know an accessibility service is running, we might want to dig a little deeper into what type of services are running. To see if we need to make changes, we need to know the service's capabilities. We can do this by querying the Accessibility Manager. There is no direct request to detect if TalkBack is enabled, for example, as your customer may be using a screen reader from their handset vendor or a third-party screen reader from the Google Play Store. Instead, we query based on the service's capabilities. Android then returns a list of all running services with that feature.

For a list of currently enabled accessibility services, we can use the `AccessibilityManager`'s `getEnabledAccessibilityServiceList()` method (Listing 5-22). We need to pass a constant representing the type of service we want to know about.

Listing 5-22. Getting a list of all running screen readers

```
val accessibilityManager = LocalContext.current.
    getSystemService(Context.ACCESSIBILITY_SERVICE) as AccessibilityManager
val enabledServices = accessibilityManager.getEnabledAccessibility
ServiceList(
        AccessibilityServiceInfo.FEEDBACK_SPOKEN)
```

The `FEEDBACK_SPOKEN` constant passed as the argument to this method returns any service that can provide spoken-word feedback, such as TalkBack. We can pass different constants to this method to return different types of service as needed. These constants are divided by the type of feedback the service provides to your user, or the capabilities the accessibility service has. To return any services that can provide any kind of feedback, pass `AccessibilityServiceInfo.FEEDBACK_ALL_MASK`. To return any running service regardless of capability or feedback type, pass `AccessibilityServiceInfo.DEFAULT`. We'll cover all the constant values here.

Feedback

These constants characterize how services provide feedback to your user. Fetching services by the type of feedback they can provide means the service is currently running. It doesn't necessarily mean that feedback type is presently enabled or active. Services can fall into multiple feedback types.

- `FEEDBACK_ALL_MASK`

  All services that provide any type of accessibility feedback to your customer.

- `FEEDBACK_AUDIBLE`

  Services that provide auditory, but not spoken, feedback.

- `FEEDBACK_SPOKEN`

  Spoken word services such as TalkBack.

- `FEEDBACK_BRAILLE`

  Braille services.

- `FEEDBACK_GENERIC`

  A catch-all property for services that don't fit into other feedback categories.

- `FEEDBACK_HAPTIC`

  Services providing haptic feedback.

- `FEEDBACK_VISUAL`

  Visual services such as overlays, color filters, etc.

Capabilities

These constants allow us to request accessibility services grouped by their abilities. Fetching services by their ability doesn't necessarily mean this capability is currently enabled or active. Services can fall into multiple capability categories.

- `CAPABILITY_CAN_CONTROL_MAGNIFICATION`

  Accessibility services that can control screen zoom levels.

- `CAPABILITY_CAN_PERFORM_GESTURES`

  Services that can mimic touch gestures on the device's screen.

- `CAPABILITY_CAN_REQUEST_FILTER_KEY_EVENTS`

  Any service that can request to filter the events received by your app from keys. This includes device hardware keys such as a camera button but also from connected devices such as keyboards and game pads.

- `CAPABILITY_CAN_REQUEST_FINGERPRINT_GESTURES`

  Accessibility services that can capture events and gestures from the device's fingerprint sensor.

- `CAPABILITY_CAN_REQUEST_TOUCH_EXPLORATION`

  Accessibility services, such as TalkBack, that allow users to explore UI elements by tapping them without necessarily activating them. This feature can also prevent certain touch gestures from being passed to your app if running.

- `CAPABILITY_CAN_RETRIEVE_WINDOW_CONTENT`

  These services can access the content of your app when presented in the current active window.

- `DEFAULT`

  The default value if no other capability is presented by the service. Passing this will return any running services.

Summary

- Android accessibility features vary by device and vendor. Extra accessibility services can be downloaded from the Google Play Store.
- Always use Android's provided UI elements, extending them where needed. Avoid creating your own controls, as it's almost impossible to match the accessibility features of the standard controls.

- Listen to your customers' preferences and respect them; failure to do this can cause frustrated customers.
- Try out the accessibility features available on your device; what's the worst that could happen? You might find something that helps you.

This chapter gave us an overview of the accessibility features and services available on Android phones. We also covered ways we, as developers, can support them better, ways the features might affect our apps, and how we can detect and respond to our customers' preferences. In the next chapter, we'll move on to iOS and start looking at how the accessibility system works for that platform.

CHAPTER 6

SwiftUI Accessibility Model

As with Apple's approach on all platforms, accessibility on iOS is locked down. There is no visibility into the accessibility subsystem and no way for developers to create custom assistive technologies. This provides strong security, since assistive technologies have hugely privileged access, having the ability to access all on-screen content and act on behalf of the user. However, this does mean that for users with specific requirements, it is not possible to build a custom assistive technology tailored to meet their exact needs.

The authors of SwiftUI have thought deeply about accessibility. Using system-provided controls will get you a lot of the way toward creating an accessible app. SwiftUI includes a comprehensive array of accessibility modifiers and APIs. Unfortunately, among some SwiftUI developers, this knowledge has somehow been misinterpreted as "SwiftUI is accessible by default" and therefore requires no further work. This is not true – SwiftUI is no more or less accessible than any other UI framework. While Apple's design provides strong foundations, it's your responsibility as a developer to use those APIs thoughtfully and test your app with real users and assistive technologies.

Accessibility Tree

As with Android, and indeed other platforms such as the Web, iOS creates a proxy representation of your app's views to expose data, metadata, and interaction details to assistive technologies. Commonly known as an Accessibility Tree, Apple sometimes refers to this as an "accessibility user interface" or "accessibility representation."

As is typical of Apple platforms, the details of this are hidden from us. The closest we can get is when running XCUI tests, when our test runner interacts with a modified version of the accessibility tree – something we'll return to in the later chapter on testing (Chapter 11).

R. Whitaker, *Developing Inclusive Mobile Apps*, https://doi.org/10.1007/979-8-8688-2809-6_6

As such, going any deeper into the implementation of the iOS accessibility system is neither helpful nor likely to remain accurate over time. But it is accurate to say that the declarative and state-driven nature of SwiftUI provides a great basis for the system to construct such a representation.

While we can't access or manipulate the accessibility tree directly, we can define how our views appear in the tree using a comprehensive set of accessibility modifiers to define our view's expected values and behaviors.

Custom Controls

The designers of SwiftUI's standard controls have provided all the accessibility properties they can to ensure the in-built controls, used in standard ways, will be more or less accessible. So, if you take one thing away from this chapter, let it be this: Use standard controls as the basis, then modify them as needed to achieve your desired look and behavior. Test your control with assistive technologies and make targeted accessibility adjustments where needed.

When making something custom, begin with the control that's closest in behavior to what you're creating. Then, where possible, apply a custom style (Listing 6-1) - this maintains much of the accessibility behaviors while allowing for customization of appearance.

Listing 6-1. Creating a custom style for a toggle

```
Toggle(isOn: $toggleOn) {
    Text("Tea")
}
.toggleStyle(ChecklistToggleStyle()) // applying a custom style
...
struct ChecklistToggleStyle: ToggleStyle {
    func makeBody(configuration: Configuration) -> some View {
        // Customize your toggle appearance here
    }
}
```

If you do need something entirely custom, the `accessibilityRepresentation` modifier is an incredibly powerful choice. We'll cover this API later in this chapter.

Adding or Removing Elements from the Tree

Any SwiftUI view can take part in the accessibility tree. However, by default, elements that don't present content, such as shapes and layout containers, aren't presented to assistive technologies – we'll look at cases where you may want to override this later in this chapter. Elements that generally do present content or are interactive are presented to assistive technologies by default.

The simplest way to add or remove an element from the accessibility tree is using the `.accessibilityHidden()`[1] modifier (Listing 6-2), passing `true` to hide an element that would otherwise be presented or `false` to show an element hidden by default.

Listing 6-2. Presenting a Circle to assistive technologies that would otherwise be hidden

```
Circle()
    .accessibilityLabel("Enabled")
    .foregroundStyle(.green)
    .accessibilityHidden(false)
```

If unhiding an element, such as in Listing 6-2, ensure you also add other accessibility properties as appropriate – in the example above, I have added a label. Otherwise, your accessibility tree will contain an empty node. The fundamentals of this are Name, Role, Value.

Name, Role, Value

As with the Android accessibility model (Chapter 4), we'll try to understand the iOS model by using the fundamental WCAG (Chapter 3) Success Criterion (SC) 4.1.2: Name, Role, Value. The essence of this SC is that any assistive technology must be able to determine a name, role, and value for any given element on screen.

In SwiftUI parlance, Name, Role, and Value to `accessibilityLabel`, `accessibilityAddTraits`/`accessibilityRemoveTraits`, and `accessibilityValue`. A common mistake I see is adding everything into the label – including the control type and value. There is a reason these attributes are separate: different assistive technologies and

[1] `https://developer.apple.com/documentation/swiftui/view/accessibilityhidden(_:)`

different configurations use each in different ways. Understanding when and where to apply each modifier is the fundamental building block of improving the accessibility of your SwiftUI code, so let's look at each in turn.

Accessibility Label

An element's Accessibility Label is the first string read by VoiceOver when an accessible element receives focus.[2] It identifies what that element is or does - think of this as your element's name. By default, most views already have an accessibility label - this is often your element's text. You'll need to add one if your view has no text value, such as an image button, or if your label wouldn't make sense when spoken aloud.

Ideally, labels should convey the meaning in one word, such as "Play" or "Like," for example. Your labels should be capitalized, and don't end them with a period.

Setting an element's accessibility label is done using the `.accessibilityLabel()` modifier, as in Listing 6-3.

Listing 6-3. Setting an accessibility label on an image

```
Image(systemName: "heart.fill")
    .accessibilityLabel("Like")
```

Traits

Trait values represent the type of a given element, or in WCAG parlance, the role. Traits provide data used by assistive technologies to determine how to interact with or how to present an element.[3] The key to traits is to keep them current - as the lifetime of your view changes, you may need to change traits along with it.

For example, if you create a stopwatch app, the time label will update every second, or millisecond, when the stopwatch is running. Here it would make sense to use the trait `.updatesFrequently`. When the user presses the Lap button and we freeze the readout, marking the label as `.updatesFrequently` no longer makes sense. Instead, we should set the trait to `.staticText`.

---

[2] https://developer.apple.com/documentation/swiftui/view/accessibilitylabel(_:)-5f0zj

[3] https://developer.apple.com/documentation/swiftui/accessibilitytraits

Use `.accessibilityAddTraits()` to add new traits, or `.accessibilityRemoveTraits()` to remove inherited ones as shown in Listing 6-4.

Listing 6-4. Adding and removing traits. A common need for this is buttons that open external links; these should have the link trait applied and the button trait removed

```
Button("Visit our website", action: openWebsite)
    .accessibilityAddTraits(.isLink)
    .accessibilityRemoveTraits(.isButton)
```

One trait is slightly different from the others: `.isSelected` represents state rather than a role. It should be applied to anything that is selected, such as a radio button or selectable row. It must be removed - or more likely in SwiftUI, not applied - as soon as the element is no longer selected.

Traits are numerous, and their behavior is not always intuitive, so I have covered them all here at a high level.

Button

This element is an interactive button. This trait causes VoiceOver to announce "button" after reading the text of the item. It also makes the element visible to assistive technologies that can interact with the screen.

Link

Link behaves like button but VoiceOver announces "link." This is an important distinction for screen reader users, so they know to expect this object will take them to a new context.

Search Field

A text field that allows your customer to enter a string to search. This trait differentiates this field from a standard text field. It hints to the user that entering text here should cause the UI to update elsewhere.

Image

Any image or visual element that has no text and no actions, that is, you shouldn't apply this trait to an image button. This enables AI-powered image exploration features in VoiceOver. See the discussion on Alternative Text for Images in Chapter 3 for guidance on when to make images accessible.

Selected

An item that is currently selected, such as a tab or item on a segmented control.

Plays Sound

An element that will trigger sound once activated. This tells VoiceOver to stop any utterances when this element is activated.

Keyboard Key

An item that acts as a key in an on-screen text input keyboard. Use this only when building a custom keyboard to ensure VoiceOver treats each key correctly.

Static Text

Text that is not editable and does not change throughout the life cycle of your view.

Summary Element

A summary element trait characterizes an area that provides an overview of the information on the screen. The best example of this is Apple's built-in Weather app (Figure 6-1). On opening a location, VoiceOver focuses on the top area, which is marked as a Summary Element. VoiceOver then reads a summary of the current weather conditions in the selected location.

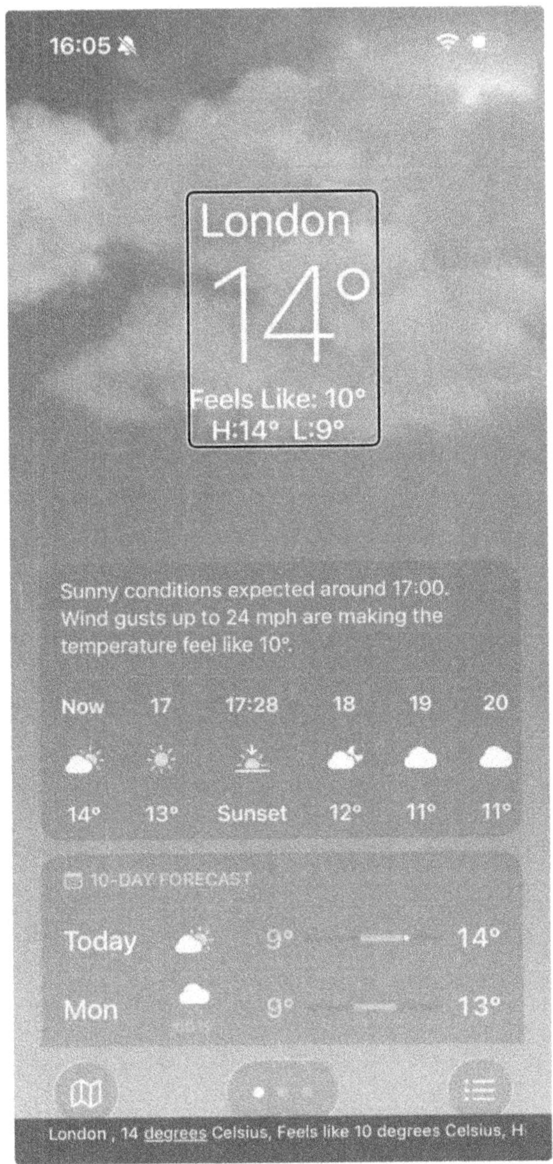

Figure 6-1. *Apple's Weather app with VoiceOver highlighting the top Summary Element*

Updates Frequently

This trait is for elements that update either their label or value frequently. This tells your user's chosen assistive technology to poll this element for value and label changes at suitable intervals.

Starts Media Session

Used for an element that starts playing or recording media once activated. This trait causes VoiceOver speech to be paused once the element is activated, preventing the media session from being interrupted.

Allows Direct Interaction

Allows Direct Interaction tells VoiceOver to provide a rotor option (See Chapter 8) to allow for direct touch interaction.

Imagine you have created a music app that provides a piano keyboard for the user to play (Figure 6-2). Using the VoiceOver paradigm of swiping to a key and double-tapping would not produce much of a tune. Allows Direct Interaction provides the option for your user to play the keyboard by tapping the keys without disabling VoiceOver for the rest of the UI.

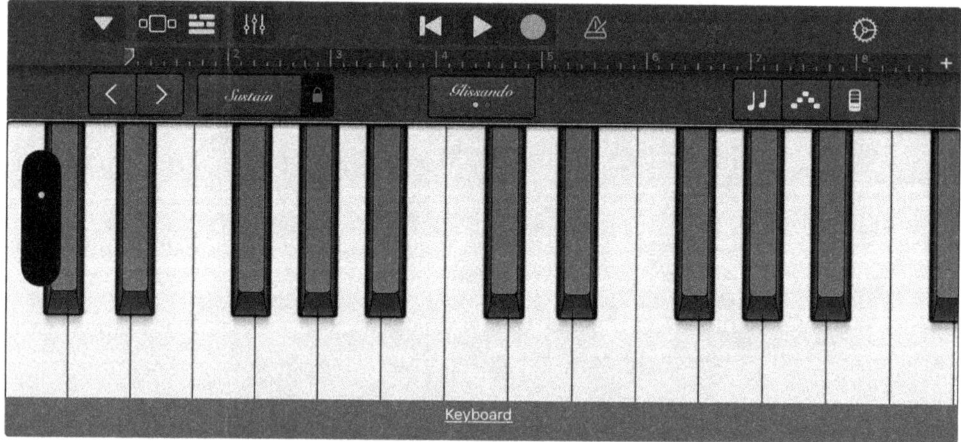

Figure 6-2. *Apple's GarageBand app with VoiceOver highlighting the keyboard view. This view has the trait "Allows Direct Interaction." Allowing multi-touch interaction on the keyboard while maintaining VoiceOver navigation of the controls above the keyboard*

Causes Page Turn

This trait indicates to screen readers that this content represents one page out of a set of pages, such as an eBook.

This trait causes a screen reader to call the `.accessibilityScrollAction{}` closure on this view immediately after completing reading the current content and will then begin to read any new content. Reading will stop if the content does not change after calling this function.

Header

The title of a navigation bar or any large text header element that divides content.

By swiping vertically, VoiceOver users can leverage this trait to skim your content. This helps determine which content is relevant to their needs without having to scan the whole screen.

Tab Bar

This trait indicates a view that is not directly interactive but contains tab buttons.

Modal

This trait causes assistive technologies to ignore the contents of any views that are not direct descendants of this view.

Accessibility Value

The accessibility value is the current value, or state, of an element.[4] This could be text entered in a text field, the current value of a slider, or the status of a switch, for example.

You'll need to set this yourself if you're creating a custom control, when you're grouping views with multiple values, or when the value provided by your chosen control may not make sense in the current context.

For example, a slider will always present a float value, but in many cases, we may want to resolve this to something more meaningful, such as an int or string. In Listing 6-5, I am setting an accessibility value using the `.accessibilityValue()` modifier to resolve a slider's float value to an appropriate string.

[4] `https://developer.apple.com/documentation/swiftui/view/accessibilityvalue(_:)-z9mo`

Listing 6-5. Setting an accessibility value for a slider

```
@State var value: Double = 0.0
Months = [
    "January", "February", "March", "April", "May",
    "June", "July", "August", "September", "October",
    "November", "December"]

var body: some View {
    Slider(value: $value, in: 0...11, step: 1)
    .accessibilityValue(months[Int(value)])
}
```

Adding or Removing from the Accessibility Tree

At times, it may be necessary to hide views from assistive technology that SwiftUI would generally expose. Decorative images are the most common example: if an SF Symbol or other image is used for visual emphasis rather than additional content, then it must be hidden from assistive technologies. Conversely, when building custom controls, you may need to expose elements that would generally be hidden, for example, shapes or stacks.

You can achieve both with the `.accessibilityHidden()` modifier shown in Listing 6-6, passing `true` to remove the element from the accessibility tree or `false` to add it.

Listing 6-6. Hiding a decorative SF Symbol is a common pattern in SwiftUI

```
Image(systemName: "heart.fill")
    .accessibilityHidden(true)
```

Navigation Order

Assistive technologies present the screen in natural reading order, from top left to bottom right in most languages. While this is correct in most instances, designs with staggered layouts or vertically stacked "value above label" patterns can produce an illogical reading order with VoiceOver.

A common design pattern for headline data is to present a large font statistic with the label below. This allows for great glanceability, especially if you're already familiar with the application, but when navigated linearly with VoiceOver, these elements will be out of order, and the meaning confusing.

To resolve this, one option is to adjust the navigation order. The modifier for this is `.accessibilitySortPriority()`. It takes a double as an argument, with higher numbers being sorted and therefore navigated before lower numbers. Sort priority is resolved on a peer level amongst elements in the same container. The default value is 0, so higher will be navigated first, and anything below that will come later. This means in many cases we may only need to set the value for a single object. In Listing 6-7 the text "Greeting" will be navigated before "Hello World!".

Listing 6-7. Setting navigation order of a label before a value

```
VStack {
    Text("Hello World!")

    Text("Greeting")
        .accessibilitySortPriority(1.0)
}
```

Accessibility Actions

Standard SwiftUI controls expose their primary action as the default accessibility action. Overriding the default accessibility action yourself is almost never required, and if you do reach the point where you feel you may need to do this, it could be a sign that the underlying construction of your control needs reconsideration. Still, the API as used in Listing 6-8 is valuable for other uses we'll cover below - so still worth touching on here.

Listing 6-8. Setting a custom default accessibility action

```
let action = { print("This button was tapped") }
let accessibilityAction = {
    print("This button was triggered with assistive technology")
}

Button("Button", action: action)
    .accessibilityAction(.default, accessibilityAction)
```

Escape

For many reasons, navigating an application with assistive technology is often slower than without. To reduce navigation effort, Apple provides some global shortcuts. Probably the most powerful of these is the Escape action.

Escape can be triggered with any assistive technology and either dismisses the current context or navigates back in the navigation stack, depending on what is currently presented. This behavior is provided automatically if you're using a regular navigation stack and system-provided modals such as alerts and sheets. However, if you present custom navigation or modals, it is important to implement the accessibility escape yourself as in Listing 6-9.

Figure 6-3. *Switch Control's Escape command on a modal screen*

Listing 6-9. Supporting the accessibility Escape command

```
VStack {
    // Your custom modal view
}
.accessibilityAction(.escape) {
    // dismiss the modal
}
```

Custom Actions

One great way to speed up accessibility navigation and create a far better experience for accessibility users is to use custom accessibility actions to expose additional actions. Custom actions allow us to provide access via assistive technology to actions that would otherwise be difficult to trigger - for example, actions requiring physical gestures. They also allow us to tidy up repetitive navigation steps by removing common actions from individual navigation.

These actions are available through any assistive technology. In Switch Control, they are presented in a HUD when an element is activated (Figure 6-4).

Figure 6-4. *Multiple custom accessibility actions on an item in the Files app. Note that the Delete action provides an icon. Other actions show a letter taken from the label as a visual differentiator*

To add a custom accessibility action, use a slightly different version of the `accessibilityAction` modifier. This version, shown in Listing 6-10, takes the action as the first argument; the second is a closure where you should provide exactly one Text item and one Image item. The text is the label that is announced by VoiceOver or shown in menus; the image is presented as an icon for Switch Control, as seen for the Delete action in Figure 6-4.

Listing 6-10. Adding a custom "Like" action to an image

```
HStack {
    // View content
}
// The element must be an accessible element to add a custom action
.accessibilityElement()
.accessibilityAction {
    likePost()
} label: {
  Text("Like")
  Image(systemName: "heart")
}
```

Adjustable

A further type of action is *Adjustable*. This gives assistive technologies the ability to increment and decrement a control's value; think of a volume slider or stepper control (Figure 6-5).

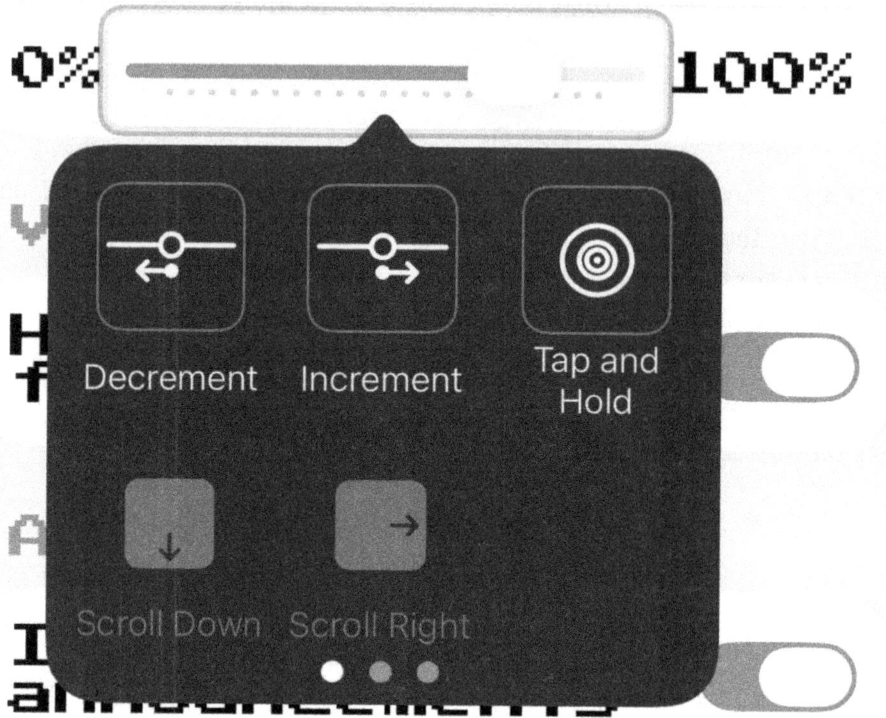

***Figure 6-5.** Switch Control's Increment and Decrement controls*

This capability can be added to any control by using the `accessibilityAdjustableAction` modifier shown in Listing 6-11. The modifier takes a single closure that is called with an `AccessibilityAdjustmentDirection` argument when the user adjusts the control with their assistive technology. Inside the closure, switch on the direction and update the value accordingly.

Listing 6-11. Adding an adjustable action to a custom stepper control

```
MyCustomStepper("Quantity", value: $value)
    .accessibilityAdjustableAction { direction in
        switch direction {
            case .increment:
                value += 1
            case .decrement:
                value -= 1
            }
    }
```

As with many standard controls, the correct functionality comes for free if you use the SwiftUI-provided Slider and Stepper. This modifier is only required when creating a custom control.

Further Actions

SwiftUI includes a couple of additional accessibility actions that follow a similar pattern to `accessibilityAdjustableAction`. `accessibilityZoomAction` provides you details about the zoom location and direction for you to handle, and `accessibilityScrollAction` passed details of the edge the user is scrolling toward.

While neither modifier is commonly used, if you're implementing a pull-to-refresh mechanism, you may need to add an `accessibilityScrollAction` that listens for scrolling at the top edge to trigger a refresh.

Focus

Any element exposed to the accessibility tree is focusable with VoiceOver. Other assistive technologies – Full Keyboard Access, Switch Control, and Voice Control – will only focus on interactive elements. In most cases, this works as expected if your controls, actions, and traits are correctly applied. If you do need to set this yourself, `.accessibilityRespondsToUserInteraction()` is the modifier you want.

Interactive elements don't automatically become focusable with the keyboard, however, meaning every interactive element which accepts input should have the `.focusable()` modifier applied. This is where having a strong design system for your app will pay dividends.

Detecting Focus

Both assistive technology focus and keyboard focus can be detected if necessary. Generally, it's best avoided, but there are valid use cases – for example, drawing a clearer focus highlight. You must not change the meaning or content of an element when it becomes focused, as this would likely fail WCAG SC 3.2.1.[5]

[5] https://www.w3.org/WAI/WCAG22/Understanding/on-focus.html

Focus detection uses parallel APIs (Listing 6-12) with different property wrappers: `@FocusState` for keyboard focus[6] and `@AccessibilityFocusState` for assistive technology focus.[7]

Listing 6-12. Detecting the focus status of a field in a set of fields

```
@FocusState var focusState
@AccessibilityFocusState var accessibilityFocusState

var body: some View {
    Button("Button", action: action)
        .focused($focusState)
        .accessibilityFocused($accessibilityFocusState)
// Note: Changing content based on focus is not recommended, this is purely
illustrative

    if focusState {
        Text("This view is focused with the keyboard")
    }
    if accessibilityFocusState {
         Text("This view is focused with an assistive technology")
   }
}
```

If your accessibility focus state only applies to certain assistive technologies, specify this in the property wrapper initializer, for example, Listing 6-13 shows how to detect focus for Switch Control only:

Listing 6-13. Defining focus state for Switch Control only

```
@AccessibilityFocusState(for: .switchControl)
```

This powerful API can adapt to work with multiple views. In Listing 6-12, we are checking the focus state for a single button using a Boolean check, but it is easy to conceive of a view where this would result in many focus properties in a single View struct. Both property wrappers also support using enums to identify views. In Listing 6-14, I have included only the accessibility focus state, but the same applies for the keyboard focus state.

[6] `https://developer.apple.com/documentation/swiftui/focusstate/`

[7] `https://developer.apple.com/documentation/swiftui/accessibilityfocusstate/`

Listing 6-14. Detecting the focus status of a field in a set of fields

```
enum MyFocusableElements {
    case field1, field2
}

@AccessibilityFocusState var accessibilityFocusState: MyFocusableElements?

var body: some View {
    VStack {
        TextField("Field 1", text: $field1Value)
            .accessibilityFocused($accessibilityFocusState, equals:
            .field1)

        TextField("Field 2", text: $field2Value)
            .accessibilityFocused($accessibilityFocusState, equals:
            .field2) // Note: Changing content based on focus is not
            recommended, this is purely illustrative

        switch accessibilityFocusState {
            case .field1:
                Text("Field 1 is focused")
            case .field2:
                Text("Field 2 is focused")
            case nil:
                Text("No field is focused")
        }
    }
}
```

Setting Focus

Setting focus on an element programmatically is something you can do using SwiftUI. It is, however, something you should never do. Moving a user's focus is at best a jarring change of context and is arguably an abuse of your user's trust. It is also not required for WCAG compliance. I include the APIs here as it is something I am commonly asked for; use of this should be reserved for the most exceptional circumstances.

Using the exact APIs we covered in Listings 6-12 and 6-14, you can move a user's focus by setting the property wrapped value. In our Boolean example, 6-12, set `accessibilityFocusState = true`. In our enum example, 6-14, set the enum that corresponds to the view on which you want to set focus: `accessibilityFocusState = .field1`.

Semantic Views

Creating semantic views is necessary if you want to take your app's accessibility to the next level. A semantic view is a view made of multiple elements grouped together for accessibility because they have meaning, or a semantic, together. This technique is about pulling together all the tools we have covered in this chapter. The aim is to make an interface that is simpler to understand and faster to navigate for accessibility customers.

You'll notice semantic views used regularly throughout iOS when you navigate using an assistive technology. Look at the table cell in Figure 6-6 from iOS's Files app. There are several pieces of information here: the file name, date, size, and a button to download. If these were presented individually, that would be four swipes with VoiceOver. And it wouldn't be clear which file would be downloaded if we activated the download button. Instead, VoiceOver presents the row as a single element, reducing navigation effort and clarifying context.

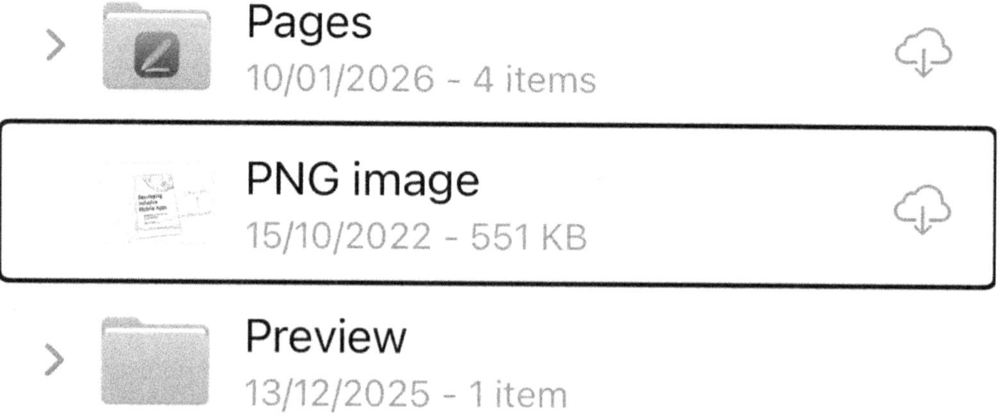

Figure 6-6. *VoiceOver highlighting a row and its content as one semantic view*

Fortunately, SwiftUI makes creating these views simple. Often, adding just one modifier to your existing views will make a massive difference. The key to this is using SwiftUI's system of Stacks, or a Group if you have no suitable Stack already. Once you know which Stack will be the frame for your semantic view, the modifier to apply is `.accessibilityElement(children: )`[8] with the appropriate child behavior enum value. Once you've defined your container, you can further refine its accessibility by applying other modifiers beneath.

Combine

Using an argument of `.combine` will take all the accessibility properties - labels, values, actions, etc. - of the contained views and apply them to the view to which this modifier is applied, creating a single accessible element. The code for Figure 6-6 could look something like Listing 6-15:

Listing 6-15. Combining views into a single accessible element

```
HStack {
    VStack {
        Text("PNG image")
        Text("15/10/2022 - 551 kilobytes")
    }

    Button {
        // Download action
    } label: {
        Image(systemName: "icloud.and.arrow.down")
    }
    .accessibilityLabel("Download")
}
.accessibilityElement(children: .combine)
```

[8] https://developer.apple.com/documentation/swiftui/view/accessibilityelement(children:)/

If you navigate this with VoiceOver, you'll notice SwiftUI has added a comma between the first and second Text elements to create the accessibility label "PNG image, 15/10/2022 – 551 kilobytes." This works fine for simple cases; if we wanted to refine the label only, we could add an `.accessibilityLabel()` modifier. However, for more complex cases we probably want a little more control; this is where the next argument comes in.

Ignore

The child behavior argument of `.ignore` turns our stack into an element that appears on the accessibility tree, as above, but discards any of the accessibility properties inherited from child elements. Ideal when we need to do something custom, but this does require that you manually apply all the required accessibility information, and you'll need to remember to update this if anything changes in the child elements.

Contain

The final argument is `.contain`. This provides a powerful option to add clarity and speed of navigation to groups of content. One of the most common uses for this is horizontally scrolling carousel-type elements. For example, Figure 6-7 shows a list of search filter options.

***Figure 6-7.** A horizontal scrolling list of search filter options*

Visually, we can determine the purpose of these options by glancing at each label, and we don't have to scroll new content on to the screen to determine this. But for VoiceOver users, they may need to navigate through each individual item to gain that context. Plus, VoiceOver or Full Keyboard Access users may have to navigate through each item in the, possibly very long, list to be able to reach content underneath.

We can resolve both issues by creating an accessible container. This is done by adding the `.accessibilityElement(children: .contain)` modifier and an accessibility label (Listing 6-16).

Listing 6-16. Creating an accessible container

```
HStack {
    // Horizontally scrolling content
}
.accessibilityElement(children: .contain)
.accessibilityLabel("Filters")
```

The exact behavior this gives your user varies by their settings and assistive technology. But by containing the elements, the entire group becomes easily skippable, while the label provides crucial context when the group, or an item inside it, first receives focus with VoiceOver.

CREATING SEMANTIC VIEWS

Apple makes use of semantic views in the App Store. When looking at a listing page for an app or game, we see a row of boxes under the app's icon (Figure 6-8). These boxes contain details such as the app's rating, developer, and age rating. The first item, the app's rating, displays "1.6M ratings," then on a new line "4.9," and finally "★★★★★." Additionally, each of these boxes is a button. If you access these elements with VoiceOver enabled with no changes to the accessibility tree, VoiceOver might behave something like this:

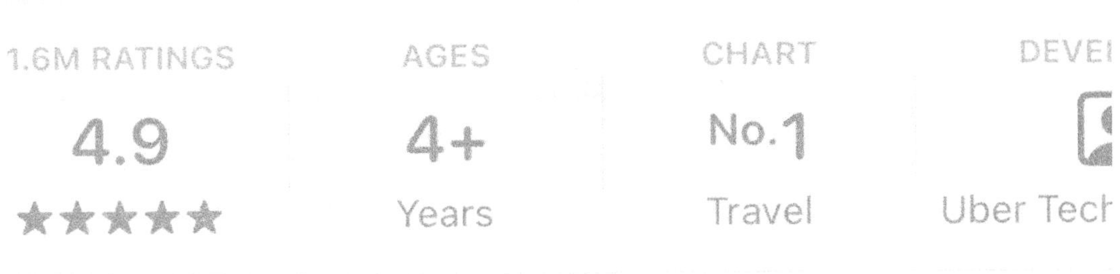

Figure 6-8. *App Store app info*

"1.6M ratings" Swipe.

"Ages Swipe

"Chart" Swipe.

"4.9, Button" Swipe.

"4+, Button" Swipe.

"No. 1, Button" Swipe.

"star star star star star" Swipe.

"Years" Swipe

"Travel" Swipe

That's a lot of swiping. For example, on one swipe we only hear the word "years" with no context provided. What does 4.9 refer to? Fortunately, this isn't how VoiceOver actually presents this view. The App Store developers have improved their accessibility tree to provide a better experience. Instead, this is the interaction:

"1.6M ratings, 4.9, Button" Swipe.

"Ages, 4 plus, Years, Button." Swipe.

"Chart, 1, No, Travel, Button"

Grouping these elements together has several benefits. Firstly, it significantly reduces the number of swipes needed to navigate the section. Grouping-related elements like the app review value and the number of reviews provide better context to what each value means.

In the GitHub repo for this book, open the Exercise 6-1 folder. I've built something that looks similar using SwiftUI. Put the techniques we've learned in this chapter to use to make a more accessible experience than what we get for free with SwiftUI, something closer to what you can experience in the App Store. I think there are further refinements to be had here, so I've included my solution too, if you want to compare it.

Labeled Content

There is one semantic view that SwiftUI provides for you that is a small addition but can make a big improvement for VoiceOver users. A very common pattern on iOS is to provide a value along with a label; this is often achieved by using two `Text`s in an `HStack`, but this requires two navigation interactions with VoiceOver. And if you have multiple pairs, it's not always clear which label corresponds to which value.

SwiftUI provides a construct for this pattern: `LabeledContent` (Listing 6-17).[9] Using this joins the label and value together for VoiceOver, resulting in more efficient and clearer navigation.

Listing 6-17. Linking a label and value

```
LabeledContent("Beans", value: "5")
```

If the appearance isn't for you, you have the option to create a `LabeledContentStyle`. This custom style will retain the accessibility benefits of using LabeledContent but allow the customization needed to get the appearance that matches your design. In Listing 6-18, we're creating a `LabeledContent` that will switch between a `VStack` and an `HStack`, depending on the user's chosen text size.

Listing 6-18. An adaptive LabeledContent

```
struct ContentView: View {
    var body: some View {
        LabeledContent("Beans", value: "5")
            .labeledContentStyle(MyLabeledContentStyle())
    }
}

struct MyLabeledContentStyle: LabeledContentStyle {
    @Environment(\.dynamicTypeSize.isAccessibilitySize) var
    accessibilitySize

    func makeBody(configuration: Configuration) -> some View {
        if accessibilitySize {
            VStack {
                configuration.label
                configuration.content
            }
        } else {
            HStack {
                configuration.label
```

[9] https://developer.apple.com/documentation/swiftui/labeledcontent/

```
                configuration.content
            }
        }
    }
}
```

Accessibility Representation

An incredibly powerful API that SwiftUI provides us is `accessibilityRepresentation`.[10] But remember – with great power comes great responsibility – this API has a specific use case.

You're in the situation I warned about earlier in this chapter, and you have no choice but to make a custom control to get the exact look and feel that works best for your application. We could use the techniques we discussed above to add the correct properties and behaviors to our control. Before doing that, consider the core functionality of your control. If it's a behavior that SwiftUI provides in a standard control, wouldn't it be great if we could just swap our custom control for a standard one in the accessibility tree? That's precisely what `accessibilityRepresentation` affords us.

A common use for this is when creating a custom Stepper – in part because they are often custom designs, but also because the Stepper in SwiftUI has no style modifier. You can construct a stepper easily with two buttons and a text element to show the current value, but making this accessible would require several modifiers. The system Stepper already exposes the correct adjustable actions, traits, and value updates for free.

As with the semantic views, ensure your custom stepper is inside a Stack or Group, and apply `.accessibilityRepresentation { }` passing a Stepper in the closure as in Listing 6-19.

Listing 6-19. Replacing a custom control's accessibility representation with a new one

```
HStack {
    Button("+") {
```

[10] `https://developer.apple.com/documentation/swiftui/view/accessibilityrepresentation(representation:)/`

```
            value += 1
        }
        Text("\(value)")
        Button("-") {
            value -= 1
         }
}
.accessibilityRepresentation {
    Stepper("Quantity", value: $value)
}
```

Summary

- The system that controls how assistive technologies interact with your app is shared across all iOS's assistive technologies and uses a representation of your view commonly known as an accessibility tree.
- iOS does a lot for us out of the box; stick with standard iOS controls for your views, and your app's accessibility will be okay. Test your app, ideally with real accessibility users, to find out where you need to make tweaks.
- SwiftUI provides a comprehensive range of accessibility modifiers to add or change accessibility properties, such as adding traits, labels, and actions.
- Semantic views are created by adding accessibility values to stacks and are an essential technique to take your app's accessibility to the next level.

Now that you know how iOS accessibility works under the hood, let's cover some of the accessibility tools iOS has available for your customers. We'll find out how you can best support them and what considerations you might need to make if you find your customer has enabled one of these features.

CHAPTER 7

iOS Accessibility Features – General

Apple's Human Interface Guidelines[1] (often known as the HIG) are essential reading for anyone creating mobile apps for iOS – not just designers. The HIG sets out how Apple has worked to make SwiftUI flexible for you as an app developer to create a distinctive look and feel while building clear, meaningful, and consistent interactions for our users.

The section on Accessibility[2] is the starting point when considering how to introduce accessibility to your iOS app. The HIG gives you the best overview of using iOS's built-in accessibility considerations. Keeping your apps consistent with this guide (not just the accessibility section) will help your users feel at home within your app, as many of the system patterns designed by Apple will carry over into your app and others. Plus, following this guide and ensuring a high level of accessibility improves your chance of getting featured on the App Store.

> *When you design for accessibility, you reach a larger audience and create a more inclusive experience. An accessible interface allows people to experience your app or game regardless of their capabilities or how they use their devices. Accessibility makes information and interactions available to everyone.*
>
> —Apple Human Interface Guidelines: Accessibility

In this chapter, we'll cover iOS system-wide accessibility features, why someone may enable them, and how having them enabled might affect your app. This is not an exhaustive list of accessibility settings; for more details on what's available from an

[1] `https://developer.apple.com/design/human-interface-guidelines/`

[2] `https://developer.apple.com/design/human-interface-guidelines/accessibility/overview/introduction/`

R. Whitaker, *Developing Inclusive Mobile Apps*, https://doi.org/10.1007/979-8-8688-2809-6_7

end-user perspective, see the accessibility section of Apple's website.[3] Instead, this chapter focuses on accessibility settings that might change the way your app looks or works or settings that might require you to add code or make decisions to best support them.

SwiftUI will do much of the accessibility work for you but will still require some customization. If you're creating a non-native app through web views or another cross-platform system, accessibility tools will often ape those of the system you're compiling for. Ultimately, as with anything cross-platform, features will vary and may be limited.

The Accessibility menu is a top-level menu in the system settings (Figure 7-1), grouped under four headings covering the class of impairment the technology is aimed to help with - general, vision, hearing, and physical and motor.

[3] www.apple.com/uk/accessibility

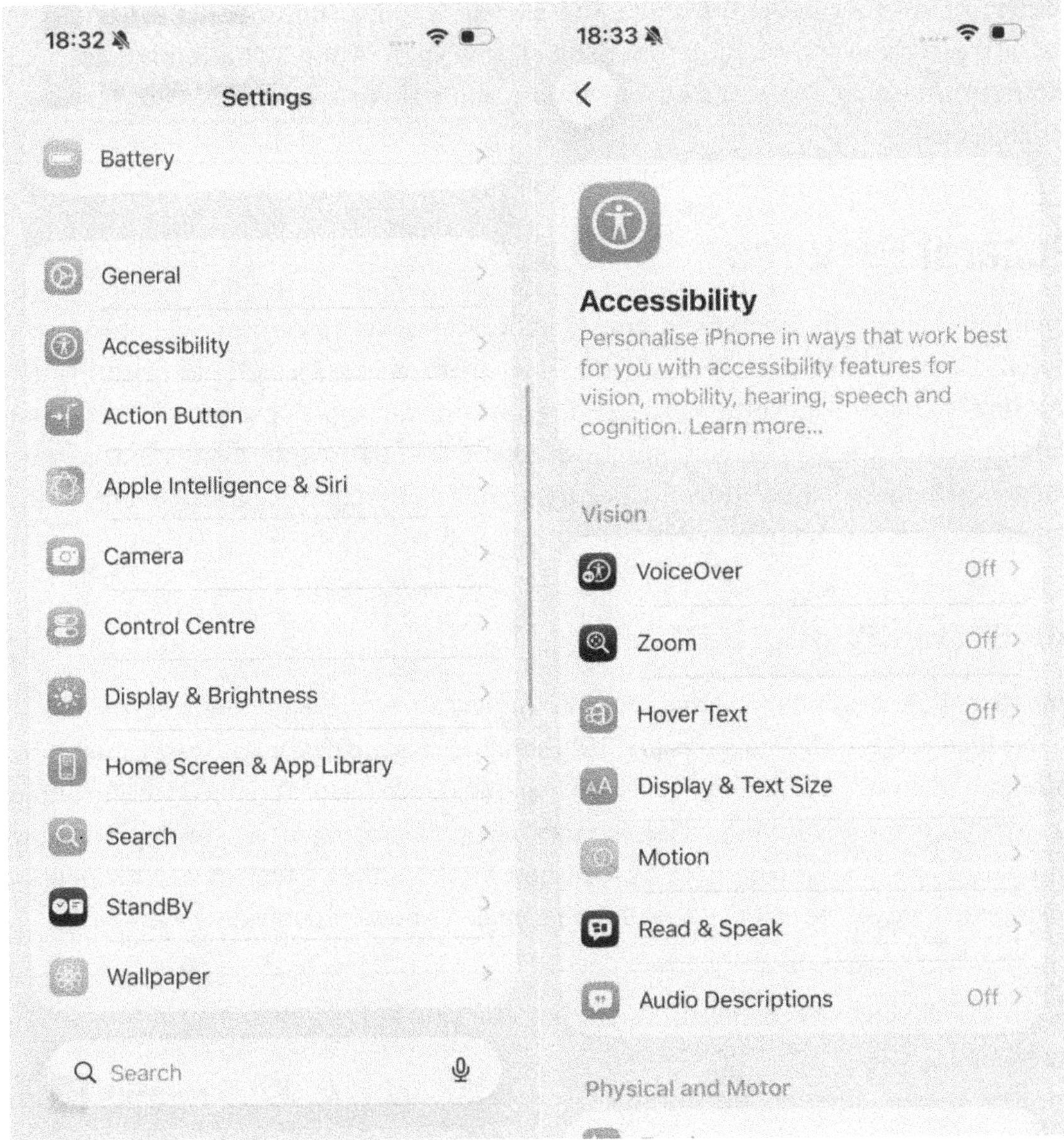

***Figure 7-1.** Accessibility settings in iOS*

Each accessibility option in this menu provides a short description of what enabling this option does. Each option is instantly enabled and present system-wide once triggered. Guided Access requires an additional step to activate the feature once enabled.

Take some time to go through this menu, enabling each one, navigate through your app, and see how each option changes how your app looks and behaves. No setting is destructive and can be instantly disabled. Some settings, however, such as VoiceOver, do change how your device functions. So it's worth reading a little about the features first, at least so you know how to turn them off when you're done. This menu is all about customizability, so you may find options you want to keep enabled on your personal device.

General Features

Apple breaks down its accessibility considerations into four categories - cognitive, motor, vision, and hearing. For this reason, I have broken the accessibility settings into four similar categories. Motor, vision, and hearing mirror Apple's categories. While there aren't specific settings to benefit those with cognitive impairments, many other settings will also help those falling into this category. In this first section, we'll cover some of the general settings and features of iOS.

Accessibility Shortcut

I mention the Accessibility Shortcut[4] first, as this will allow you a quick and easy way to enable many accessibility features on iOS. Therefore, it is the best way to test your apps' work with many iOS accessibility tools. Having this simple feature enabled will encourage you to activate these features as a regular part of your development and testing workflows. Importantly, it's also the simplest way to disable these features, which can save a lot of frustration once you've enabled a feature that changes how your device works.

Tip Enable the Accessibility Shortcut before trying out anything else in this chapter.

Enable the accessibility shortcut in the accessibility settings on your device by going to Settings ➤ Accessibility ➤ Accessibility Shortcut. You'll find the Accessibility Shortcut option near the bottom of the list. I highly recommend enabling nearly every item on the list (Figure 7-2), so you can try these out quickly when needed. Keeping them enabled gives you pain-free access to accessibility tools when you want to check something out. The options available on this menu vary depending on the settings for your device and OS version.

[4] https://support.apple.com/en-us/111771

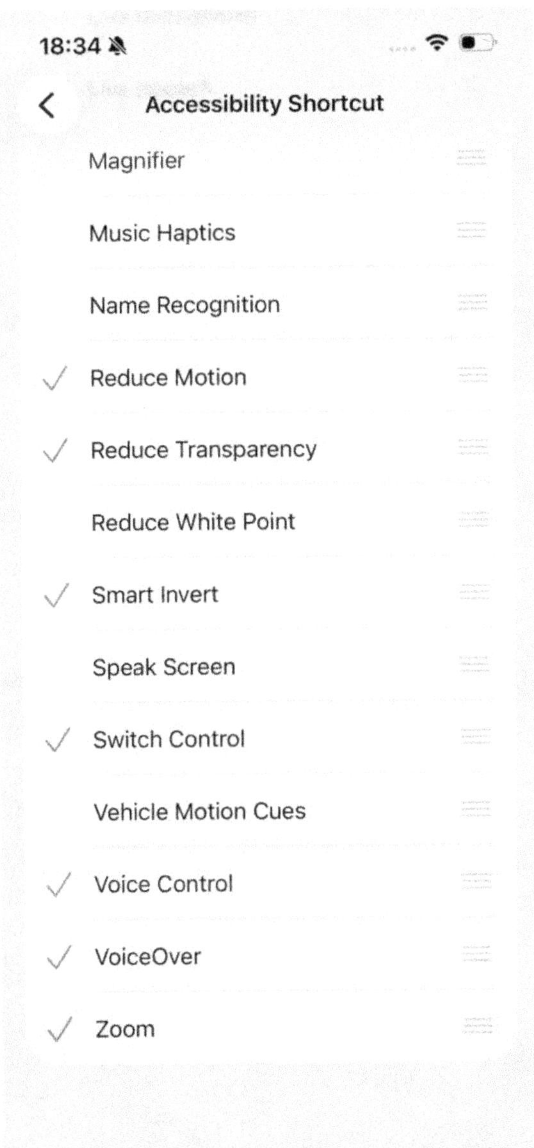

Figure 7-2. *Enable every option in this list that you may want easy access to later*

You can then activate the accessibility shortcut when required by triple tapping the side button. This presents a modal menu (Figure 7-3) where you can activate or deactivate the features you chose from the preceding list.

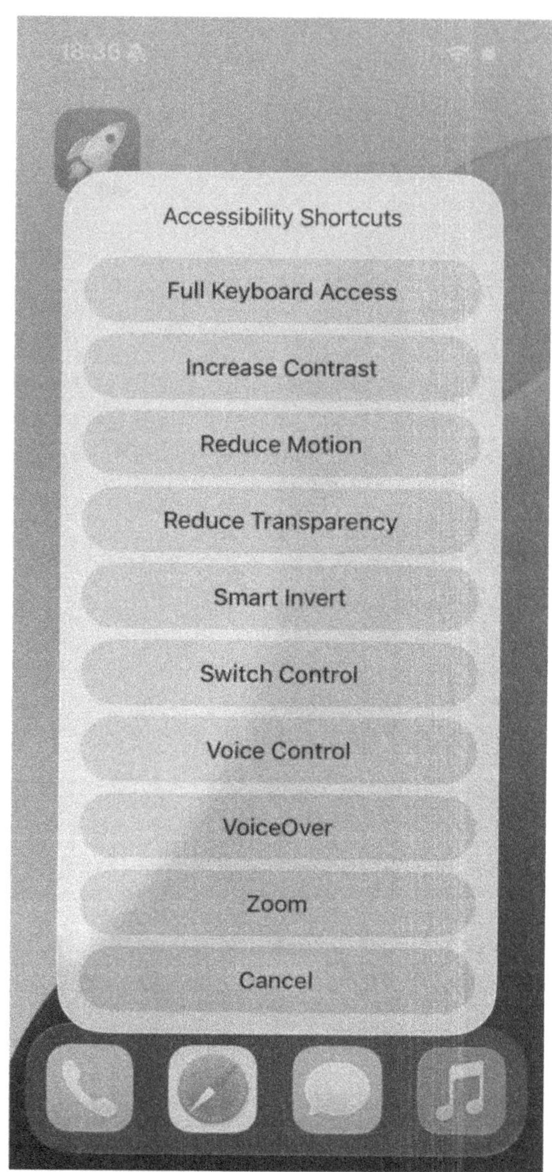

Figure 7-3. *Accessibility shortcut activated after pressing the side button three times*

Control Center

A second quick access way to toggle accessibility features is through Control Center. Swiping down from the top of the screen will show a bunch of buttons providing quick access to common device controls (Figure 7-4). The controls displayed are customizable via a long press gesture. Some accessibility settings are adjustable here directly; for others, you can add the Accessibility Shortcut tile, providing the same options we enabled in settings in the previous section.

Figure 7-4. *Control Center with accessibility controls on the bottom four rows. L–R: Dark mode, accessibility shortcut, Full Keyboard Access, Voice Control, Increase Contrast, Switch Control, Reduce Transparency, Reduce Motion, Smart Invert, Hover Text, text size slider, Hover Typing, Speak Screen, VoiceOver*

Guided Access

Guided Access[5] allows a device to be locked only to the current app and to disable certain app and system features. Guided Access makes the device into a standalone kiosk device and is often used in retail settings where you might not wish to give the public unrestricted access to a device. Guided Access is primarily designed, however, to be helpful for people with a range of needs: by preventing accidental input and settings changes, it ensures consistent device behavior and eliminates the possibility of the device getting into a state where the user can't interact with it.

Guided Access needs to be enabled in the device's accessibility settings. Once enabled, it can be activated by using the accessibility shortcut of pressing the side button three times (Figure 7-5). Guided Access is enabled per-app session and must be disabled to exit the app.

[5] https://support.apple.com/en-us/111795

Figure 7-5. *Setting up Guided Access*

There is no SwiftUI API for Guided Access at the time of writing, but you can detect if Guided Access is activated by checking `UIAccessibility.isGuidedAccessEnabled` and receive updates from `guidedAccessStatusDidChangeNotification` (Listing 7-1) when this setting is changed. In your app, you can use the status of this setting to decide whether to lock down individual features, such as settings, or destructive actions.

Listing 7-1. Registering for notifications in guided access status

```
import UIKit
class MyViewController: UIViewController {
    var guidedAccessStatus: Bool {
        get{
            return UIAccessibility.isGuidedAccessEnabled
        }
    }
    override func viewDidLoad() {
        super.viewDidLoad()
        NotificationCenter.default.addObserver(
            self,
            selector: #selector(guidedAccessChanged),
            name: UIAccessibility
                .guidedAccessStatusDidChangeNotification,
            object: nil
        )
    }
    @objc
    func guidedAccessChanged() {
      // check guidedAccessStatus for current value.
      // Hide features as appropriate.
    }
}
```

A better way to use this is to implement the `UIGuidedAccessRestrictionDelegate`[6] on startup of your app. This delegate allows you to set custom actions that can be enabled or disabled on request when a customer enables guided access within your app. For example, you might add restrictions for accessing Settings or destructive actions like Delete. This could then be configured by the person setting up guided access to enable the guided access user to customize settings to their preferences but not allow them to delete any items.

[6] https://developer.apple.com/documentation/uikit/uiguidedaccessrestrictiondelegate

First, we need to create unique strings for each feature our users might want to disable. Creating these as an enum (Listing 7-2) allows us to keep this type safe and provide the additional data we need.

Listing 7-2. Providing unique strings for Guided Access features

```
enum Restriction: String, CaseIterable {
    case settings = "com.myCompany.myApp.restriction.settings"

    case delete = "com.myCompany.myApp.restriction.delete"

}
```

Next, we need human-readable strings for iOS to display to our customer – a short string used as a button label, then a longer descriptive string. Let's extend our enum in Listing 7-3 to associate those values with the unique string.

Listing 7-3. Associating human-readable strings with our restrictions enum

```
extension Restriction {
    var title: String {
        switch self {
        case .settings:
            return "Settings"
        case .delete:
            return "Delete"
        }
    }
    var detail: String {
        switch self {
        case .settings:
            return "Allow changing settings"
        case .delete:
            return "Allow permanent deletion of items"
        }
    }
}
```

Now we need to provide these strings to iOS in our app delegate by conforming to the `UIGuidedAccessRestrictionDelegate` (Listing 7-4). There are two protocol methods and one property we need to implement. The `guidedAccessRestrictionIdentifiers` variable is an array of unique strings for iOS and our app to identify features. Then we have two functions, `textForGuidedAccessRestriction` and `detailTextForGuidedAccessRestriction`, where we provide our human-readable strings. To keep things neat in our app delegate, let's do this in an extension.

Listing 7-4. Providing our Guided Access strings to iOS

```
extension AppDelegate: UIGuidedAccessRestrictionDelegate {
    var guidedAccessRestrictionIdentifiers: [String]? {
        return Restriction.allCases.map { $0.rawValue }
    }

    func textForGuidedAccessRestriction(
        withIdentifier restrictionIdentifier: String)
        -> String? {
            return Restriction(
                rawValue: restrictionIdentifier
            )?.title
    }

    func detailTextForGuidedAccessRestriction(
        withIdentifier restrictionIdentifier: String)
        -> String? {
            return Restriction(
                rawValue: restrictionIdentifier
            )?.detail
    }
}
```

Finally, we need to handle iOS's callbacks when our user changes the Guided Access status of a feature (Listing 7-5). For this, we need to conform to another delegate function in our extension, `guidedAccessRestriction(withIdentifier restrictionIdentifier: didChange: )`. This function provides us with a `newRestrictionState` enum value of either `.allow` or `.deny`.

Listing 7-5. Handling user changes in Guided Access feature status

```
    extension AppDelegate: UIGuidedAccessRestrictionDelegate {

...

func guidedAccessRestriction(
    withIdentifier restrictionIdentifier: String,
    didChange newRestrictionState: UIAccessibility
        .GuidedAccessRestrictionState
    ) {
        switch restrictionIdentifier {
        case Restriction.settings.rawValue:
            if newRestrictionState == .deny {
                // remove settings feature
            } else {
                // add settings feature
            }
        case Restriction.delete.rawValue:
            if newRestrictionState == .deny {
                // remove delete feature
            } else {
                // add delete feature
            }
        default:
            preconditionFailure()
        }
    }
}
```

Additionally, your app can query the `guidedAccessRestrictionState(forIdentifier: String)` function on the `UIAccessibility` API at any time to determine the status of a restriction (Listing 7-6). This can then be used to decide whether to deny an action or perhaps, preferably, hide an option altogether.

Listing 7-6. Detecting the status of a Guided Access restriction

```
import UIKit
class MyViewController: UIViewController {
    override func viewDidLoad() {
        super.viewDidLoad()
        let deleteFeatureState = UIAccessibility
        .guidedAccessRestrictionState(
            forIdentifier: Restriction.delete.rawValue
        )

        switch deleteFeatureState {
        case .allow:
            // enable the delete feature
        case .deny:
            // disable the delete feature
        @unknown default:
            preconditionFailure()
        }
    }
}
```

Assistive Access

Assistive Access[7] is a more modern feature intended to allow people with cognitive disabilities to use their device independently. Rather than locking down the device to a single app as Guided Access does, it entirely changes the look and feel of the software on the device to a much more pared-down and consistent interface. In this mode, the person who sets up Assistive Access can choose which apps are available. Any iOS app can be supported, but apps that aren't optimized for Assistive Access are relegated to a "more apps" section.

Supporting Assistive Access may not be appropriate for all apps, but before you rule out your app, consider whether by streamlining the experience, you can create a version of your app optimized for Assistive Access.

[7] https://support.apple.com/en-gb/guide/assistive-access-iphone/welcome/ios

If your app is already intended for use by those with cognitive impairments, add the `UISupportsFullScreenInAssistiveAccess` key to your app's info.plist and set the value to true. This enables your app to run in Assistive Access mode with no further modifications. To support this, you will need to ensure your app's layout is adaptive, as the frame in which your app is displayed will be reduced compared to regular iOS.

Assistive Access Scene

For other apps, you can create an `AssistiveAccess` scene (Listing 7-7) explicitly providing your optimized Assistive Access experience. First, add `UISupportsAssistiveAccess` to your app's info.plist and set the value to true. Then add your AssistiveAccess scene with the optimized Assistive Access view to your app as below.

Listing 7-7. Adding an Assistive Access scene to your application

```
@main
struct MyApp: App {
  var body: some Scene {
// Your existing app scene
    WindowGroup {
      ContentView()
    }
    // Add an assistive access scene
    AssistiveAccess {
        // Add your new assistive access optimized view
        AssistiveAccessContentView()
    }
  }
}
```

Importantly, the view you pass to your `AssistiveAccess` scene should be a separate, paired-down version of your app's UI. While still using SwiftUI, the UI of your app is rendered differently compared to regular SwiftUI interfaces, and the exact appearance may vary depending on your users' Assistive Access settings (Figure 7-6).

Figure 7-6. *Camera as an Assistive Access app*

This Assistive Access experience should include your app's core functionality. Aim to reduce cognitive load by reducing the requirement for making decisions, simplifying the UI, and removing opportunities for accidental actions.

To achieve this, avoid branching navigation, instead preferring a refined, linear navigation stack that guides users through any required choices. Remove destructive actions where possible, or if not, ensure these have a double confirmation mechanism to prevent accidental destruction. Meaningful UI should be represented in both text and images, allowing people to infer meaning in the mode that most suits them. Remove any timing-based UI.

If you need to determine if assistive access is enabled to remove or adjust functionality, you can do this by querying the `accessibilityAssistiveAccessEnabled` environment property as in Listing 7-8.

Listing 7-8. Detecting the status of Assistive Access

```
@Environment(\.accessibilityAssistiveAccessEnabled) var
accessibilityAssistiveAccessEnabled
```

Localization

Localization is built throughout iOS. While translating your app into different languages can be complex and nuanced, the coding to support this is not. You may feel your app doesn't need localization as your business is currently only available in one country, but this doesn't reflect our global society. A sizable number of people in any market will not have the market's primary language as their first.

SwiftUI APIs mean the technical work of localization is nearly all done. In many cases, creating a String Catalog and hitting ⌘ + B may be all that's needed. For strings that are not in views, you will need to update the String initializer you're using - see Making Strings localizable.

The first step is adding a String Catalog. In your project hit ⌘ + N and search for "string" (Figure 7-7). Ensure you select "String Catalog" and not one of the legacy options.

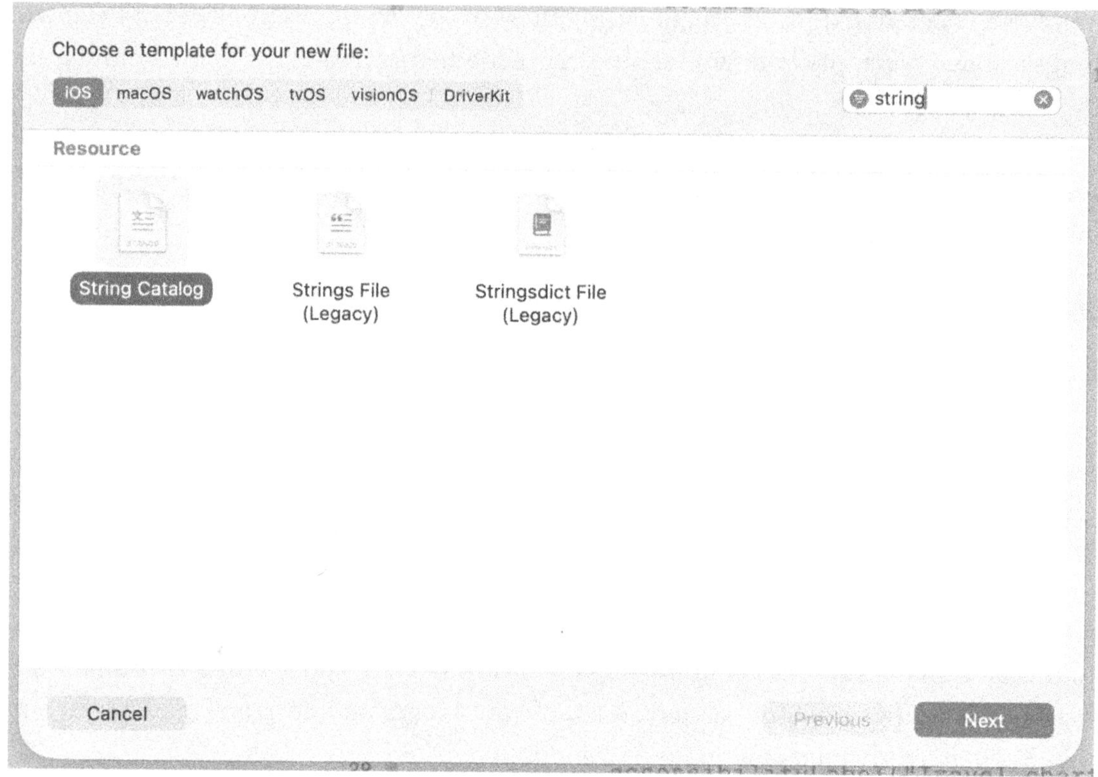

Figure 7-7. *Creating a String Catalog*

Hit ⌘ + B to build your project, and all strings used directly in standard SwiftUI views will be added to your new catalog. To add a new localization, hit the + button in the bottom left and select your language (highlighted in Figure 7-8). This presents your strings in a tabular format, showing exactly which strings have been localized and what the localization is. Xcode also shows you the percentage progress of your localization. You can then choose File ➤ Export to generate a catalog to send to a localization service.

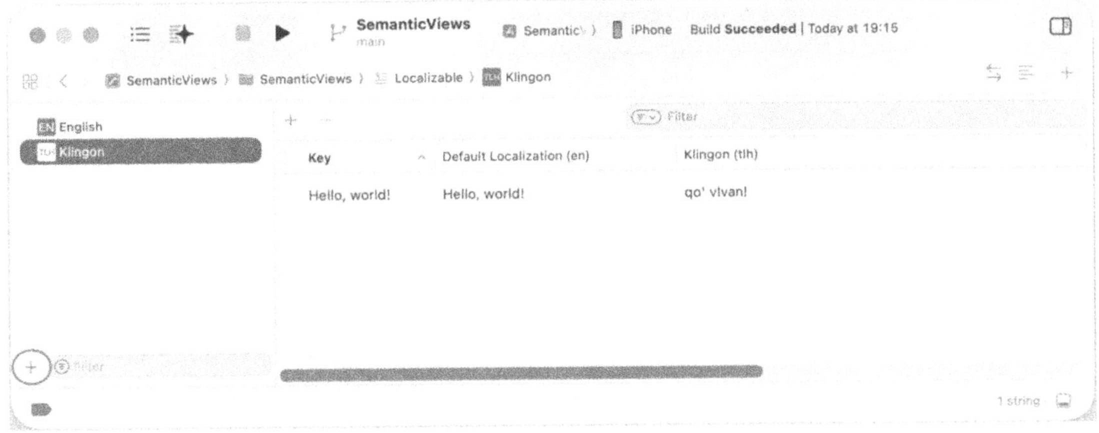

Figure 7-8. *A string catalog with translation added*

Making Strings Localizable

Strings used directly in SwiftUI initializers for elements such as Text and Button will appear in the String Catalog automatically when you build your project. For any strings created outside of these initializers, you'll need to use a specific String initializer (Listing 7-9). This will then appear in your String Catalog to be localized, and the string can be used in your code the same as the non-localized version.

Listing 7-9. Creating a localizable string

```
let bannerHeadline = String(
    localized: "Fresh for you",
    comment: "Headline for what's new section"
)
```

This initializer includes a comment; this is context you provide to your translation service to help the translator, or AI, understand the usage of the string and produce the most accurate translation. Comments can also be added to strings in initializers for SwiftUI Text elements (Listing 7-10), allowing you to provide a comment anywhere in your view code - for example, a Button initializer.

Listing 7-10. Providing a comment for your localization service

```
Text(
        "View details",
        comment: "Button label to show more information about an item"
    )
```

Views

Localizing views is all about following good layout practices, much like supporting dynamic type. It is not possible to guarantee that the visual length of your string will be the same for each localization. Many languages take up much more space than English. English's 12-character localization becomes the 13-character Lokalisierung in German, while in simplified Chinese, it's the 3-character 本土化. You can test this using pseudolanguage; we'll cover this in Chapter 11.

Ensure your designs, and the way you have built those designs in code, provide space for text to grow or shrink. Truncating text is acceptable, providing you can tap on it to view in full on a detail screen. For example, making a full table view showing all text would cause a lot of scrolling. If you have text that is not inside a scroll view, that won't have the space needed to grow.

Accessibility Nutrition Labels

Accessibility nutrition labels[8] were introduced in iOS 18. They are not part of your app but part of your app's App Store listing. They allow users to make informed decisions before downloading an app about whether an app will be suitable for their needs. Users can also specify these labels when searching the app store, meaning if your app supports accessibility features, it may be ranked higher in search results.

Nutrition labels cover the following features: VoiceOver, Voice Control, Larger Text, Dark Appearance, Differentiate Without Color, Sufficient Contrast, Reduced Motion, Captions, and Audio Descriptions - more on supporting each of these in the following chapters.

[8] https://developer.apple.com/help/app-store-connect/manage-app-accessibility/overview-of-accessibility-nutrition-labels

Guidance on how to test and when it is appropriate to show your app supports each feature can be found in Apple's documentation[9]; we will cover this more in chapter 11. The key guideline Apple provides is that these flags should apply to "common tasks." What a common task means in your app will depend on its functionality, but as guidance, Apple suggests primary functionality; features that appear in your app store listing description or screenshots; mandatory tasks, such as onboarding and account login or signup; or anything that you would ship a hotfix for if it were broken.

Ensure you keep the label status accurate and up to date. As with the rest of your App Store metadata, if Apple finds any of your responses to be inaccurate, your app could be rejected or delayed during app review.

Summary

- Read Apple's Human Interface Guidelines. It's the last word in making your app feel at home on iOS for all your users. Follow the advice Apple set out here, and you're more likely to have your app featured on the App Store and less likely to get an app review rejection.
- Enable the accessibility shortcut before continuing with the book, and keep it enabled even after you've finished reading. It gives you quick access to popular accessibility tools and will help with pain-free accessibility testing.
- Preparing your app for localization is good practice as it removes hard-coded strings from your code and makes it easier to change them in the future. If you do decide to localize your app, a bunch of work is already done.
- Even if your app is only available in one market, you still stand to increase your market by localizing your app.

[9] https://developer.apple.com/help/app-store-connect/manage-app-accessibility/overview-of-accessibility-nutrition-labels

- Accessibility Nutrition Labels are a powerful tool that allows users to make informed choices before downloading apps. Good accessibility support can result in improved visibility and increased downloads. But the information you provide must be current and accurate to prevent issues at app review.

Over the next three chapters, we'll dive a little deeper into the accessibility features Apple has created to benefit people with specific disabilities or requirements. The following chapter will cover the broadest range of features: vision considerations.

CHAPTER 8

iOS Accessibility Features – Vision

The following features Apple primarily designed to aid people with visual impairments. These features help blind and low-vision users, including long-sightedness, low vision, color impairments, and others. Some configurations can also be beneficial to people with cognitive impairments, ADHD, low literacy, or people who prefer their text a little larger or colors a little more muted. Some people enable the grayscale color filter just because it looks cool. Vision considerations make up the largest group of accessibility features currently available on iOS.

VoiceOver

The iOS accessibility feature with which developers are most likely familiar is VoiceOver. VoiceOver is Apple's built-in screen reader that is available across all its screen-based platforms and works with your app without requiring developers to enable its use. VoiceOver is far more than a basic screen reader; it also serves as a navigation tool for low-vision users to enable them not just to know what text is on the screen but also what buttons or actions are available to them and allows them to perform those actions.

iOS also features a more basic screen reader for reading content only; this feature is referred to in iOS as Spoken Content. This requires no specific developer intervention.

Caution Don't enable VoiceOver until you've read "Navigating with VoiceOver."

VoiceOver will change how you interact with your device, as users employ a series of swipes to navigate your app in a natural direction (top left to bottom right in English). A cursor is drawn on the screen to add a visual highlight to the element currently

R. Whitaker, *Developing Inclusive Mobile Apps*, https://doi.org/10.1007/979-8-8688-2809-6_8

focused (Figure 8-1). On focus, VoiceOver reads the element's information to the user in the following order: Accessibility Label ➤ Accessibility Value ➤ Accessibility Traits ➤ (after a short pause) Accessibility Hint. However, the exact order and inclusion of each is determined by your users' settings, so you can't guarantee this behavior. Each of these four values is determined for you as part of your app's accessibility tree, covered in Chapter 6.

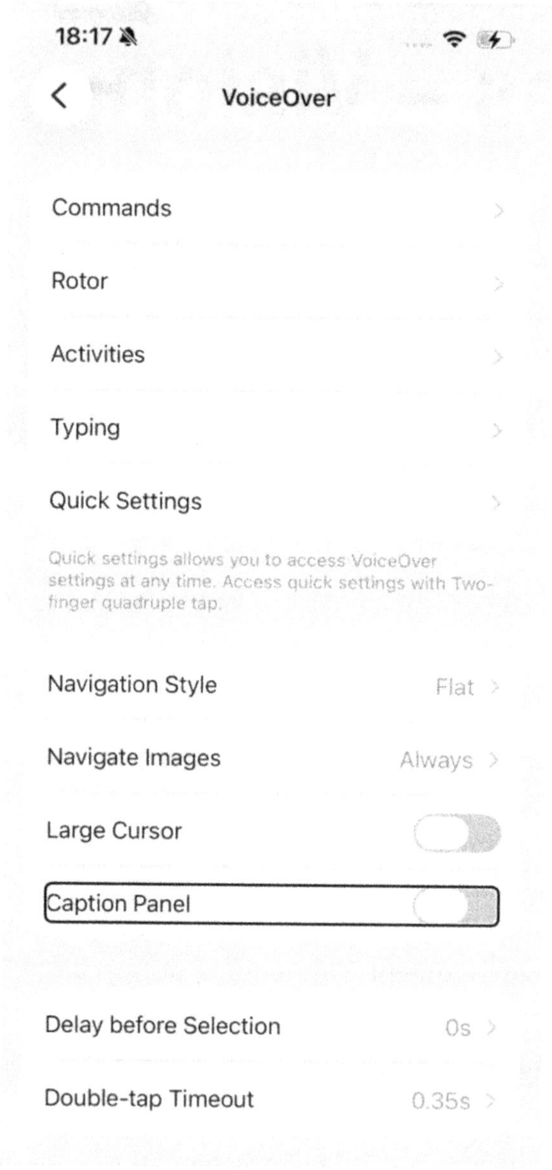

Figure 8-1. *VoiceOver selecting Caption Panel. Double tap anywhere on the screen to activate this control*

If you have built your interface using standard controls and patterns, iOS will be able to determine most of the accessibility tree for you, but it cannot infer your intent. Because of this, you should always test with VoiceOver and make tweaks to the accessibility tree as needed. Common pitfalls include missing or incorrect accessibility values, labels, or traits, and elements accessed in a nonlogical order.

Remember too that VoiceOver users will likely not have the full-screen context that a sighted person would. Their context may be limited to the currently selected element and those immediately surrounding it, so each element should make sense on its own. Semantic views covered in Chapter 6 are an excellent solution for this contextual problem.

You can check if VoiceOver is currently running by checking `accessibilityVoiceOverEnabled` environment property (Listing 8-1).

Listing 8-1. Detecting VoiceOver status and changes

```
@Environment(\.accessibilityVoiceOverEnabled) var voiceOverEnabled
```

Announcements

At times it may be necessary to ask VoiceOver to make an announcement to the user. This would be in the case where something on the screen has changed, outside of the user's current focus.[1] This is similar to the Live Region feature available on Android and the Web.

A common example would be when searching within an application. The user is focused on the search field to enter their query, but the number of results updates elsewhere on the screen. If someone is unable to see the results have been updated, this could lead to a frustrating experience. A user may have to use trial and error, navigating in and out of the search field and results, to refine their search. Instead, we should post a debounced announcement to inform the user that results have been updated and how many are present (Listing 8-2).

---

[1] https://developer.apple.com/documentation/accessibility/accessibilitynotification

Listing 8-2. Posting a VoiceOver announcement

```
Text("\(results.count) results")
    .onAppear {
      let announcement = AttributedString("\(results.count) results")

     AccessibilityNotification
         .Announcement(announcement)
         .post()
}
```

If something critical happens, you can define the announcement as high priority using the `accessibilitySpeechAnnouncementPriority` property (Listing 8-3).

Listing 8-3. Posting a high-priority VoiceOver announcement

```
Text("An error occurred")
    .onAppear {
        var importantAnnouncement = AttributedString("An error occurred")
         ImportantAnnouncement
             .accessibilitySpeechAnnouncementPriority = .high
         AccessibilityNotification
             .Announcement(importantAnnouncement)
             .post()
}
```

Posting a notification in this way will interrupt any current utterances, so it's best if you use this technique only when absolutely necessary, if at all. Announcements of any kind can be noisy and disruptive. Plus, notifications are easily missed if another VoiceOver utterance takes precedence. Before reaching for an accessibility announcement, consider if the need can be resolved by adjusting the design, behavior, or structure of your screen.

Adjusting VoiceOver Utterances

For some specific use cases, it may be desirable to have a little more control over exactly how VoiceOver reads a piece of text. A common example is that of a reference number, where instead of reading "One thousand, two hundred and thirty-four," the meaningful utterance would be "One, two, three, four." Other examples include code, text emphasis, and using content in different languages.

Depending on the attribute you wish to change, there are different approaches. Some options have modifiers; in many cases we can use attributed strings.

Much like attributed strings for displaying rich text visually, you can also add accessibility-specific attributes. These strings can be passed to announcements, as in the previous section, or used in place of regular strings in components such as `Text` or passed to accessibility modifiers.

For example, in Listing 8-4, an attributed accessibility string is applied to a `Text` element that will add emphasis to our announcement by speaking "hello" at a lower pitch and "world" at a higher one.

Listing 8-4. Setting an attributed accessibility label

```
Text("Hello, World!")
    .accessibilityLabel { _ in
        var hello = AttributedString("Hello")
        hello.accessibilitySpeechAdjustedPitch = -1

        var world = AttributedString("world!")
        world.accessibilitySpeechAdjustedPitch = 1

        return Text(hello + world)
}
```

Pitch

The `accessibilitySpeechAdjustedPitch` attribute, as used above in Listing 8-4, allows us to adjust the vocal pitch that VoiceOver uses to read this text. A value of 0.0 is the user's chosen VoiceOver pitch. Values less than 0.0 lower the pitch, and values greater than 0.0 raise the pitch. This can be useful for adding emphasis to a section of speech.

You can achieve the same using a modifier on your text as in Listing 8-5.

Listing 8-5. Adjusting speech pitch down

```
Text("Hello")
    .speechAdjustedPitch(-1)
```

Spell Out

Many apps will include reference numbers at some point - account numbers, purchase references, card numbers, and phone numbers - numeric or alphanumeric strings that are never intended as full words. But VoiceOver can't infer you intended this behavior, which can result in a garbled announcement that is difficult to understand. Instead, we must make our intention explicit.

A common approach I have seen to resolve this issue, and one I used myself before I knew the correct solution, is to add spaces between characters in the accessibility string. While this produces the correct VoiceOver announcement, it creates a worse experience for other assistive technology users - especially Braille display users, for whom this will take up significantly more space[2] and require more navigation.

Instead, Spells Out reads each character of the string individually while keeping the appearance as an unbroken string. We can add this using the `.speechSpellsOutCharacters`[3] modifier as in Listing 8-6 or using an attributed string as in Listing 8-7.

Listing 8-6. Telling VoiceOver to read an account number as digits with a modifier

```
Text("1234")
    .speechSpellsOutCharacters()
```

Listing 8-7. Telling VoiceOver to read an account number as digits with an attributed string

```
struct ContentView: View {

   private var referenceNumber: AttributedString {
       var referenceNumber = AttributedString("1234")

        referenceNumber.accessibilitySpeechSpellsOutCharacters = true
        return referenceNumber
    }
```

[2] Braille formats vary, but as an example, a space occupies one cell and a numeric character also occupies a single cell but requires a numeric indicator before it to clarify the character is a number rather than a letter. So the 4-character string "1234" in Braille is the 5-cell sequence "⠼⠁⠃⠉⠙". When spaces are added between characters, this becomes the 11-cell sequence "⠼⠁ ⠼⠃ ⠼⠉ ⠼⠙". Braille displays commonly have around 20 cells, so it doesn't take a long number before scrolling is required when using this technique.

[3] https://developer.apple.com/documentation/swiftui/text/speechspellsoutcharacters(_:)/

```
    var body: some View {
        Text(referenceNumber)
    }
}
```

Phonetic Notation

VoiceOver doesn't always have the correct pronunciation for every word, particularly for brand names. Using International Phonetic Alphabet, or IPA, notation, we can specify exactly how we want a word pronounced without affecting how the accessibility label is presented to non-speech users. This is done with an attributed string using the key `accessibilitySpeechPhoneticNotation` (Listing 8-8).

Listing 8-8. Using IPA notation to specify pronunciation of a brand name

```
private var brandName: AttributedString {
    var brandName = AttributedString("brndnm")
    brandName.accessibilitySpeechPhoneticNotation = "brændneɪm"
    return brandName
}
```

Punctuation

If your app contains code or other text where punctuation is important, you can use `accessibilitySpeechIncludesPunctuation` attributed string key (Listing 8-9) or the `.speechAlwaysIncludesPunctuation()`[4] (Listing 8-10) modifier to force VoiceOver to read each individual punctuation mark.

Listing 8-9. Requesting VoiceOver to announce punctuation for code using an attributed string

```
private var codeSample: AttributedString {
    var codeSample = AttributedString("print(\"Hello, world!\")")
    codeSample.accessibilitySpeechIncludesPunctuation = true
    return codeSample
}
```

[4] https://developer.apple.com/documentation/swiftui/text/speechalwaysincludespunctuation(_:)/

Listing 8-10. Requesting VoiceOver to announce punctuation for code using a modifier

```
Text("print(\"Hello, world!\")")
    .speechAlwaysIncludesPunctuation()
```

Language

If your app includes strings that are in a language other than the current localization, for example, a language learning app, you ensure VoiceOver can announce these strings correctly. This is done by using the localization system, as covered in Chapter 7, in addition to the SwiftUI environment.

As the environment modifier allows us to apply different environment values to a view, we can specify the locale for a single view or group of views. This allows VoiceOver to determine which language to use (Listing 8-11). But to allow this, you must have the string defined for the correct language in your strings catalog (Figure 8-2).

Listing 8-11. Setting the locale for a view to force VoiceOver to use the correct language

```
Text("Hello, World!")
    .environment(\.locale, .init(identifier: "es"))
```

Figure 8-2. *A strings catalog with a localization specified to match the explicit locale in Listing 8-11*

Magic Tap

Magic Tap is a special accessibility action (accessibility actions are covered in Chapter 6), only available to VoiceOver. It provides fast access to the most important action on your screen. For example, in the Timer app, Magic Tap starts or stops a timer. VoiceOver users perform a magic tap by double tapping anywhere on the screen with two fingers.

Not every screen or app is suited to having a Magic Tap action, but if there is a clear primary action, adding one can be a valuable power feature.

You can add a magic tap action anywhere in your view's hierarchy (Listing 8-12). Each screen can only support a single magic tap action.

Listing 8-12. Supporting Magic Tap

```
VStack {
    // View content
}
.accessibilityAction(.magicTap) {
    pauseGame()
}
```

NAVIGATING WITH VOICEOVER

Once you toggle the feature on in Settings ➤ Accessibility ➤ VoiceOver, VoiceOver is immediately active. VoiceOver changes how navigating your iPhone works, so it's important not to enable it and start tapping around without knowing first how you can disable it.[5] Many times, when I was working at an Apple reseller, customers would bring in iPhones they had been unable to use for days, as idle thumbs had led them to enable VoiceOver and they were not able to turn it off again. I even heard of people who wiped their phone entirely to try to disable it.

For testing and learning, I'd also recommend enabling the Caption Panel. You can find this in the VoiceOver settings. This shows a panel at the bottom of the screen showing the current utterance as it is spoken. This should help you to understand precisely what you are presenting to your customer.

VoiceOver navigates accessible elements in the natural reading order of your user's language setting – top left to bottom right in English – and highlights one element at a time. A single tap no longer activates the item, as you would expect when tapping a button, but instead causes the element to be read aloud. The screen can also be navigated by swiping, as elements may not always be visible or large enough for partially sighted people to accurately tap. A swipe right will move to the element next toward the bottom right, while a swipe left will navigate toward the top left. The newly focused element is then read.

[5] https://support.apple.com/en-gb/guide/iphone/iph3e2e415f/ios

To activate an element – toggle a switch, tap a button, etc. – the gesture now becomes a double tap. The control will respond to this double tap, regardless of where on the screen you tap and what is under your finger at the time. This is beneficial for people with visual impairments, who may struggle to figure out the exact location of a tap target – so dropping the requirement for precise targeting means more reliable activation of controls.

Swipe navigation also facilitates the use of the screen curtain. The screen curtain blanks out the iPhone's screen entirely, so the phone looks to anyone else as if it were asleep. In addition to saving battery life, this also provides extra privacy for blind and visually impaired users. As well as having their personal content read aloud, blind users may not be aware of the full visual content of the screen and could inadvertently display sensitive personal information to those around them.

The rotor control (Figure 8-3) can be used to configure how a secondary VoiceOver gesture behaves. Swiping vertically rather than horizontally will perform the function chosen on the rotor. One of the most common uses is the headings option; this feature will skip over content and move focus only to items with the heading accessibility trait. This is helpful to skim the content of a screen without having to navigate through every element.

Figure 8-3. *The VoiceOver rotor control selecting the Headings option*

Other rotor controls allow users to navigate by accessibility containers, cycle through available accessibility actions, control the speaking rate, or read text by individual character or word. Adding custom rotors is a powerful advanced technique that we won't cover in this book, but the WWDC video "VoiceOver efficiency with custom rotors" is a great place to find out more.[6]

Zoom

Screen zoom is useful for people experiencing tunnel vision. But you may also find that other people use it if your Dynamic Type support is lacking or VoiceOver utterances are unclear. When you perform user testing, if you find visually impaired participants are firing up zoom on a specific screen, this could be a sign you need to make accessibility improvements there.

Zoom can be used in one of two modes: firstly, window zoom, where a viewfinder appears on the screen magnifying the content underneath (Figure 8-4). This mimics using a magnifying glass against the screen but without showing the underlying RGB pixels you'd see with a real-world magnifying glass. Secondly, full-screen zoom, where the entire screen is zoomed and no longer fits within the device's display.

[6] https://developer.apple.com/videos/play/wwdc2020/10116/

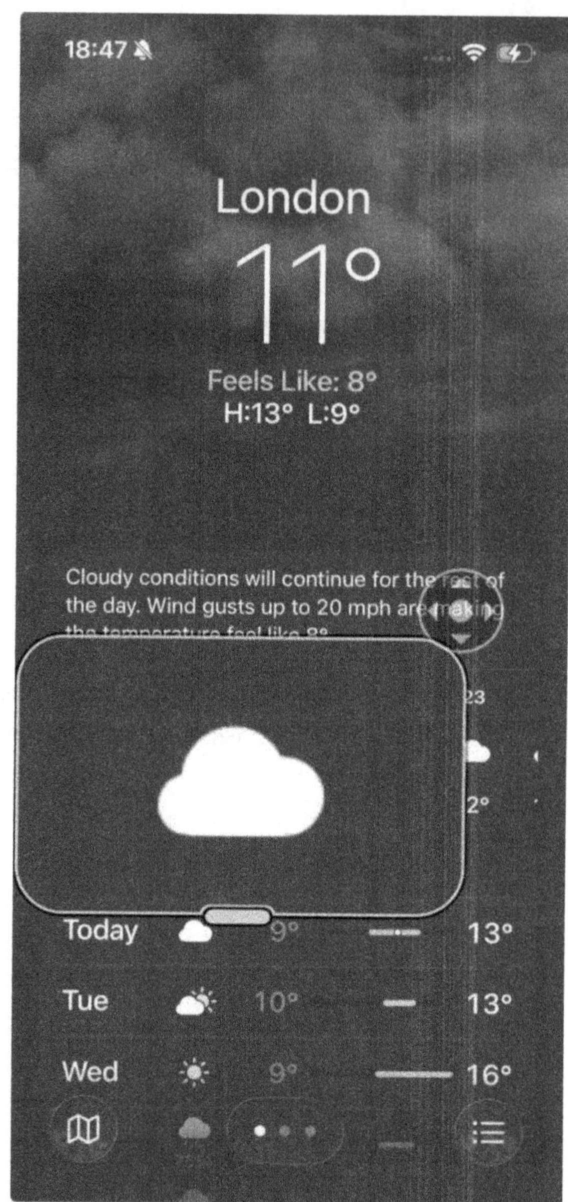

***Figure 8-4.** Zoom enabled in window mode*

Here's what makes it a secondary choice for some visually impaired users – in either mode, the content visible is effectively reduced to around a quarter of the full screen. Meaning three-quarters of your content is no longer visible, most notably content on the non-natural reading side (right in English). To use zoom, users must move a finger around the screen to follow content, making elements easy to miss and losing the surrounding context. The content also then becomes pixelated and blurry, so it is harder to determine.

To move the zoomed area around your screen, three-finger swipes are used, meaning that if you employ three-finger gestures at all in your app, these will be consumed by zoom and not passed to your app.

Bold Text

Bold text does what it says on the tin (Figure 8-5). The SwiftUI font system will nearly always provide this for you for free, even when using custom fonts, provided your font has a bold variant included. But you should also consider increasing the weight of some UI elements, such as icons. If you use SF Symbols, again, you'll get this behavior for free.

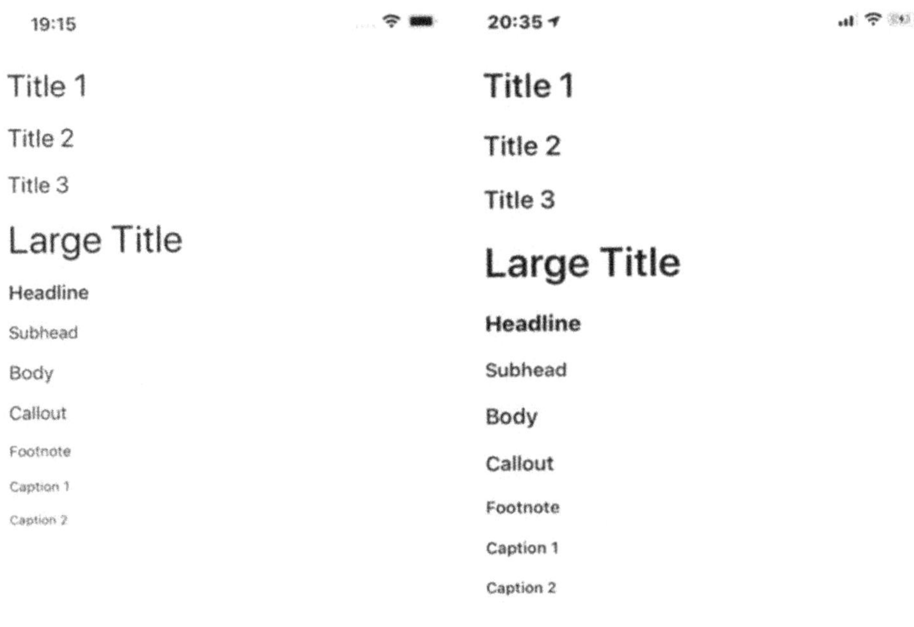

Figure 8-5. *iOS text styles with standard text (left) and bold text (right)*

If you're using custom icons, consider providing a heavier weight version and switching to that when Bold Text is enabled. Bold is not one of the variants; the asset catalog will switch for us automatically. Instead, we must reference two separate images and switch them in code. Listing 8-13 shows how to listen to the `legibilityWeight` environment property and switch our image weight as needed.

Listing 8-13. Switching icons based on the user's chosen Bold Text setting

```
struct ContentView: View {
    @Environment(\.legibilityWeight) var legibilityWeight

     var body: some View {
       VStack {

           switch legibilityWeight {
               case .bold:
                   Image("MyIcon-Bold")
               default:
                   Image("MyIcon")
           }
       }
    }
}
```

Larger Text or Dynamic Type

Larger text is the friendly human-readable name for what, in code, is often referred to as dynamic type. Dynamic type allows the user to adjust the text size to one better suited to how they use their device (Figure 8-6). In the manner of the best accessibility features, this isn't just about people who need larger text to be able to read the screen but about customization - this feature allows text sizes below the default, allowing more content to fit the screen without scrolling. This can range from xSmall (extra small) with a body text size of 14pt to AX5 (accessibility size 5) with a body text size of 53pt. See Table 8-1 for the full range of body text point sizes.

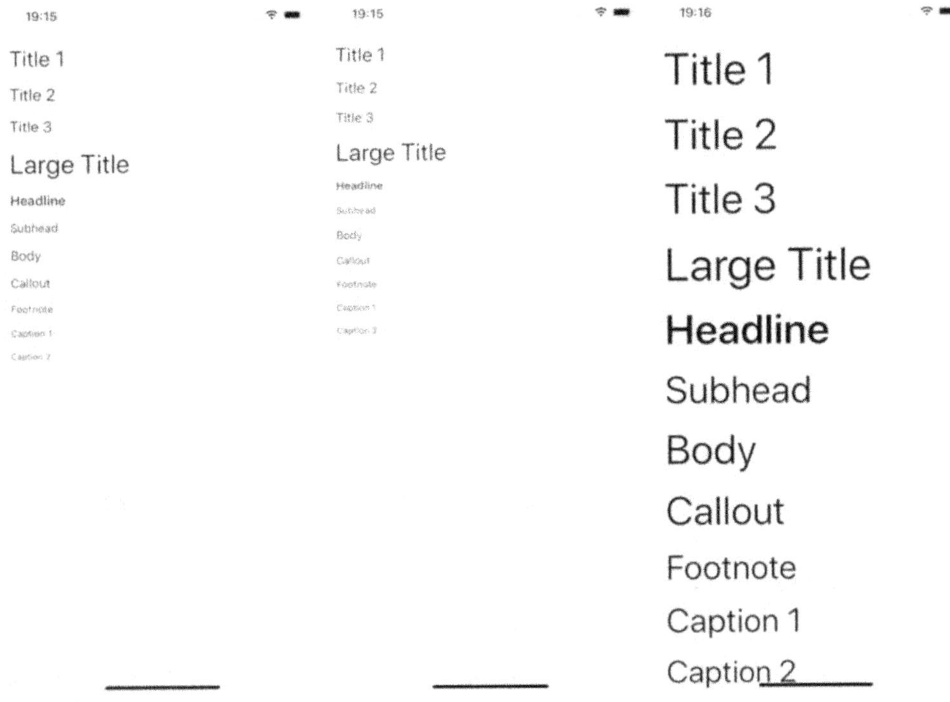

Figure 8-6. *Dynamic Type text styles at standard sizes (left), smallest sizes (center), and the largest accessibility size (right)*

Table 8-1. *Dynamic Type text sizes*

Dynamic type size	Body text size (points)	%age of default
xSmall	14	82
Small	15	88
Medium	16	94
Large (Default)	17	100
xLarge	19	112
xxLarge	21	124
xxxLarge	23	135
AX1	28	165
AX2	33	194

(continued)

Table 8-1. (*continued*)

Dynamic type size	Body text size (points)	%age of default
AX3	40	235
AX4	47	276
AX5	53	312

The full range of dynamic text sizes matched to text styles are available as part of the HIG.[7]

Dynamic Type support is native throughout SwiftUI, and as with bold text, this scaling will almost always be provided for free. But there is one common mistake I see made that prevents text scaling: specifying a fixed-size font. Using `.font(.system(size: 17))` should be reserved only for instances where you must have a fixed font size. Instead, prefer text styles provided by SwiftUI.

SwiftUI provides 11 font styles that scale proportionally to your user's chosen text size – not just in the font size but also in spacings and other metrics – providing a thorough and consistent approach to scaling. Applying `.font(.subheadline)` will give you a 17pt, semibold font that scales in both directions and will provide a far better look and feel compared to an explicit `.font(.system(size: 17, weight: .semibold))`. Listing 8-14 applies the SwiftUI provided headline style to a title.

Listing 8-14. Creating Text with Dynamic Type support

```
// For body style, no font modifier is needed.
Text("Screen Title")
    .font(.headline)
```

Line Limit

The `.lineLimit()` modifier is commonly overused. Its purpose is to fix the maximum number of lines of text to prevent unbounded scaling where this would create difficulty navigating the app. For example, this is often appropriate in a list view (Figure 8-7). Applying a `.lineLimit(2)` modifier should provide all users with enough context to make a judgment about whether the current element is worth diving into further detail.

[7] https://developer.apple.com/design/human-interface-guidelines/ios/visual-design/typography/

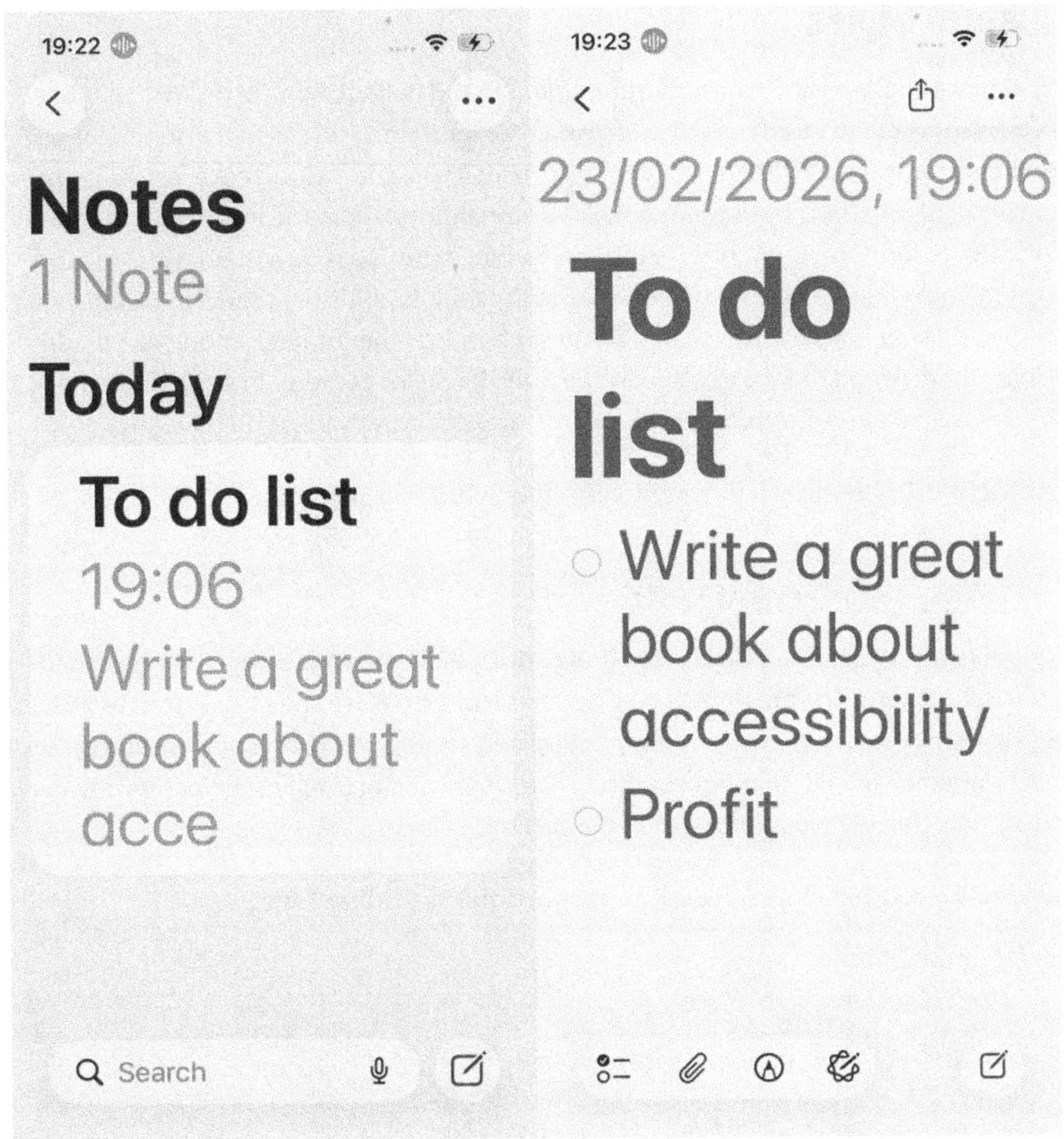

Figure 8-7. *The Notes list shows truncated content (left) but shows the full content scaled appropriately in the detail screen*

`.lineLimit()` should almost never be used on detail screens where someone would expect to be able to see the full content. Using it here would mean people are blocked from reading the full text. Instead, ensure the content is wrapped inside a scroll view and allowed to scale.

Custom Styles

What if your design calls for a font other than the iOS default, San Francisco? Or what if you want your standard body text size to be larger than 17pt? SwiftUI also provides modifiers for this that will respect a user's chosen text scale. I won't cover adding custom fonts to your app here, but Apple provides a straightforward guide in their developer documentation.[8] Once you have your custom font ready, pass an instance of your custom font, with the desired default size, to the font modifier, as shown in Listing 8-15.

Avoid using `fixedSize` except in views such as a tab bar or navigation bar, where scaling them would reduce the screen space available for content. In such situations, you should use the Large Content Viewer to offer an alternative - more on that later.

Listing 8-15. Creating a dynamic text style with a custom font

```
Text("Hello, World!")
    .font(.custom("MyFont", size: 17))
```

In Listing 8-15, our font will scale proportionally in line with the SwiftUI-provided body style, where 17 is the default text size. In Listing 8-16, we specify a text style with the `relativeTo` argument to provide a more targeted scaling behavior. This is useful for text that is larger or smaller than regular body text where at larger scales the body-provided values may provide too much or too little scaling.

Listing 8-16. Specifying a custom proportionally scaling font

```
Text("Hello, World!")
    .font(.custom(
        "MyFont",
        size: 17,
        relativeTo: .subheadline
    ))
```

[8] https://developer.apple.com/documentation/swiftui/applying-custom-fonts-to-text

Scaled Metric

Aside from specifying font styles and sizing that will scale, it's important to consider how your layout is constructed overall. Specifying fixed sizes for elements will result in clipped or truncated text when scaled, even if everything looks great at regular sizes. Instead, prefer adding spacing and padding values to achieve your required layout, and any text is ultimately contained within a scroll view somewhere above it in the view hierarchy to allow space for growth.

In some layouts, it may be necessary to scale padding, image sizes, or other values proportionally to the font size. This can be done using the `@ScaledMetric` property wrapper. In Listing 8-17, we're scaling a colored Rectangle proportionally to the subheadline text size.

Listing 8-17. Specifying a custom proportionally scaling icon size

```
struct ContentView: View {
    @ScaledMetric(relativeTo: .subheadline) var headlineIconSize = 50.0
    var body: some View {
        VStack {
            Rectangle()
                .fill(.red)
                .frame(
                    width: headlineIconSize,
                    height: headlineIconSize
                )
        }
    }
}
```

Responding to Text Sizes

If you need to respond to text size changes for any other reason, SwiftUI provides an `@Environment` property that exposes the user's current chosen size (Listing 8-18).

Listing 8-18. Detecting the user's current chosen text size

```
@Environment(\.dynamicTypeSize) var dynamicTypeSize
```

The most common usage of this is to detect if the text is set to an accessibility size, at which point you may decide to make some adjustments to your design. Such adaptions may include increasing any line length limits or switching from an `HStack` to a `VStack` when laying out text. The simplest way to detect this is to use the `isAccessibilitySize` property on the `dynamicTypeSize` environment value.

Listing 8-19 shows a pattern I use in nearly every project I create that I call an "adaptive stack." This view shows the enclosed content in an `HStack` at regular text sizes but switches to a `VStack` when a large accessibility size would mean horizontally stacked text could be difficult to read.

Listing 8-19. An adaptive stack responding to accessibility text sizes

```
struct ContentView: View {
    var body: some View {
        AdaptiveStack {
            Text("Beans")
            Text("5")
        }
    }
}

struct AdaptiveStack<Content: View>: View {
    @Environment(\.dynamicTypeSize) var dynamicTypeSize

    private let content: Content

    init(@ViewBuilder content: () -> Content) {
        self.content = content()
    }

    var body: some View {
        if dynamicTypeSize.isAccessibilitySize {
            VStack {
                content
            }
        } else {
```

```
            HStack {
                content
            }
        }
    }
}
```

Large Content Viewer

While text content in your app should scale, the size of fixed bars, such as the tab bar and navigation bar, should not scale. If they did, there would be little room for your content. For such bars, fixing or limiting the amount of available growth of content within them is desirable to prevent clipping and truncation. You should then support the Large Content Viewer (Figure 8-8), providing users of accessibility text sizes with a fallback to see the content at a larger scale. The large content viewer is shown when an accessibility text size is enabled, and the user performs a long press on the element.

Figure 8-8. Large content viewer triggered by a long press on the "..." button in the toolbar of Notes

If you use standard SwiftUI bars, this behavior is provided for you. But for a custom UI, the following may be needed: First, restrict the dynamic type scale to one that allows the content to grow without clipping or truncating. Then, add the

`.accessibilityShowsLargeContentViewer()`[9] modifier. For example, for a button that includes an icon and text label, as we might find in a tab bar, our code might look like Listing 8-20.

Listing 8-20. Adding the Large Content Viewer to a non-scaling button

```
Button(action: {
    navigateToFavorites()
}, label: {
    Image(systemName: "star")
    Text("Favorites")
})
// allow the smallest text scale
// up to the maximum before clipping occurs
.dynamicTypeSize(.xSmall ... .large)
.accessibilityShowsLargeContentViewer()
```

The large content viewer is intended for short text labels, not for long-form content. Labels should be paired with an icon where one exists in your regular UI. Usually, the `.accessibilityShowsLargeContentViewer()` modifier will pick this up correctly, but if you need to customize this, use the `.accessibilityShowsLargeContentViewer {}` modifier with a closure that includes your `Text` and `Image` items (Listing 8-21).

Listing 8-21. Passing a custom view to the Large Content Viewer

```
// ... your view
.accessibilityShowsLargeContentViewer {
    Image(systemName: "star")
    Text("Favorites")
}
```

[9] https://developer.apple.com/documentation/swiftui/view/accessibilityshowslargecontentviewer()/

Show Borders

Show Borders was known as Buton Shapes prior to iOS 26. It helps make button tap targets more visible and obvious by adding an outline, background, or underlined text (Figure 8-9). This is a powerful feature for those with visual or cognitive impairments.

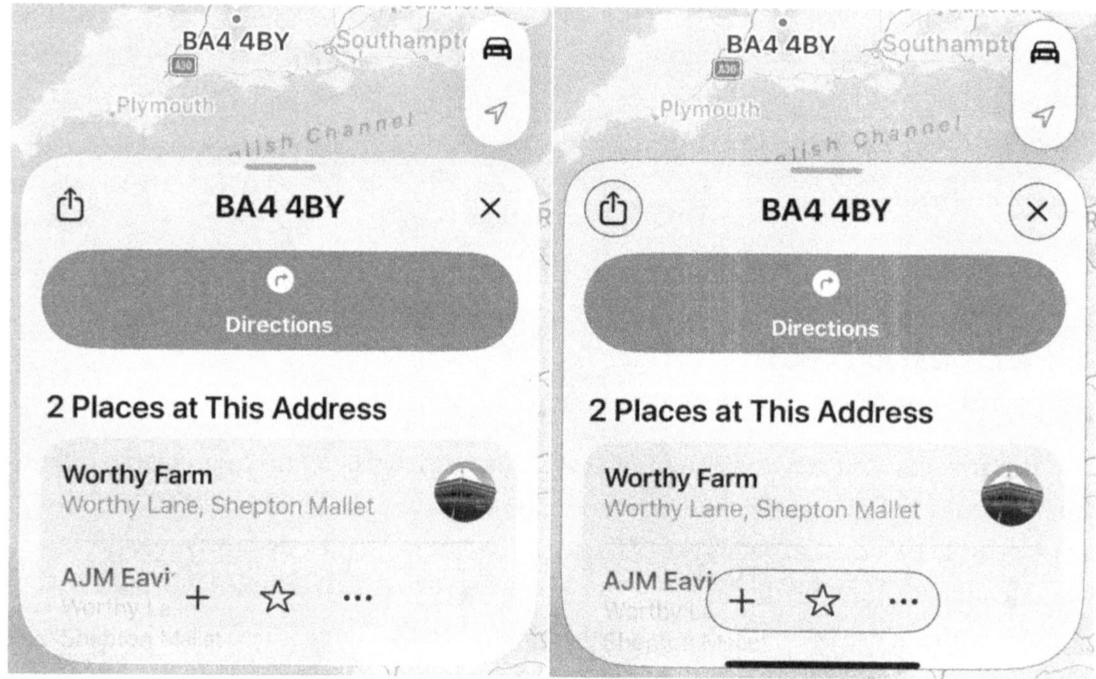

Figure 8-9. *A maps bottom sheet with Button Shapes disabled (left) and enabled (right)*

This behavior is provided for you by SwiftUI's standard Button controls and in many cases will need no tweaking. But if instead you have used an `.onTapGesture` to respond to activation on a non-button element, you'll need to listen to the `accessibilityShowBorders` environment property and add an accommodation of your own. In Listing 8-22, I am adding an underline to my view when Show Borders is enabled.

Listing 8-22. Adding an underline to a view with a tap gesture

```
struct ContentView: View {
    @Environment(\.accessibilityShowBorders) var showBorders

    var body: some View {
       VStack {
           Text("Tappable text")
               .underline(showBorders)
               .onTapGesture {
                   print("Tapped")
               }
       }
}
```

A common pitfall with Show Borders occurs when using a custom view as a label for a button that already provides a shape accommodation. The example in Figure 8-10 shows an application with multiple buttons that provide their own shape; in these cases, enabling Show Borders adds unnecessary borders.

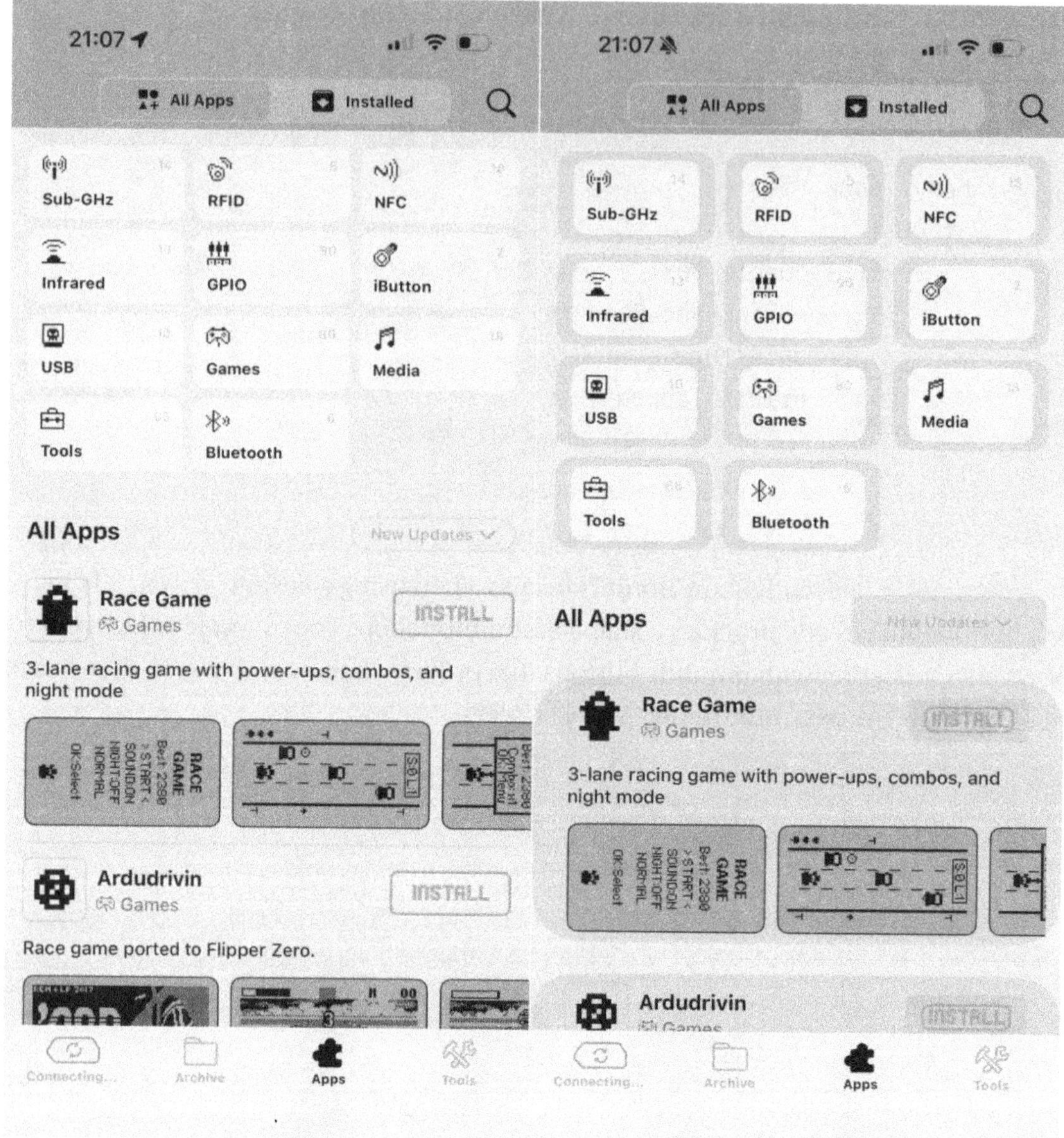

Figure 8-10. *An application with multiple buttons, all providing their own shape. The Show Borders setting is disabled on the left and enabled on the right*

The custom view already has a shape indicating that it is tappable and the tappable area. But when Show Borders is enabled, a further border is added automatically by SwiftUI. In this case the fix is to tell SwiftUI this added border is not necessary by applying the `.buttonStyle(.plain)` modifier (Listing 8-23).

Listing 8-23. Adding an underline to a view with a tap gesture

```
Button {
    selected.toggle()
} label: {
    Text("Free Shipping")
        .foregroundStyle(.black)
        .padding()
        .background {
            Capsule()
                .fill(
                    selected ? .purple.opacity(0.3)
                        : .clear
                )
                .stroke(.purple)
        }
}
.accessibilityAddTraits(
    selected ? .isSelected : .isButton
)
.buttonStyle(.plain)
```

Finally, if you want more control over the shape that SwiftUI adds for you when Show Borders is enabled, apply the `.buttonBorderShape()` modifier to your button.

Reduce Transparency

Reduce Transparency is an essential feature for some low-vision users; for those with vision already blurred, adding blur on otherwise transparent backgrounds can make it challenging to determine foreground from background. Transparency can also cause the contrast ratio to fall below an acceptable value if the background is not defined at build time.

The most immediately noticeable use of this is folders on SpringBoard (Figure 8-11). These are a great example of how to make an accessibility feature while maintaining a comparable experience, rather than a second-class one. With this feature disabled, folders have a frosted background showing the content behind. Enable this setting, and all springboard content behind the open folder is removed, keeping a dimmed springboard background image. Folders take on a darker gray appearance with no transparency.

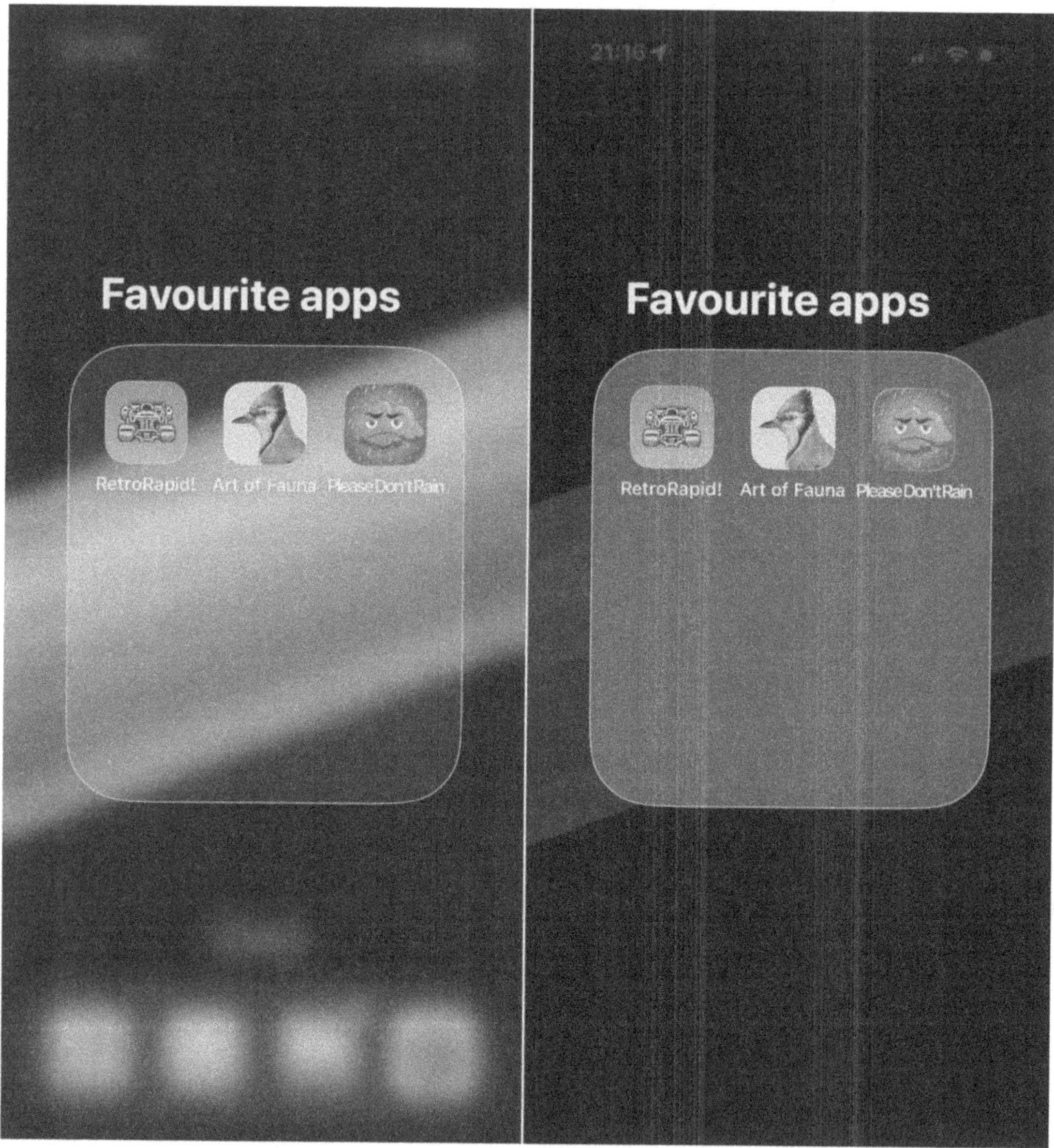

Figure 8-11. *SpringBoard folder (Left). SpringBoard folder with reduced transparency (Right)*

If you use system-provided material or glass effects, Reduce Transparency will be applied automatically. But when adding `.opacity()` modifiers, accommodations are not enabled for you by default, as Apple can't make a clear decision on how to reduce transparency based on your UI design; therefore, this is a design consideration you need to make when introducing transparency.

If your transparency layer is above a solid color that you can guarantee will not change from build time, there may be no need to respond at all. In all other cases, a compromise should be made. An easy decision would be to replace transparency with a solid color; a more polished choice would be to add a tint to your new solid background representing the content behind.

To determine whether to respond to this setting, use SwiftUI's `accessibilityReduceTransparency` environment property as in Listing 8-24.

Listing 8-24. Detecting changes in Reduce Transparency status

```
struct ContentView: View {

    @Environment(\.accessibilityReduceTransparency) var reduceTransparency

    var body: some View {
        ZStack {
            VStack {
                Text("Content")
                    .padding()
            }
            .background(
.gray.opacity(reduceTransparency ? 0.9 : 0.2)
            )
        }
    }
}
```

Increase Contrast

Increase Contrast is the user-friendly name for what, in SwiftUI, is called `colorSchemeContrast`. A good example of this setting can be seen in Messages (Figure 8-12), where the background colors on message bubbles change to increase their contrast against the message text.

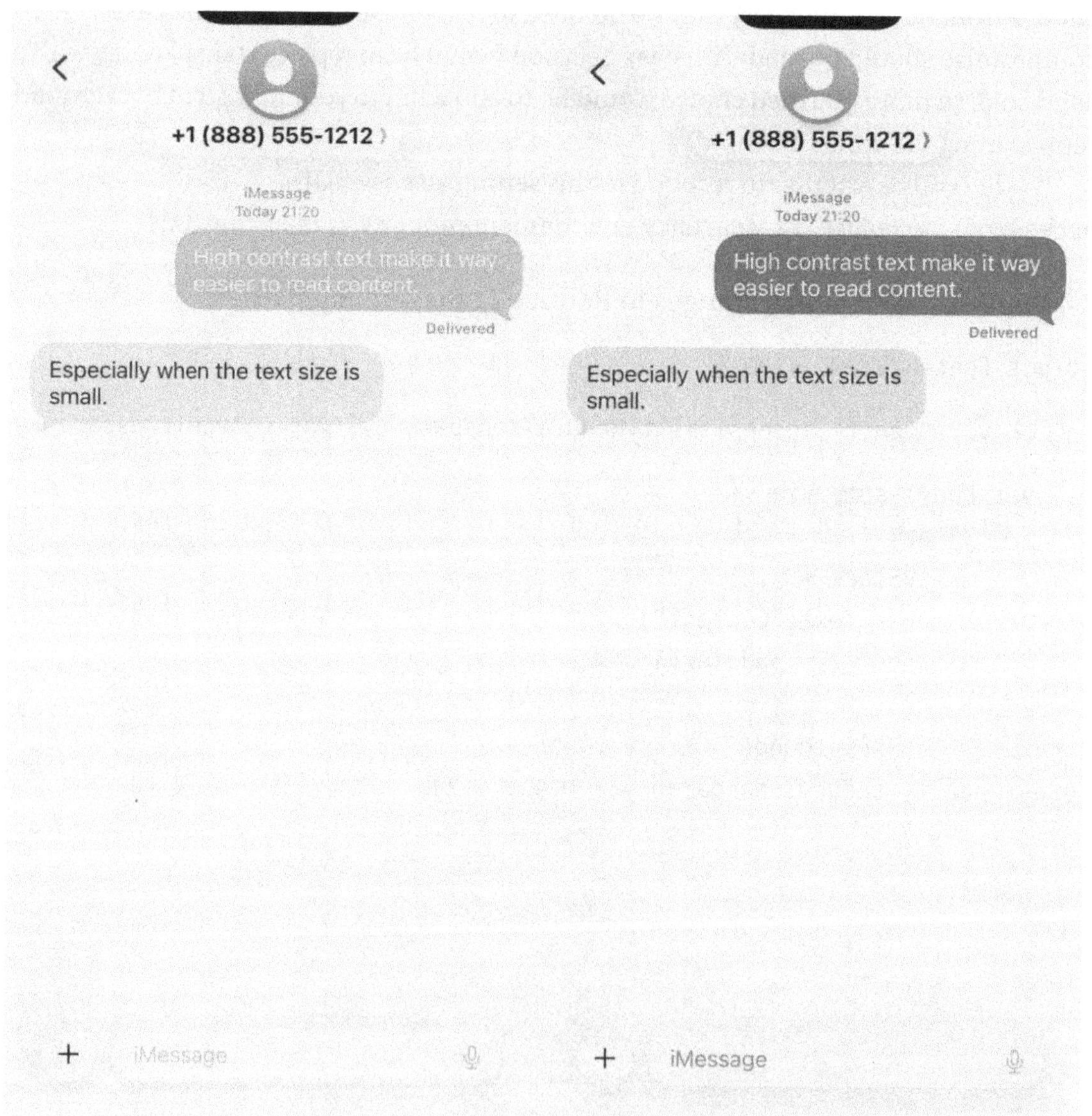

***Figure 8-12.** Increase contrast disabled in Messages (left) and enabled (right)*

The simplest choice for supporting this setting is to provide high-contrast variants for all colors and images in your asset catalog (Figure 8-13). If you haven't already added these, open your xcassets file, and select the color or image resource for which you want to create a high-contrast variant. From the attributes inspector on the right, toggle the "High Contrast" checkbox. A new variant will appear for each asset selected. Once added, iOS will automatically choose the right asset for you based on your customer's setting and will switch them out dynamically.

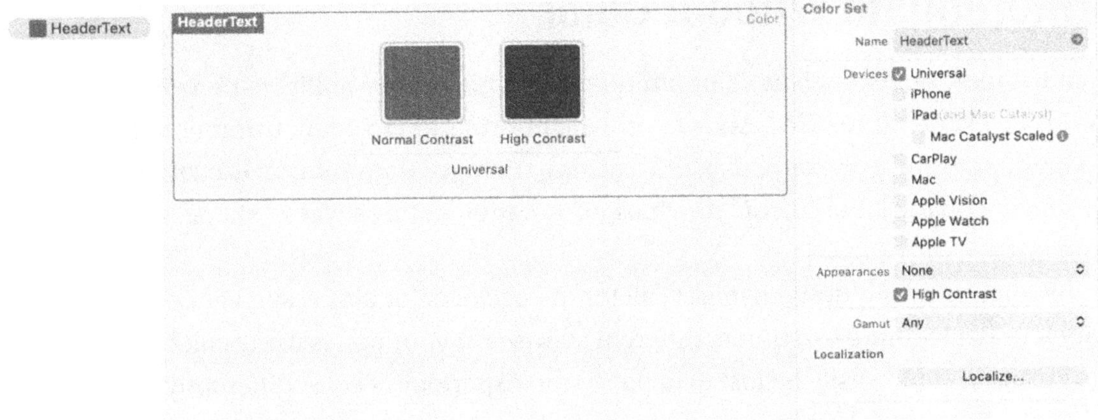

Figure 8-13. *Normal and High Contrast color variants in an asset catalog*

If you're not relying on the catalog to switch out your assets, you'll need to make the switch in code. Listen to the `colorSchemeContrast` environment property[10] as in Listing 8-25, and switch assets based on the increased or standard value.

Listing 8-25. Detecting changes in Increase Contrast status

```
struct ContentView: View {
    @Environment(\.colorSchemeContrast) var contrast

    var body: some View {
        switch contrast {
        case .increased:
            Image("MyIcon-HighContrast")
```

[10] https://developer.apple.com/documentation/swiftui/colorschemecontrast/

```
        default:
            Image("MyIcon")
        }
    }
}
```

Differentiate Without Color

Some impairments, such as color blindness, can hinder our ability to perceive colors. As such, a key feature of WCAG is to provide information to your customer in multiple redundant forms. For example, a red warning triangle containing an exclamation, grouped with the label "Error," provides information in three ways – shape, color, and text.

Sometimes your designs might call for the use of color alone, such as coloring text labels or backgrounds, to hint at different statuses. If your app is using color in this way, its meaning could easily be lost to anyone who experiences color differently, either for biological or cultural reasons.[11]

To determine if you should be providing additional forms of furnishing this information, listen to the `accessibilityDifferentiateWithoutColor` environment property and add additional content if needed as in Listing 8-26.

Listing 8-26. Detecting changes in differentiate without color status

```
struct ContentView: View {

    @Environment(\.accessibilityDifferentiateWithoutColor) var
    differentiateWithoutColor

    var status: Status = .good

    var body: some View {
        Circle()
            .fill(status.color)
```

[11] Remember also that if you are changing background or text color in this way, each possible color combination should pass the WGAG guideline of at least 4.5:1 contrast ratio.

```
          .overlay {
              Text(
                differentiateWithoutColor ? Status.icon
                : ""
              )
          }
    }
}
```

I am not aware of anywhere within iOS that this consideration is used. If you can add another mode such as shape or text when this setting is enabled, it would likely benefit a wider audience and be simpler to maintain if added permanently for all users.

Invert Colors

Some users find reading dark text on a light background difficult to distinguish, or even painful to read. Dark Appearance will fill this need in most cases, but for apps where content is presented only in a dark-on-light scheme, inverting colors can help (Figure 8-14).

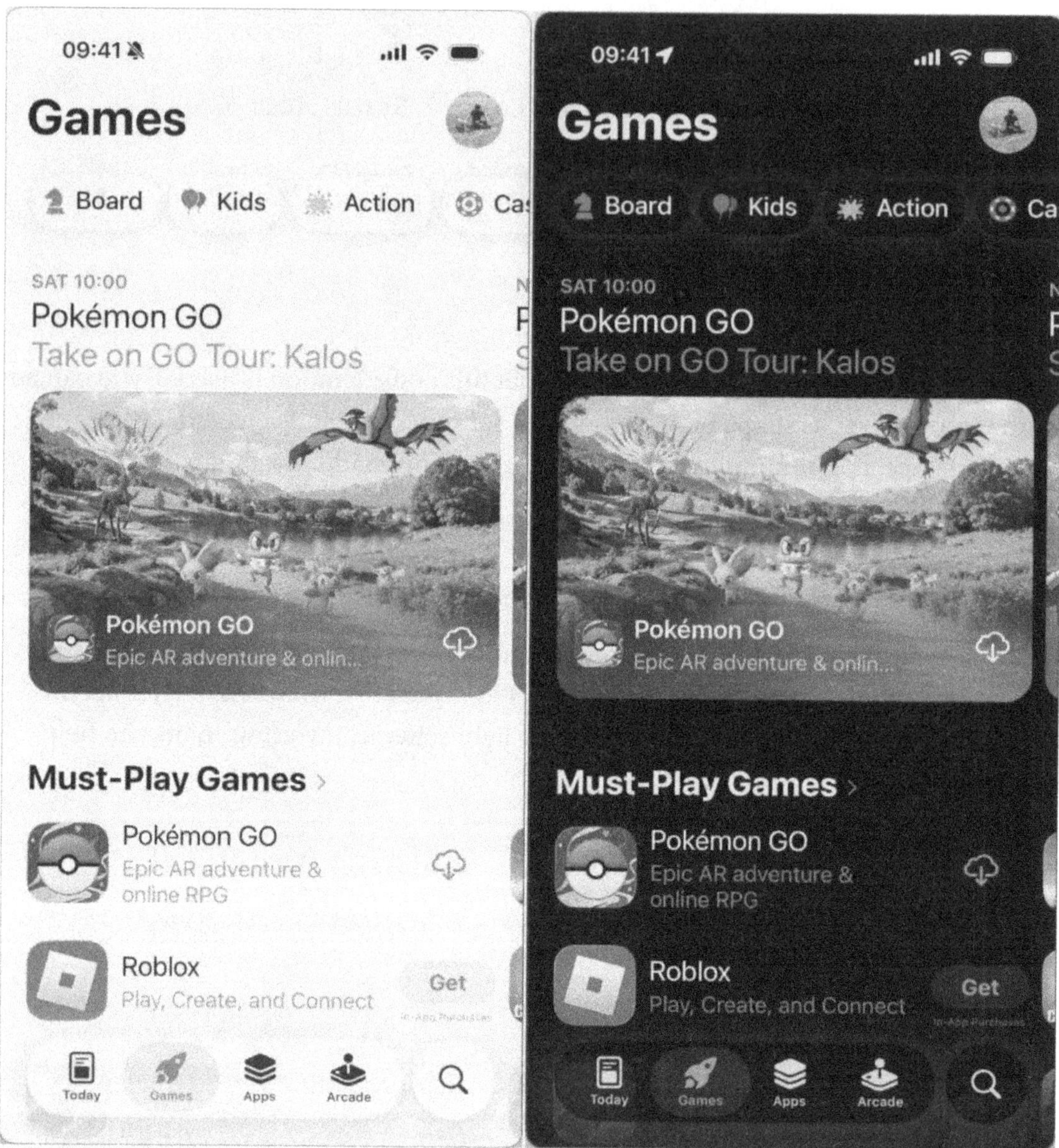

Figure 8-14. *Smart invert (right) - text, icons, and backgrounds are inverted; photos and full-color images are kept at their original color*

Classic Invert changes everything, including images, meaning these will often look wrong and potentially lose meaning. With Smart Invert, iOS will invert all views except for those explicitly exempted.

For full-color images and videos, apply the `.accessibilityIgnoresInvertColors()` modifier to present the content in regular colors.[12] Icons, UI elements, and text content should not have this modifier applied.

Reduce Motion

The Reduce Motion option is essential for people affected by motion sensitivity, where specific animations can trigger dizziness and nausea. It's also invaluable for people with anxiety disorders, ADHD, and autism, among others. For these users, large amounts of motion, especially in the periphery, can be distracting and upsetting.

To get an idea of the kind of animations that can trigger, enable this option on your phone. As you use your phone, keep an eye out for which animations Apple has disabled – for example, the zooming animation when launching an app. Fast animations, animations in multiple planes, and zooming animations can all have a negative impact, so if you make use of these, consider listening to the `accessibilityReduceMotion` environment property. Remove or reduce the prominence of the animation; crossfading is often a good choice. If your animation is repeating, consider limiting it to 3 iterations or fewer.

Play Animated Images

Many users may find animated images and videos distracting but may not want them removed entirely. Imagine social media without any GIFs; it would be a boring place. Instead, if someone has toggled Play Animated Images off, this shows that they wish to make an explicit choice about whether to view animated content, likely because it could trigger a motion disorder, an attention-related condition, or an anxiety disorder. Listen to the `accessibilityPlayAnimatedImages` environment property and, if this is false, disable any autoplay of videos, GIFs, or similar content within your app – but crucially, don't remove them entirely; instead, offer playback controls.

The origin of this setting stems back to when iMessage gained message effects – users who had Reduce Motion enabled would never see the message effect, resulting in a degraded experience. To resolve this, Apple added an explicit 'Autoplay Message Effects'

[12] `https://developer.apple.com/documentation/swiftui/view/accessibilityignoresinvertcolors(_:)`

setting to iOS for more fine-grained control. This is a great example of how adding customization options allows you to meet accessibility needs while still delivering a polished, non-degraded experience.

Dim Flashing Lights

While all accessibility considerations are important, not supporting the Dim Flashing Lights setting on iOS is one that could directly result in causing serious harm to your users. If a user has enabled this setting, it is likely because they experience photosensitive epilepsy, and flashing lights could trigger seizures. iOS can, in some instances, automatically detect flashing content and dim it once this setting is enabled. But if you provide flashing images through a custom animation or video player, it is essential that you listen to the `accessibilityDimFlashingLights` environment property and either remove that animation or reduce the prominence.

You may also wish to present additional UI if this setting is enabled, informing users before upcoming flashing content.

Audio Descriptions

`AVFoundation` contains built-in support for audio description tracks. Using an `AVPlayer` instance for your media will give you this functionality for free when your customer has this setting enabled - provided you ensure your videos have audio descriptions embedded in your videos. Any good video-editing software will allow you to add caption tracks and secondary audio tracks for descriptions.

Appearance

If you use only system-provided colors, your app will automatically switch between light and dark depending on the user's setting. But realistically, if you haven't been routinely checking your app in both light and dark appearances during development, some things are going to look a bit weird when you toggle between them.

Dark mode, while also looking neat and saving battery life, is an essential accessibility feature for people with light sensitivity, and for some users, light text on dark is easier to distinguish than the inverse. But this doesn't mean you should only support dark mode - many people find the opposite is easier to read text.

Appearance is not found in the Accessibility settings. Instead, you can toggle it through the Settings app under Display and Brightness. Toggle the appearance now and test your app to see where you might need to make changes. You may need to add dark variants of some colors and image assets. We'll cover this below.

Dark (or light) variants of colors and images can be added to any assets stored in asset catalogs. Select the color or image you want to add a dark variant of, and in the appearance section of the attributes inspector choose "Any, Dark." (Figure 8-15). The 'Any' option here will effectively be the color used in light appearances - the name is a function of legacy asset catalog formats.

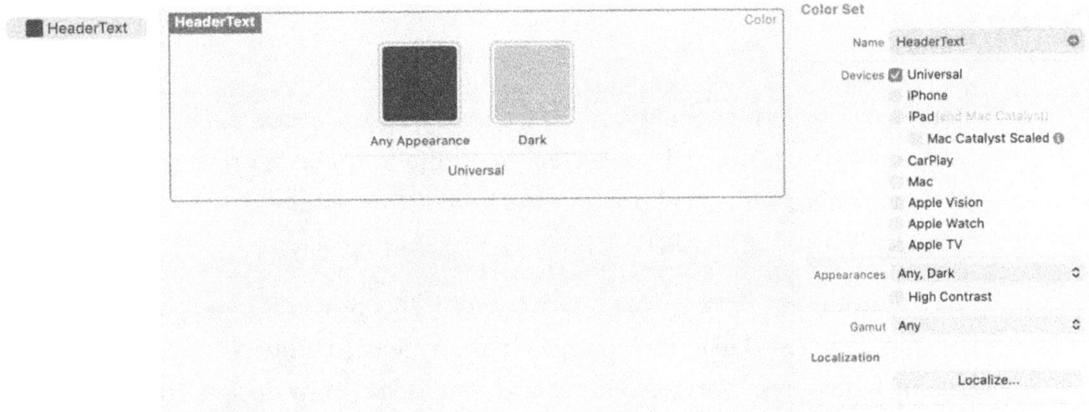

Figure 8-15. *Dark and Any color variants in an asset catalog*

By specifying Any and Dark variants in your asset catalog, iOS will switch your colors and images automatically. But if you need to handle this yourself in code, listen to the `colorScheme` environment property[13] and load assets based on the light and dark values (Listing 8-27).

Listing 8-27. Checking Dark Mode status on a view

```
struct ContentView: View {
    @Environment(\.colorScheme) var colorScheme

    var body: some View {
        switch colorScheme {
```

[13] https://developer.apple.com/documentation/swiftui/colorscheme/

```
        case .dark:
            Image("MyIcon-dark")

        default:
            Image("MyIcon-light")
        }
    }
}
```

Summary

- Visual considerations make up by far the largest selection of iOS accessibility features, so it could feel daunting trying to support them all. But sticking with good practices - using iOS-provided controls, adaptive layouts, and asset catalogs - will go a long way.
- The environment properties system is incredibly powerful; you can use it to detect and listen to changes in many accessibility settings. Exactly which ones you respond to will depend on your design. In the later chapter on testing, we'll discover how you can use this system to support accessibility testing too.
- VoiceOver can seem confusing when you first use it, but you'll pick up the basics quickly and can make it a regular part of your development workflow.
- Dynamic Type and Dark Appearance are essential parts of any modern iOS app. If you don't support them, your app won't feel at home on iOS, and your customers will notice.

In the next chapter, we'll continue our look at iOS accessibility features. We'll move on to the considerations iOS makes for people with limited movement and cover what you can do as a developer to make these customers feel at home in your app.

CHAPTER 9

iOS Accessibility Features – Physical and Motor

Physical and motor considerations assist people who may not be able to perform multi-touch gestures; for example, someone with three fingers may need assistance to perform a four-finger gesture. People who may have very little motor control may use Switch Control or Voice Control to make the best use of what movement they have available to them.

The key API to be aware of for all motor technologies is the `.accessibilityRespondsToUserInteraction()`[1] modifier. This modifier indicates that an element is interactive and therefore should be focused by assistive technologies that allow for interaction. If you have built a custom control and find Switch Control, Voice Control, and Full Keyboard Access can't focus or activate it, adding this modifier should be the first thing you reach for.

Users with motor impairments will appreciate careful consideration of control size and input accuracy. Aim for all controls to have a minimum size of 44 x 44 points. Avoid requiring complex gestures or precise timing. Test your interface with Switch Control and ensure all functionality is accessible.

[1] `https://developer.apple.com/documentation/swiftui/view/accessibilityrespondstouserinteraction(_:)`

R. Whitaker, *Developing Inclusive Mobile Apps*, https://doi.org/10.1007/979-8-8688-2809-6_9

Switch Control

Switch Control[2] is intended for use by those with limited movement but who can accurately and repeatedly perform one or more simple movements. This movement can be harnessed by a "switch." This switch can be a number of things – from external physical devices such as push switches and suck/blow tubes to input detected by the iOS device such as eye tracking or sounds.

Caution Don't enable Switch Control until you have read "Navigating with Switch Control."

Using the accessibility tree, Switch Control will automatically scan the screen, highlighting accessible elements with a focus indicator, similar to the appearance of VoiceOver.

There are two differences you may initially notice when comparing Switch Control's default operation to that of VoiceOver. Instead of highlighting every accessible element in turn, as is the standard setting on VoiceOver, elements are automatically grouped into meaningful areas to reduce the number of presses needed to access any given element. Secondly, content-only elements are skipped, focusing only on controls, as Switch Control is intended as a tool to allow interaction.

On selecting an element with Switch Control, available actions are presented in a popover (Figure 9-1). If you use iOS's built-in controls, these actions will be populated for you. Accessibility actions will also be shown in this menu – details of these are available in Chapter 6.

---

[2] https://support.apple.com/en-gb/119835

***Figure 9-1.** Switch Control showing actions available for an interactive element*

Navigating an interface in this way can be time-consuming. As a result, your users with Switch Control enabled are most likely to be the ones most affected by time-outs, so consider removing them entirely, or if not possible, significantly increasing their duration, if you detect Switch Control is enabled. You may also wish to remove the requirement for any multi-touch gestures or increase the prominence of gesture alternatives and reduce the prominence of destructive actions.

You can get the status of Switch Control from the environment using the environment property in Listing 9-1.

Listing 9-1. Detecting Switch Control status from the environment

```
@Environment(\.accessibilitySwitchControlEnabled) var switchControlEnabled
```

When elements are highlighted by Switch Control, they are usually done so individually (Figure 9-2). When elements are inside a collection, or multiple items are closely arranged, they will often be focused as a group for more efficient navigation (Figure 9-3). Switch Control will usually make this determination for you, but we can have greater control over this by creating a semantic view. By grouping related elements either inside a Stack or a Group we can add the modifier `.accessibilityElement( children: .contain)` to that group.

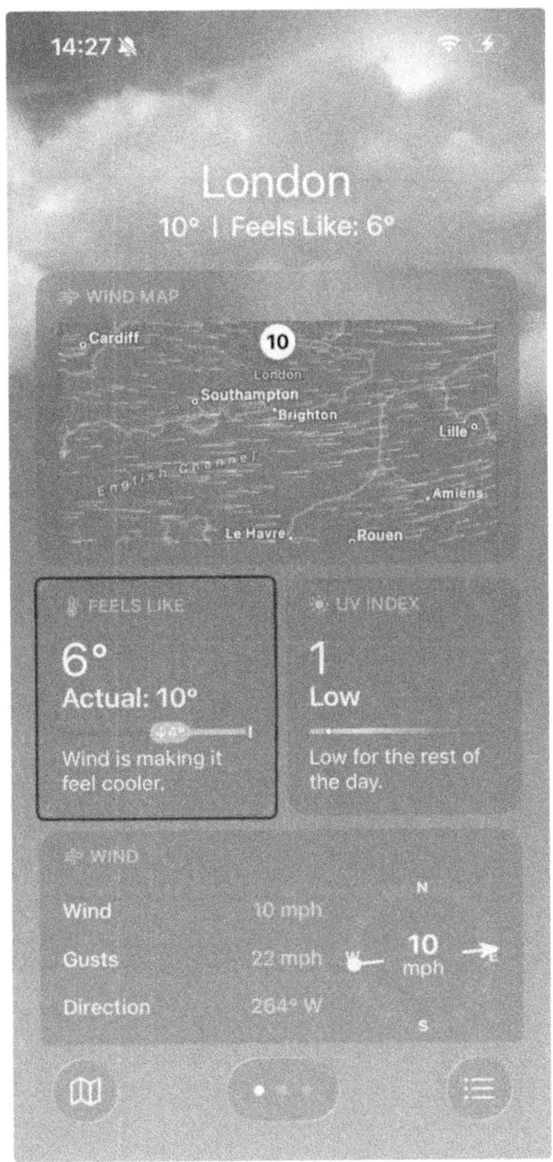

Figure 9-2. *Switch Control focusing on an individual element*

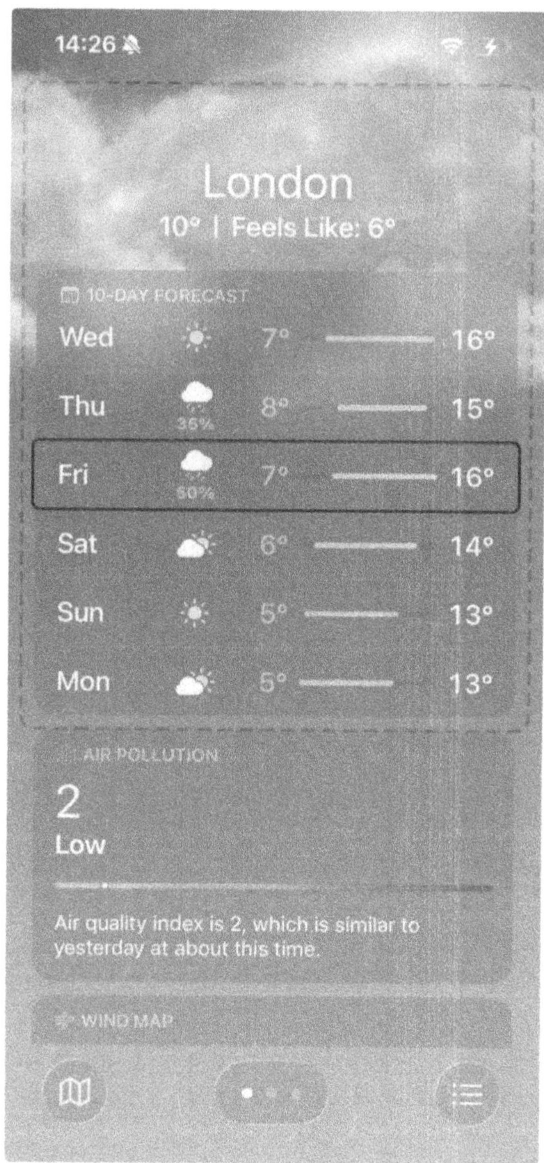

***Figure 9-3.** Switch Control focusing on an element inside a group*

The `contain` argument causes Switch Control to navigate this group as a top-level element (Figure 9-3). Users can then choose to navigate into this area if they wish to activate a control contained within. This makes navigating the full screen considerably more efficient if used effectively. Further detail on semantic views can be found in Chapter 6.

NAVIGATING WITH SWITCH CONTROL

Before enabling Switch Control, you need to add a switch to your device. Your screen is probably the simplest choice to use in a testing situation, although I'd also recommend trying this out using head movements and sounds. Under the Switch Control menu in Accessibility settings, tap Switches ➤ Add New Switch… ➤ Screen ➤ Full Screen ➤ Select Item.

Now enable Switch Control through the Accessibility settings or, in the future, by activating the Accessibility Shortcut we set up in Chapter 7. You'll see a blue focus ring appear at the top of the screen; after a moment, this indicator will move down the screen to the next group of selectable elements; after another pause, the box will make another jump, and so on. To activate the highlighted area, tap anywhere on the device's screen. If this highlight contains a group of items, the scanner will begin to cycle through the elements.

Once you have used Switch Control to activate a single element, you are presented with a popover of possible actions. These actions are cycled in the same method as the screen itself, meaning you can tap anywhere on the screen to perform the highlighted action or move focus into the highlighted group. The first action highlighted in the popover is always Tap.

Disable Switch Control by triple-tapping the sleep button on your device to activate the Accessibility Shortcut, then double-tap the screen once Switch Control is highlighted.

Voice Control

Voice Control allows full control of your app using only voice, making it ideal for people with the most limited movement. Voice Control uses the same accessibility tree as VoiceOver, Switch Control, and many other assistive technologies, meaning your app supports it by default.

Voice Control can be enabled with the accessibility shortcut. But the most straightforward way to activate it is to say "Hey Siri, turn on Voice Control." To disable it you can simply say "Turn off Voice Control" followed by "Tap Confirm".

Navigation should come naturally, as the most common command you will use is "Tap" followed by the label of the button. If you're unsure of a button's label, say "Show names" (Figure 9-4) to present bubbles with the first word of the accessibility labels for each control. Most users prefer saying "Show numbers" and referencing each control using the presented index.

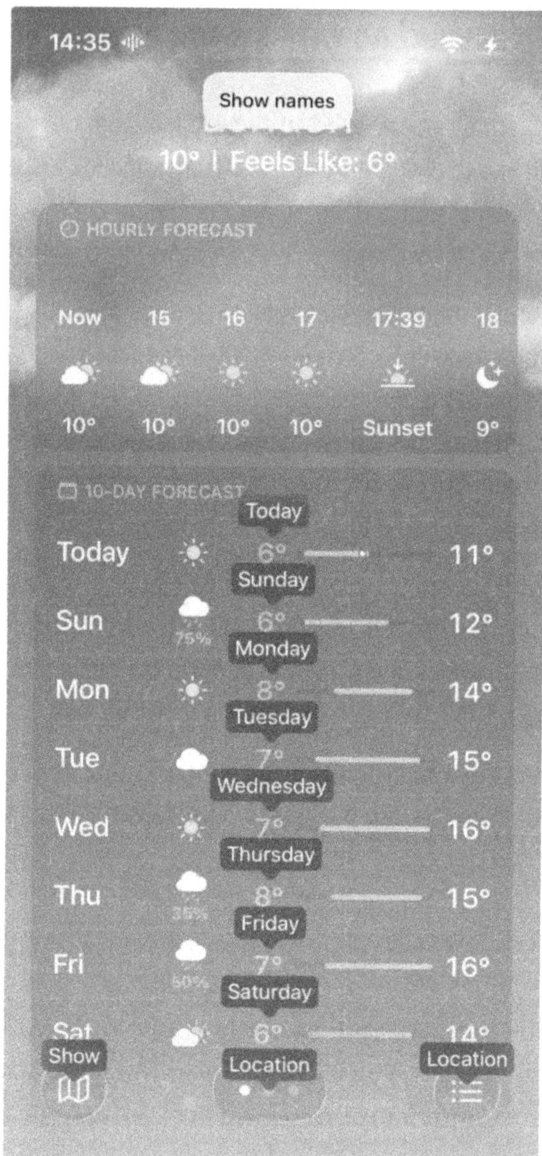

__Figure 9-4.__ Voice Control displaying names

Ensure your accessibility labels for controls are accurate and brief, as this will be the phrase used by your Voice Control customers to activate the control in question.

If your element contains a long label or may have other valid labels, you can offer a group of shorter or alternative labels that your user may speak. This is done by adding the `.accessibilityInputLabels()`[3] modifier to your control and passing an array of alternate strings (Listing 9-2), ensuring the primary label is listed first.

Listing 9-2. Providing friendly labels for Voice Control to listen for to activate a "play" control

```
Button(action: {
    play()
}, label: {
    Image(systemName: "arrowtriangle.forward.fill")
})
.accessibilityLabel("Play")
.accessibilityInputLabels([
    "Play",
    "Play song",
    songTitle,
    "Play \(songTitle)"
])
```

Full Keyboard Access

Full Keyboard Access[4] allows access to all controls using an attached physical keyboard. Like VoiceOver, Voice Control, and Switch Control, this feature uses the accessibility tree. So if your app support is good for those assistive technologies, you'll likely find Full Keyboard Access works well too. Navigating between items is done using the Tab and arrow keys, and elements can be activated with the Space bar.

[3] https://developer.apple.com/documentation/swiftui/view/accessibilityinputlabels(_:)-2upwq/

[4] https://support.apple.com/en-gb/guide/iphone/ipha4375873f/ios

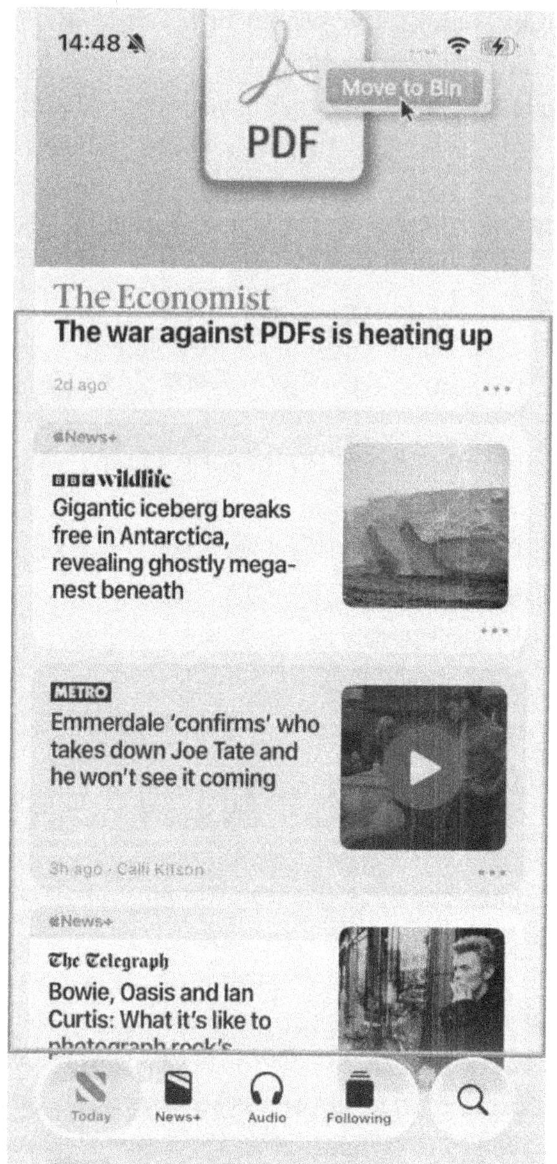

Figure 9-5. *Full Keyboard Access focusing on an element within a list*

Full Keyboard Access makes full use of accessibility actions covered in Chapter 6 to present actions that are not otherwise directly available with a simple tap. These actions can be shown by pressing Tab + Z. Pressing Tab + F shows a search UI, allowing targeting elements by name, using the `.accessibilityInputLabels()` modifier we introduced in the above section.

As with Switch Control, navigation of the screen can be made more efficient by grouping related elements using the `.accessibilityElement(children: .contain)` modifier.

Keyboard Navigation

Keyboard Navigation is a technology that doesn't use the accessibility tree but instead uses a separate focus engine. Once an external keyboard is connected, there are no activation steps needed to enable this feature; you can immediately navigate focusable elements with the Tab key and activate them with the Enter key.

Keyboard Navigation is not intended to focus on every control as Full Keyboard Access does. Instead, it is intended to navigate between elements where the keyboard can be used to input data – i.e., text fields and text views. Collections such as lists should also be focusable so their content can be navigated with arrow keys.

Any element in SwiftUI can be made keyboard focusable by adding the `.focusable()` modifier.

Tracking and Setting Keyboard Focus

Keyboard focus can be both set and read using the `@FocusState` property wrapper.[5] If you wish to know or set the focus of a single element, use the Boolean variant of this property wrapper; for multiple elements, an enum-based variant is available.

In Listing 9-3 we create a `@FocusState` var in our view; this is a Boolean value. Using the `.focused()` modifier, we can assign this `@FocusState` to our field and then read and set focus using the Boolean.

Listing 9-3. Reading and setting the focus state of a single field

```
struct ContentView: View {

    @FocusState var fieldFocused: Bool
    @State var fieldValue = ""
```

[5] `https://developer.apple.com/documentation/swiftui/focusstate/`

```
    var body: some View {
        VStack {
            TextField("Field", text: $fieldValue)
                // Assigning @FocusState to a field
                .focused($fieldFocused)
                .onAppear {
                    // Setting the field focused when it appears
                    fieldFocused = true
                }
        }
    }
}
```

In Listing 9-4, we have multiple fields we wish to track and so use an enum rather than a Boolean to set and read the current focus.

Listing 9-4. Reading and setting focus states of multiple fields

```
struct ContentView: View {
    // An enum detailing all fields on which we want to detect focus
    enum FocusableElements {
        case field1, field2

        var fieldName: String {
            switch self {
            case .field1:
                "Field 1"
            case .field2:
                "Field 2"
            }
        }
    }

    @FocusState var focusedField: FocusableElements?

    @State var field1Value = ""
    @State var field2Value = ""
```

```
    var body: some View {
        VStack {
            TextField("Field 1", text: $field1Value)
                .focused($focusedField, equals: .field1)
                .onAppear {
                    focusedField = .field1
                }
                 // Adding a border only when focused
                .border(focusedField == .field1 ? .red : .clear)

            TextField("Field 2", text: $field2Value)
                .focused($focusedField, equals: .field2)

            Text("\(focusedField?.fieldName ?? "No field") is focused")
    }
}
```

Keyboard Shortcuts

Keyboard Shortcuts are available to both Keyboard Navigation and Full Keyboard Access users, so adding these to your app's key features is extremely powerful.

Adding a keyboard shortcut to an action is a case of adding a `.keyboardShortcut()` modifier to the button that performs the action. The shortcut then becomes available while the screen containing that button is present. An enum value can be used to specify a common key – these are localized automatically where appropriate (Listing 9-5). To specify a specific keyboard key, add the key as a string (Listing 9-6). You can also specify one or more modifier keys with the `modifiers` argument. If no modifier is specified, the Command key is the default. The exceptions to this are `.defaultAction` (Enter) and `.escape`, which can be assigned to an action without requiring a modifier key (Listing 9-7). For advice on picking a combination for a keyboard shortcut, check out the Keyboard section of the Apple Human Interface Guidelines.[6]

[6] `https://developer.apple.com/design/human-interface-guidelines/keyboards#Custom-keyboard-shortcuts`

Listing 9-5. Adding a command keyboard shortcut for the common key "Space"

```
Button("Play") {
    playSong()
}
.keyboardShortcut(.space)
```

Listing 9-6. Adding a control keyboard shortcut for the key "n"

```
Button("New Playlist") {
    newPlaylist()
}
.keyboardShortcut("n", modifiers: .control)
```

Listing 9-7. Adding a keyboard shortcut for the key "escape"

```
Button("Go back") {
    navigateBack()
}
.keyboardShortcut(.escape)
```

Pointer Support

Pointer support comes for free in SwiftUI. Once your user connects a mouse, trackpad, trackball, or other pointing device, any interactions that work with a single touch are now accessible with the pointer.

While the functionality may work as expected, you may wish to confirm that pointer support also looks right. Consider adding a `.hoverEffect()` modifier to your buttons; `.lift` should generally be used for buttons with a solid background and `.highlight` for those without. Add the `.clipShape()` modifier after the hover effect to ensure the effect has the right shape and size.

Avoid triggering actions using an `.onHover {}` modifier, as these interactions can only be triggered using a pointer, not with touch or other assistive technologies.

Game Controller Support

If you have configured your Keyboard Navigation support correctly, then game controllers will also be able to navigate and activate appropriate elements in your UI with no further action needed. But for some specific applications, adding further game controller support could be a huge benefit.

Game controllers are specifically designed for fine-grained control; they are ergonomically designed, and variations, such as the Xbox Adaptive Controller, allow extensible and configurable input. Obviously, this makes sense for games, but for apps where users may want to capture accurate input or finely adjust values, adding support for controllers may be valuable.

Using the `GameController` framework, you can listen to notifications when controllers connect, then set up `valueChangedHandler` callbacks for controller buttons you care about and react accordingly.

If this sounds like a feature users would benefit from in your application, check out the Game Controller framework documentation at developer.apple.com.[7]

Summary

- Ensuring your accessibility tree is valid will ensure both Switch Control and Voice Control work as expected; make sure you test with both.
- If your app makes use of touch gestures or input timing, make sure you offer an alternative that doesn't require such accurate input, for example, by exposing these interactions as accessibility actions.
- Power users will also appreciate the consideration you give to keyboard, pointer, and game controller support.

The next chapter concludes our look at iOS's accessibility features. We'll cover the considerations iOS provides for people with hearing impairments.

[7] `https://developer.apple.com/documentation/GameController`

CHAPTER 10

iOS Accessibility Features – Hearing

If I were to offer a single piece of advice regarding improving apps for people with hearing impairments, it would be to embed captions on any video content by adding a subtitle track and using the `AVPlayer` to play the video. If your app makes prominent use of audio, consider an alternative way to provide an engaging experience, perhaps through leveraging animation, other visual cues, or haptics.

Mono Audio

Mono Audio disables stereo output for all audio on the device. This is done at a system level and requires no changes by your app. Mono Audio may be used for people who have hearing loss on one side, as stereo audio can cause them to lose content if some audio is panned to the side they struggle to hear. For instance, if a video of a conversation is panned so that one person is left and the other right, someone with hearing loss on one side will only hear half of the conversation.

You might want to know about this setting if you rely on stereo audio within your app. For example, a game that might use panned audio to hint at the presence of enemies will lose meaning with this setting enabled. If Mono Audio is enabled, consider removing the need for panned audio, such as by adding additional visual UI to indicate the direction of the audio source.

There is no SwiftUI API to query this setting, but it is available in your SwiftUI code using UIKit's `UIAccessibility.isMonoAudioEnabled` property. This returns a simple Boolean value indicating the state of the switch.

R. Whitaker, *Developing Inclusive Mobile Apps*, https://doi.org/10.1007/979-8-8688-2809-6_10

Subtitles and Captioning

Captions can be enabled in the Accessibility settings for the device. `AVFoundation` contains built-in support for both audio descriptions and closed captioning, so using an `AVPlayer` instance for your media will give you this functionality for free (Figure 10-1) - provided you ensure your videos have audio descriptions and closed captions embedded. Any good quality video editing software will include the ability to add captions and alternative audio tracks.

Figure 10-1. *AVPlayer displaying embedded captions*

In the first instance you should always add captions as caption tracks embedded in the video file, known as "closed captions," and play using `AVPlayer`. This allows your users to customize the appearance as needed in the device settings (Figure 10-2). The caption appearance settings chosen by the user are not exposed to developers, meaning a custom video player cannot replicate them. Open captions, where text is burned directly into the video, similarly cannot respect your users' preferences.

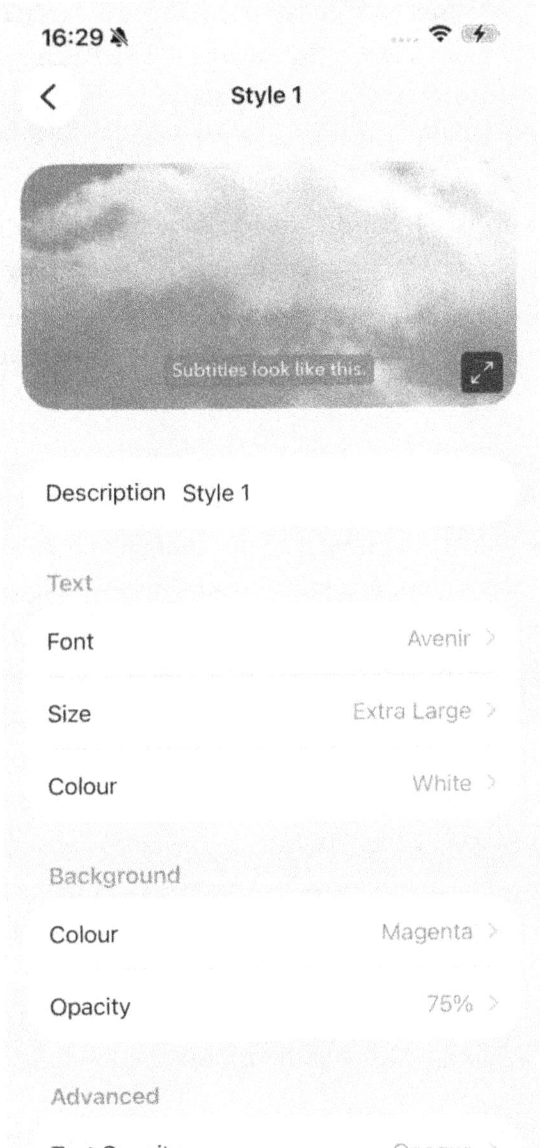

***Figure 10-2.** Customizing the caption appearance. This is only available when using AVPlayer*

What if you're not playing video with `AVPlayer`? Maybe you're using a custom video player, perhaps you want to display captions as part of your UI, or possibly you have a speech audio track played in your app. In these circumstances, you need to show the captions yourself. Bear in mind that with this option you will not only be responsible for displaying the captions but also keeping them in sync with the audio.

To decide if you should show or hide captions, there is again no SwiftUI API. But by checking `UIAccessibility.isClosedCaptioningEnabled` as part of UIKit, you can get the Boolean state of this setting at the time you query.

Most professional video-editing software will allow you to add a subtitle track to your videos. Ideally, these subtitles should be professionally transcribed, but many AI services are available to transcribe audio and do so with reasonable accuracy – just be sure to review the output before including it in your app. If you do burn the captions into the video track, avoid the TikTok style of showing a single word at a time, which prevents users from reading at their own pace and can be highly distracting.

Haptics

Haptics are one of those features of smartphones that can make an app feel polished when used correctly; sensory feedback can really bring your digital experiences into the physical world. But they are also a subtle way to draw attention to a state change, especially for people who cannot hear UI sounds – either because they have disabled the sounds, they are in a loud environment, or they have hearing loss.

Some standard SwiftUI components, such as sliders and pickers, already provide haptic feedback. But if creating custom controls, or if you wish to add some physical feedback to enforce meaning, SwiftUI includes a `.sensoryFeedback()` modifier.[1] This modifier allows us to specify a feedback type from a predefined list and specify the value that will trigger the feedback. Variations of this modifier provide more control over exactly how the feedback is triggered.

In Listing 10-1, we show a warning message in response to the `showWarning` value being set to true. A change in this same value will trigger feedback of type `.error`.

Listing 10-1. Triggering haptic error feedback when an error is shown

```
struct ContentView: View {
    @State var showWarning = false
    var body: some View {
        if showWarning {
```

[1] `https://developer.apple.com/documentation/swiftui/sensoryfeedback/`

```
            HStack {
                Image(systemName: "exclamationmark.triangle.fill")
                    .accessibilityHidden(true)
                Text("An error occurred")
            }
            .sensoryFeedback(.error, trigger: showWarning)
        }
    }
}
```

Custom Haptics

While the `.sensoryFeedback()` modifier does offer a wide range of possible feedback types that will feel familiar, if your interface makes significant use of sound, you should consider creating custom haptics based on that sound. This is possible with the Core Haptics framework.

A notable example of this in use is when paying with Apple Pay. The sounds designed to indicate success or failure of a payment have matched haptic patterns, creating a vibration effect that feels incredibly natural.

We won't go into full details of implementing custom haptics here; for that, you should read the Core Haptics documentation on the Apple website.[2] Using the framework, you can craft complex haptic patterns to match the exact feel you need.

If you are supporting game controllers as covered in Chapter 9, many controllers are also capable of generating haptic feedback using the Core Haptics and Game Controller frameworks in combination.

Music Haptics

If your application features a music player playing back commercially available tracks that are identifiable with an ISRC code, the Music Haptics framework[3] will play back synchronized haptics as generated by Apple. While this is a specific use case, when appropriate, this is a great example of a 'magical' feeling accessibility consideration.

[2] https://developer.apple.com/documentation/CoreHaptics

[3] https://developer.apple.com/documentation/mediaaccessibility/music-haptics/

Summary

- If you detect that a customer has a hearing accessibility feature enabled, they might struggle to determine speech or audio directionality. Consider offering alternatives if these are important to your app.
- Use your video-editing software to embed a subtitle track into any video content your app uses and use the `AVPlayer` control to display captions automatically.
- Add haptics to draw attention to state changes. This will help people with hearing impairments, but also those with visual and cognitive impairments.

Now that we have covered the full range of iOS accessibility features a developer might need to consider, we need to ensure our changes are having the right impact for our customers. In the next chapter, we'll consider different techniques for testing your app's accessibility.

CHAPTER 11

Testing for Accessibility

This book will give you a whole bunch of tools and practical tips you can use when creating your apps, from design and coding to the wider service. How you use this knowledge in your app must be based on your team's consideration of how best it fits what you are trying to achieve. None of these tools will have the impact needed by real people, however, unless you check your work.

Don't consider accessibility testing as an extra. As you might with unit testing, you should aim for accessibility testing to become a regular part of your workflow. Include considerations for accessibility testing as part of your existing test plan. As such, I'm not going to teach you the basics of making a test strategy; instead, I will provide tips and tools that should become second nature.

What we will cover here is a very high-level overview of different types of accessibility testing and tools and techniques you can use to help with each. It is important to remember when reading this chapter that testing accessibility is an enormous topic, one that really deserves more than a single chapter. Use all the information here as a starting point, not a destination.

Automated Testing

The question I get asked by far the most by fellow developers is how they can automate accessibility testing. This is an understandable instinct, but my answer is always a little disappointing.

Accessibility is all about humans and how they perceive and interact with your software. As such, machines don't make a great proxy for this; automated testing must never be a replacement for manual user testing.

Code can never understand your intention, so you can only validate a small subset of what is defined in WCAG. That said, anything that can be automated should be automated, as this flags issues earlier in the development cycle, making fixes faster

R. Whitaker, *Developing Inclusive Mobile Apps*, https://doi.org/10.1007/979-8-8688-2809-6_11

and cheaper. I highly recommend investigating these tools to see how they can fit into your development workflow and help you increase or improve your velocity while maintaining accessibility.

XCUI Testing

iOS's first-party UI testing framework, XCUI, performs its tests by checking against your app's accessibility tree. This means that any well-written XCUI test is also an accessibility test. It also means that an accessible app is one that is easier to write automated tests for.

XCUI tests include an accessibility audit function[1] that can run a suite of tests on your screen and output the results right in Xcode along with screenshots of any issues found. The audit is done by adding a single line to your existing UI tests as shown in Listing 11-1, making this a quick value-add.

Listing 11-1. Enabling accessibility tests in XCUI

```
@MainActor
func testAccessibility() throws {
    let app = XCUIApplication()
    app.launch()
    // Navigate to the screen you wish to audit
    try app.performAccessibilityAudit()
}
```

Espresso Testing

Android's Espresso testing framework similarly includes a group of accessibility checks that can be dropped into your existing Espresso test suite. Include these tests by importing `AccessibilityChecks`,[2] and enable them with the code in Listing 11-2.

[1] https://developer.apple.com/videos/play/wwdc2023/10035/

[2] https://developer.android.com/training/testing/espresso/accessibility-checking

Listing 11-2. Enabling accessibility tests in Espresso

```
import androidx.test.espresso.contrib.AccessibilityChecks
@RunWith(AndroidJUnit4::class)
@LargeTest
class MyWelcomeWorkflowIntegrationTest {
    companion object {
        @Before @JvmStatic
        fun enableAccessibilityChecks() {
            AccessibilityChecks.enable()
        }
    }
}
```

Tests will then automatically execute on a view and its descendants each time an action is performed on that view. Alternatively, you can instruct Espresso to run the suite of tests on the root view by adding `setRunChecksFromRootView(true)` immediately after the `enable()` call.

Vendor Tools

A range of vendors offer suites of tools to help speed up detection, remediation, and reporting of accessibility issues. I have included three here that are well-versed in mobile accessibility. As with any tool vendors, while they may be able to offer you more comprehensive coverage and more streamlined reporting, you should always beware of marketing claims. Inclusion here is informational only and does not constitute a recommendation.

Deque Axe DevTools for Mobile

Deque is a big name in digital accessibility - they offer a range of services such as training, consulting, and audits. Their website also features a big selection of blogs and resources on digital accessibility, and they hold the free Axe-Con accessibility conference every year, which is worth signing up for.[3]

[3] `https://www.deque.com/axe-con/`

Deque's Axe DevTools for mobile[4] product is an accessibility testing toolkit for iOS, Android, and cross-platform. The suite includes an analyzer that will validate your app screen by screen as you run it and an automated SDK that can drop into your existing UI test suite. Each option reports failures into a dashboard with screenshots, failure details, and guidance on how to fix the issue.

Level Access

Level Access is one of the longest-established digital accessibility specialists. Like Deque, they offer a broad range of services from audits and consulting to reporting, in addition to their automation options. Their mobile product[5] is intended to run against an app without requiring code access, making it simple for non-technical users to run.

Evinced

A challenger to Deque and Level Access, Evinced[6] focuses only on automated testing without providing other accessibility services. Like other vendors, Evinced offers both an analyzer and an automation option for Android, iOS, and cross-platform, which feed results into a dashboard that provides failure details, annotated screenshots, and fix guidance.[7]

Verification Tools

Accessibility verification tools are a middle ground between automated testing and manual testing. They can provide a little more detail than automated testing in some areas but still require manual work to run the checks. As noted above, Evinced, Deque, and Level Access provide these features in addition to their fully automated tools, so I won't cover them again here.

---

[4] `https://www.deque.com/axe/devtools/mobile-accessibility`

[5] `https://www.levelaccess.com/mobile-testing/`

[6] `https://www.evinced.com/`

[7] At time of writing, tech editor for this book, Quintin Balsdon, is employed by Evinced.

As with automated tests, it is not possible to detect all, or even most, accessibility issues with tools such as these. It is therefore important not to rely on these for full coverage; however, they can be useful for detecting issues earlier in the development process.

Reveal

Reveal[8] is an iOS developer view-debugging tool built by a team of developers to fulfill their requirements when working on apps. In addition to the view debugger, they have added an accessibility debugging mode, which shows you all entries in the accessibility tree and flags potential issues.[9]

Google Accessibility Scanner

Google's Accessibility Scanner is an app, downloadable for free from the Google Play Store.[10] The Accessibility Scanner can run an audit against your app on demand, capturing a screenshot and highlighting elements that would benefit from improvement (Figure 11-1). The report provides the identifier of the view that has failed, along with a description of why the element failed and guidance on how you might fix the error.

[8] `https://revealapp.com/how-reveal-helps/accessibility/`

[9] I provided guidance on accessibility rules applied in Reveal.

[10] `https://play.google.com/store/apps/details?id=com.google.android.apps.accessibility.auditor&pli=1`

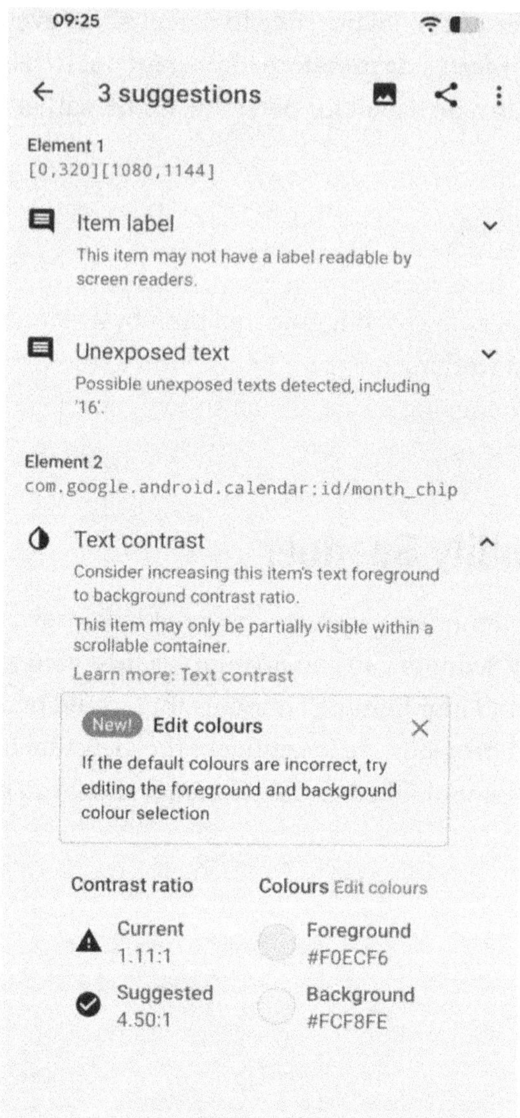

Figure 11-1. *Google Accessibility Scanner suggesting accessibility improvements*

Apple Accessibility Inspector

Accessibility Inspector[11] is part of Xcode's suite of tools; launch it from within Xcode via the Xcode menu ➤ Open Developer Tool. You can then run the Accessibility Inspector against your app on a device or in the simulator in one of two modes.

[11] `https://developer.apple.com/documentation/accessibility/accessibility-inspector`

Inspection allows you to target a user interface element to view the element's accessibility properties such as label, traits, and hint (Figure 11-2). The top of the Inspection view shows an approximation of the string that VoiceOver reads when it encounters the element - note that this is often not the same as what is announced on device.

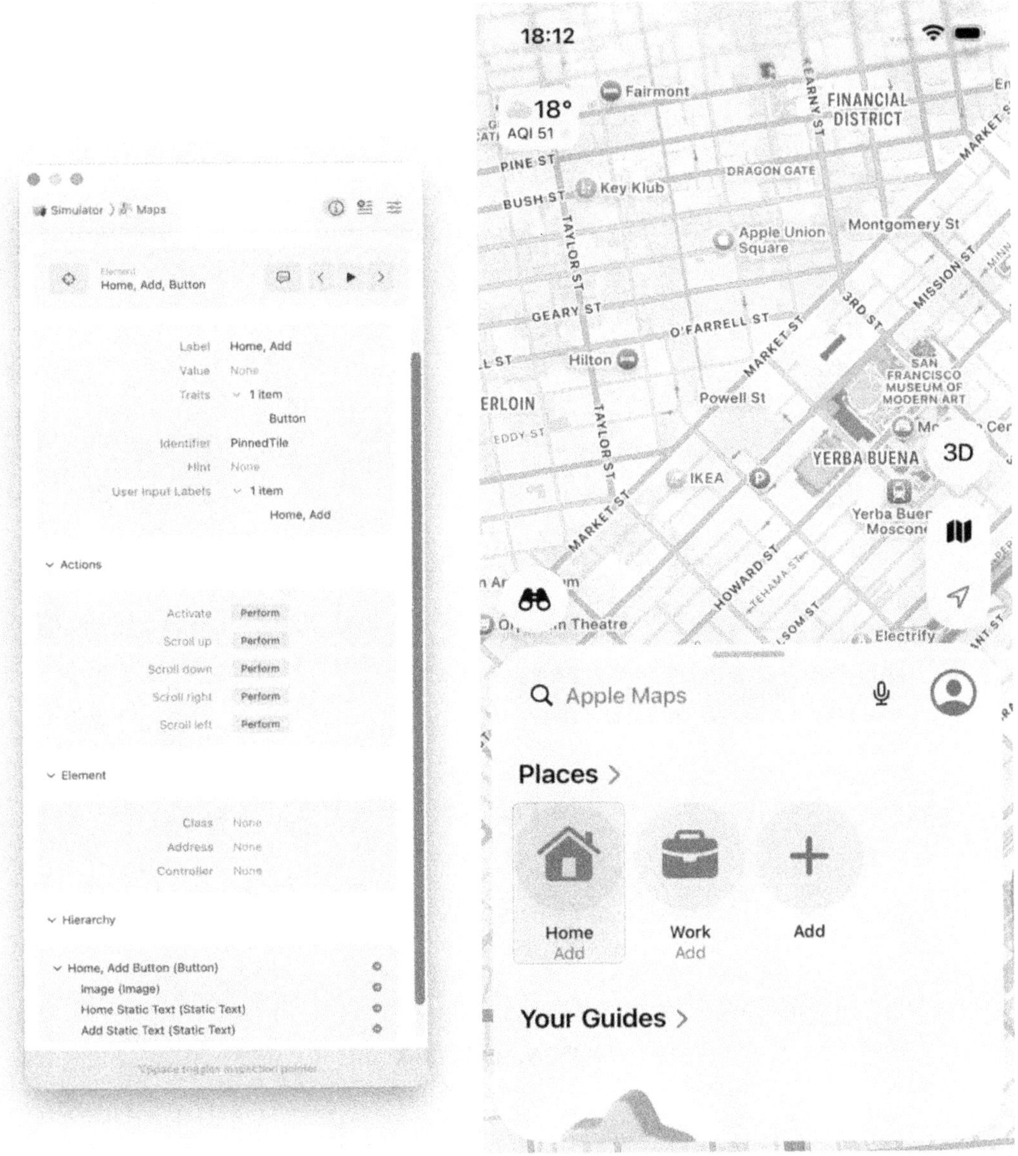

Figure 11-2. Accessibility Inspector in Inspection mode (left) displaying the accessibility attributes of the Home button in Maps, highlighted (right)

The play and forward/back buttons here will cycle through accessibility elements on the current screen in the order they would be navigated by VoiceOver, offering a quick way to discover issues with ordering or unexpectedly hidden elements.

Audit mode runs a check on the entire current view and reports on accessibility issues found (Figure 11-3), including details of why the verification failed, a screenshot of the element that failed in position, and a hint on how you might fix the failure.

Figure 11-3. *Accessibility inspector reporting in audit mode (left). The audit creates screenshots highlighting the area of the screen where there may be an issue (right)*

The Accessibility Inspector also provides quick access to toggle some accessibility features using the Settings tab (Figure 11-4).

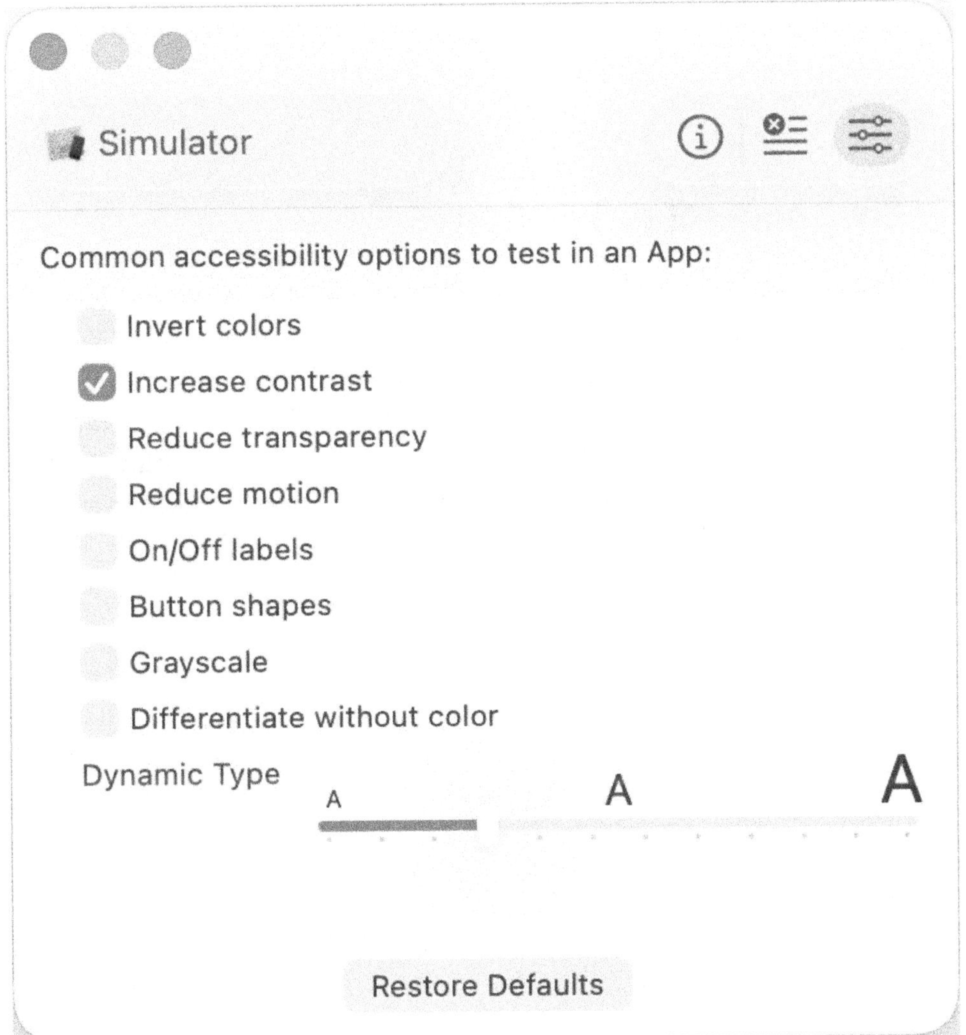

***Figure 11-4.** Accessibility Inspector Settings tab providing controls for some accessibility features*

Developer Tools

Developer tools can help check accessibility coverage while you build your UI, allowing you to detect issues before they even happen. These will generally not include validations; instead, they provide variations of your UI based on various accessibility considerations.

Xcode Environmental Overrides

Like Accessibility Inspector, Xcode features an Environmental Overrides menu for the currently running app. This works in both the simulator and on a device. You can find the button for this menu on the debugger toolbar at the bottom of the editor (Figure 11-5). Here you can effortlessly switch between dark and light appearances and adjust the Dynamic Type size. You can also toggle several accessibility features, including Increase Contrast, Reduce Transparency, Bold Text, and Reduce Motion.

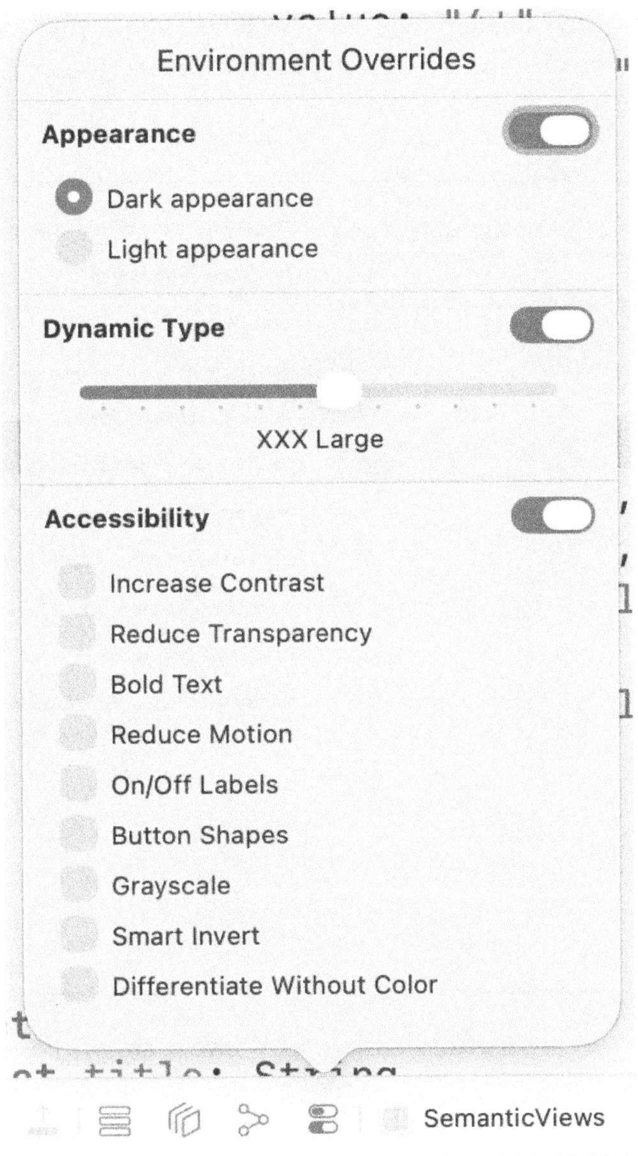

Figure 11-5. *Xcode Environmental Overrides*

Xcode Application Language

Xcode also provides overrides for testing your app in different languages, including pseudolanguages. Edit your app's build scheme by clicking the app name in the Xcode toolbar. Under Run ➤ Options, you'll find a dropdown option for App Language. Here you can choose from any language supported by iOS to check your localizations. In the list, you'll find a section of various pseudolanguage options (Figure 11-7).

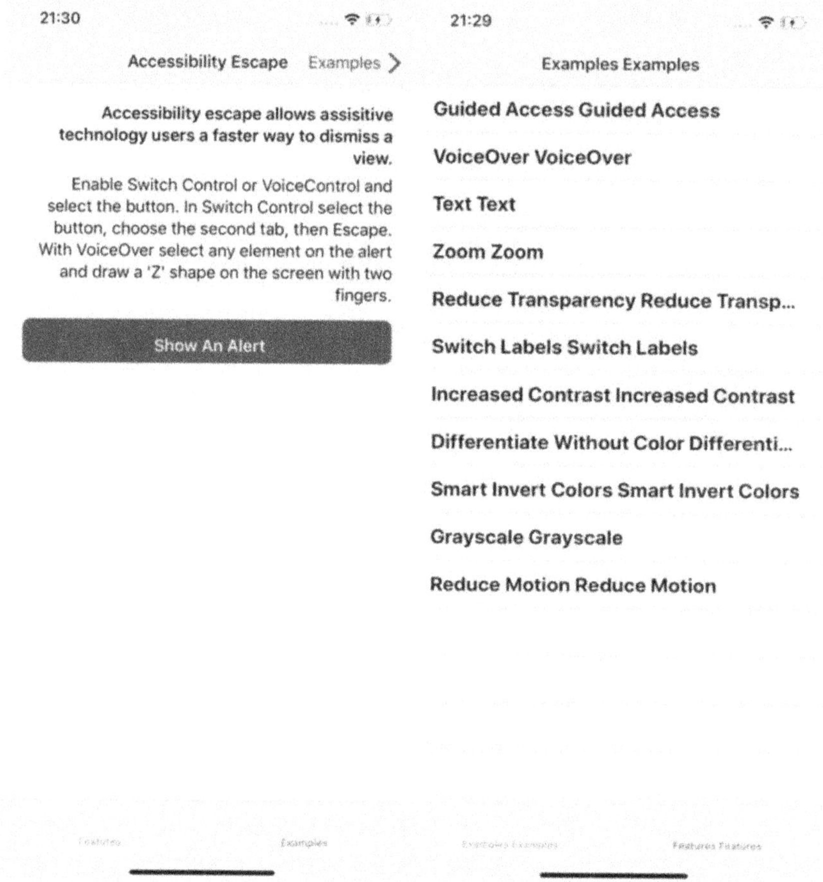

***Figure 11-6.** Selecting a pseudolanguage in Xcode's scheme editor*

Pseudolanguages are synthesized languages that mimic languages with different properties. The most useful in this list are the Right-to-Left Pseudolanguage and the Double-Length Pseudolanguage (Figure 11-7).

Right-to-Left Pseudolanguage mimics how your app will appear in a language such as Arabic that reads from the opposite direction of most languages. Double-Length Pseudolanguage duplicates your strings. These allow you to check that your layout is flexible enough to support languages that take up more space than your development language. Providing adequate flexibility in your layout will also assist with your support for Dynamic Type sizes.

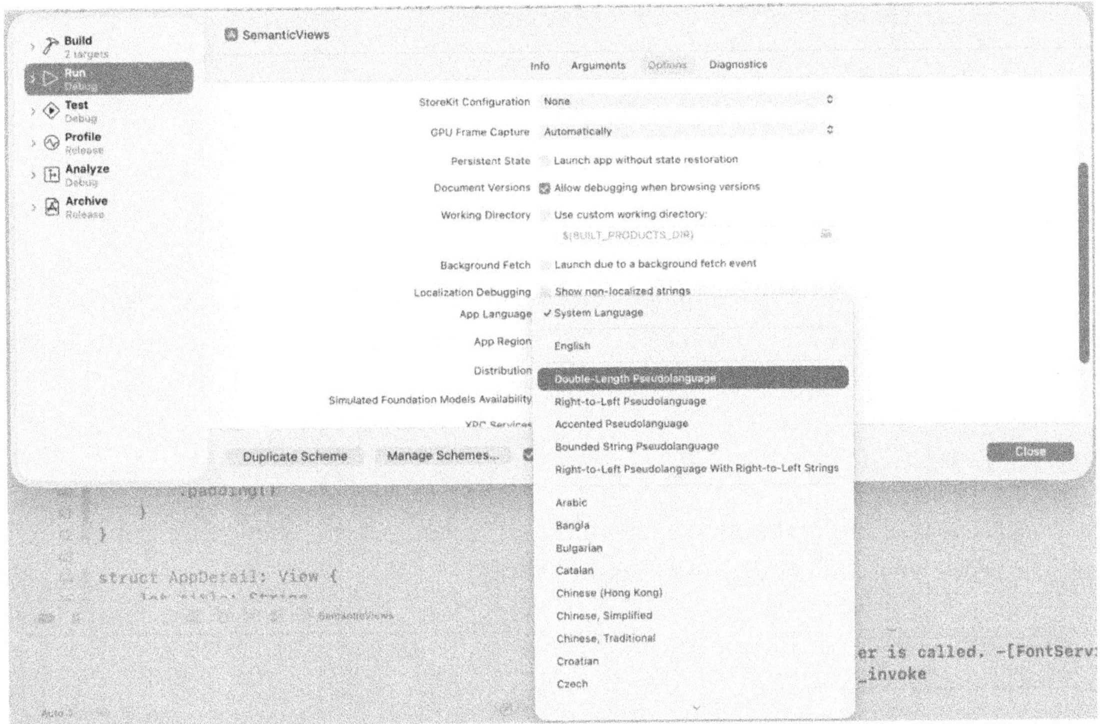

Figure 11-7. *Right-to-Left Pseudolanguage (left) and Double-Length Pseudolanguage (right)*

ADB Commands

Android can be controlled via command line using ADB. By using the `adb shell settings put system` command, you can set the text size (Listing 11-3), display inversion (`accessibility_display_inversion_enabled 1`), high contrast text (`high_text_contrast_enabled 1`), and display magnification (`accessibility_display_magnification_enabled 1`).

Listing 11-3. Using ADB to set a larger text size

```
adb shell settings put system font_scale 1.30
```

Previews

Previews are a powerful way to check your view code as you're writing it. Leveraging them to show variants based on accessibility settings is a great way to discover potential issues as you're building the UI.

SwiftUI

The canvas includes the option to show multiple variants of your view by orientation, color scheme, or dynamic type size (Figure 11-8).

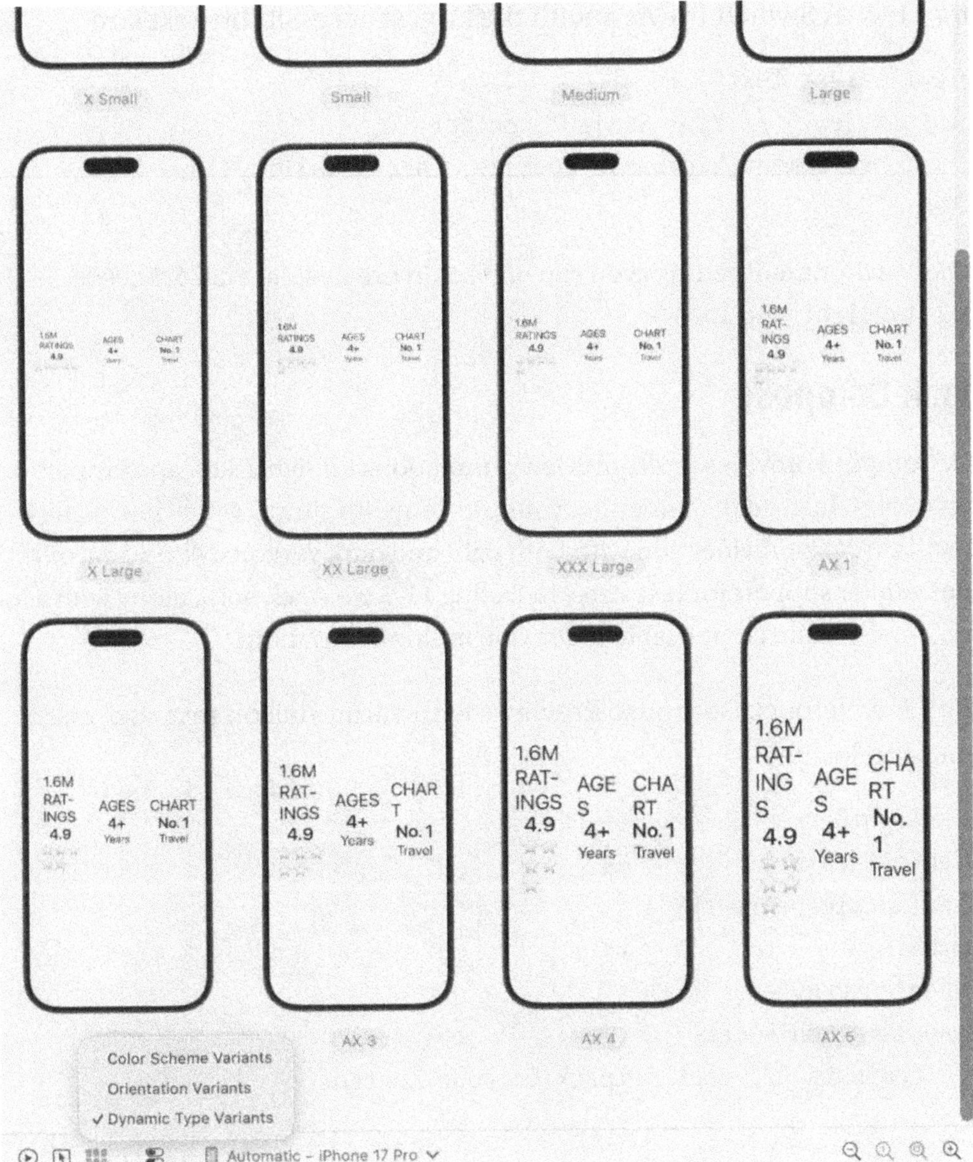

***Figure 11-8.** Xcode Canvas showing screen variations at Dynamic Type increments*

You can also use the SwiftUI environment to create previews with specific settings. In Listing 11-4, we're creating a preview with the Dynamic Type size fixed to the largest accessibility option.

Listing 11-4. A SwiftUI Preview with the largest accessibility text size

```
#Preview("Larger text") {
    ContentView() // Your SwiftUI content
        .environment(\.dynamicTypeSize, .accessibility5)
}
```

Other environment settings you can enforce in previews are `colorScheme`, `legibilityWeight`, and `locale`.

Jetpack Compose

Jetpack Compose provides multi-preview annotations for light/dark appearance and font scales. Instead of annotating your preview with simply `@Preview`, using `@PreviewLightDark` provides you with both light and dark variants. `@PreviewFontScale` provides similar support for text sizes. In Listing 11-5 we stack both, along with a locale preview, on the same composable to provide multiple variations.

Listing 11-5. Jetpack Compose Previews with variations on text size, color scheme, and locale

```
@PreviewLightDark
@PreviewFontScale
@Preview(locale = "fr-rFR")
@Composable
fun MyContentPreview() {
    MyApplicationTheme {
        Content() // Your Jetpack Compose content
    }
}
```

Manual Testing

While automated tools and inspectors are fantastic at preventing regressions and highlighting less obvious accessibility errors, there are accessibility issues that automated testing can never identify. The most common of these is determining if the accessibility tree you are presenting to your customer is logical and meaningful. While in the visual user interface we have designers do this for us, their hard work doesn't always translate to a useful accessibility tree once we have turned the designs into code. The only way to check this is to try it for yourself.

Testing Setup

Before we get to devices, you'll need a setup to record your findings and progress. Accessibility testing is complex - there are a lot of technologies and a lot of features or screens to test with each. It's easy to get lost. It's also easy to find and catalog a lot of issues - things that we could make better - but while those improvements have value, our focus should be on identifying and fixing issues that could block someone from completing a task altogether. A good recording setup can help clarify and prioritize both.

Progress Matrix

A progress matrix is a simple way to track manual accessibility testing across features and assistive technologies.

To create a matrix, list across the top all the assistive technologies and accessibility considerations you are going to test with. Then, on the vertical axis list the features you are testing. Keep these features as self-contained as possible; the larger you make them, the harder it becomes to track progress meaningfully. I suggest that in most cases you'll want to break into screens at the largest granularity and often break them down further into components.

In the matrix, record your progress with "in progress" and "complete" statuses.

In the example below (Table 11-1), I have created a testing matrix for the onboarding flow of an application and the home screen. Testing is complete for the welcome screen and currently in progress for keyboard support on the notification permissions screen. I have kept the assistive technology names generic, but you may find it simpler to track if you use the names of the technologies that are specific to the platform you are testing.

Table 11-1. *Sample testing matrix*

	Screen reader	Keyboard	Text scaling	Color contrast
Welcome	✓	✓	✓	✓
Notification permissions	✓	⧗		
Home screen				
Tab Bar				

Recording Results

Ultimately, you will likely want to enter any findings into whatever work-tracking software you are using, in the format you usually use for bugs. This will be different for every organization, so I won't give guidance beyond suggesting good practice.

When you discover a potential issue, make a note immediately. Record where you saw the issue – the screen and the component, the steps you took leading up to the issue, what you saw, and what you were expecting to see.

Once you have completed testing, you can revisit these notes to check if you are able to reproduce, judge if it is a genuine problem, and assign a severity. This part of the process may require some research – speaking to designers or developers to understand intent, investigating how other apps behave, or speaking to users or accessibility experts.

Finally, add a severity rating to your issue. The exact scale I will leave to you, but you should have three tiers – I'm calling them Blocking, Issue, and Improvement.

Blocking

An issue that prevents a user from being able to achieve something with their chosen assistive technology. For example, if the keyboard can't activate a button, a screen reader can't read some text, or text becomes unreadable at larger sizes – this issue is a blocker and should be fixed as the highest priority.

Any flashing images that could cause a seizure must fall into this category.

Issue

An issue that would fail WCAG but can reasonably be worked around. For example, if a button doesn't work with an assistive technology, there is an option in a menu that performs the same action and can be activated.

Most issues will fall into this category.

Improvement

An issue that would improve the quality of the experience for someone using assistive technologies. For example, adding synonyms for controls to access them via Voice Control, or improving the quality of accessibility labels to remove unnecessary length or detail.

Device Setup

As we have covered in earlier chapters, there are many assistive technologies and accessibility settings on both platforms. Providing a testing guide for all would be an entire book of its own. So here I have covered two technologies only - screen readers and scaled text. To be clear, testing only these will not guarantee your app's accessibility, but these will likely have the most impact for the greatest number of users and will surface issues that affect multiple assistive technologies.

If you followed the guides earlier in this book, you'll likely already have your device set up well for testing, but I'll cover these here as a reference for setting up new devices. These steps assume you haven't already made any customizations to accessibility settings.

iOS Setup

In Settings ➤ Accessibility scroll to the bottom and find the option for the Accessibility Shortcut. In this menu, enable any assistive technology you may wish to test with, but ensure VoiceOver is included. Enabling options in this menu provides ease of access later by triple-tapping the sleep/wake button on your device.

Return to the Accessibility settings, and in the VoiceOver options, enable the Caption Panel. This is an area of text that appears at the bottom of the screen when VoiceOver is enabled. This shows the exact text of the VoiceOver utterance, allowing you to detect any issues that may not be immediately obvious just from hearing the speech. It can also be useful in an office where such utterances could disrupt colleagues.

To verify text scaling, open Display & Text Size from the Accessibility settings, and tap Larger Text. Enable Larger Accessibility Sizes. Then swipe down from the top of your screen to reveal Control Center. Long-press on the screen to enter editing mode. Tap *Add a Control,* then *Text Size.* This then adds a slider to your Control Center, allowing a quick way to change the Dynamic Type size to the maximum and back again. By long-pressing on this slider, you can set the text size for the current active app only (Figure 11-9), meaning you won't affect the rest of your device.

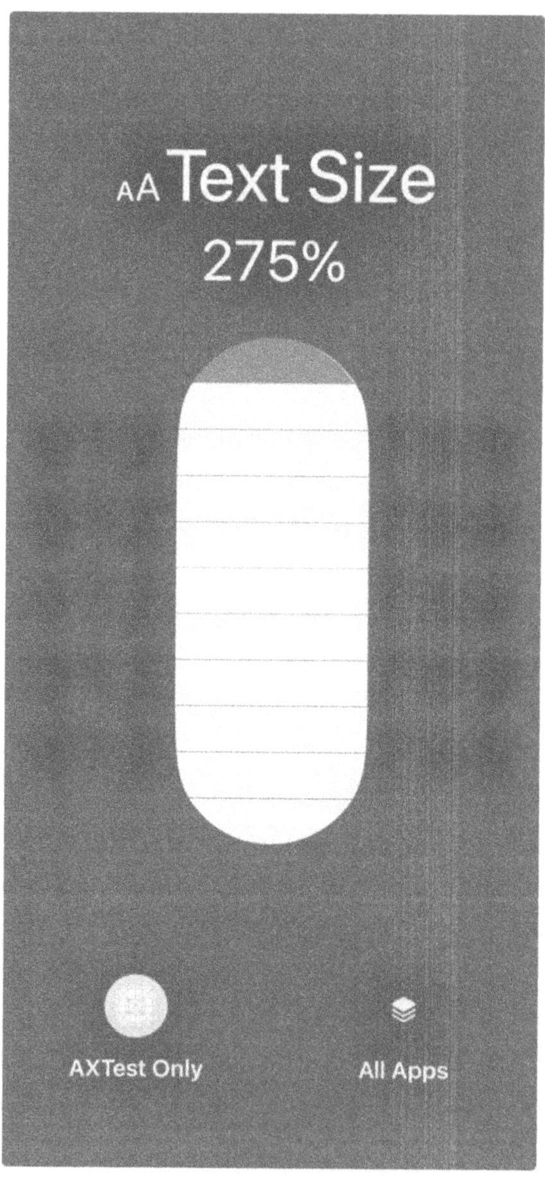

Figure 11-9. *Setting text size for the active app only in Control Center*

While you're editing the Control Center, add a button for Screen Recording so you can easily capture reproduction steps of an issue.

Android Setup

As with all Android Devices, exact setup steps will vary by model and manufacturer. As noted in earlier chapters, I am using a Google Pixel device running Android 16.

In Settings ➤ Accessibility ➤ TalkBack enable the TalkBack shortcut. This allows you to easily toggle TalkBack on and off by holding both the volume up and down buttons on your device at the same time. Then open the TalkBack Settings and enable Display speech output. This option shows a toast displaying the current text of the utterance, reducing disruptions for colleagues and allowing you to detect potential issues that may not be clear from hearing the speech alone.

Next, swipe down from the top of the screen to open the Quick Settings, tap the pencil to enter edit mode, and ensure you have Screen Recording and Font Size (represented by smaller and larger capital T characters) enabled (Figure 11-10).

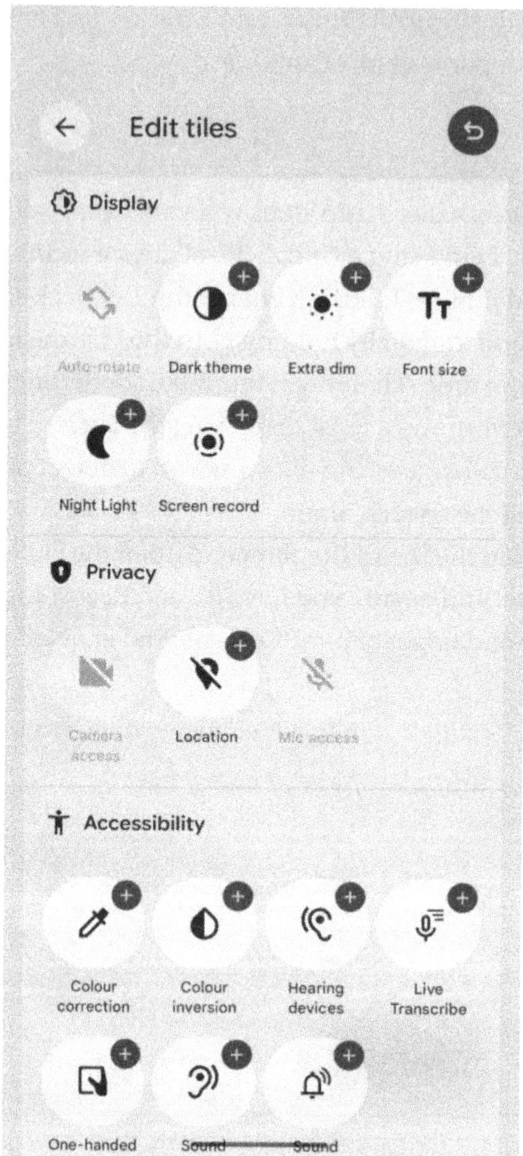

Figure 11-10. *Adding actions to the Quick Settings menu. Note Font size and Screen record in the Display section*

Tapping on the Font Size button from Quick Settings opens a slider where you can adjust text scaling to the maximum value.

Screen Reader Testing

When making a new screen or making a significant change to a screen, navigate your screen with VoiceOver or TalkBack enabled. While these screen readers make up just one assistive technology, they make the largest use of the accessibility tree, meaning you are most likely to discover an issue with a screen reader than with any other assistive technology.

Once you become familiar with how these screen readers work, this test should become a quick and essential part of your regular development workflow. For details on navigating with each, see "Navigating with TalkBack" in Chapter 5 and "Navigating with VoiceOver" in Chapter 8.

When performing manual testing with screen readers, there are a few questions to ask as you're navigating. This list is very high level but makes a good starting point.

1. **Is each element focusable and in a logical order?**

   Elements should follow each other in a meaningful way that provides context to controls. Don't present a "buy" button before the name of the item that's being purchased, for example. Are there any elements missing or elements that are focusable that shouldn't be?

2. **Are the utterances meaningful and not overly complex?**

   Does each control adequately describe its purpose in as few words as possible? A button to buy should be "Buy" or "Buy {product name}," it should not be "Button" or "Double tap this button to buy {product name} for {price}."

3. **Can I interact with each control?**

   Can you activate or otherwise interact with each control you can focus on, usually by double tapping? Can I figure out the current state or value of a control, and does this update when the control is changed - for example, the text content of a text field or the value of a slider?

Text Scaling

Set the text size to the largest possible setting supported on your device, and check the following:

1. **Is any text overlapping?**

   If any text overlaps other text and is therefore unreadable, this is a failure. Often this will happen if content is not inside a scroll view or has a fixed size.

2. **Is text clipped or truncated?**

   If text is clipped or truncated, this is acceptable in the context of a table or collection, provided I can tap on the text to see the full content elsewhere. If there is nowhere that I can see the full, non-truncated text, then this is a failure.

Accessibility Nutrition Labels

The iOS App Store features optional accessibility nutrition labels; for more on these, see Chapter 7. To find which labels you should apply, Apple provides an assessment guide.[12] Following this will not ensure you have a "fully accessible" app, but it does go a long way. If you're starting out making your app accessible, following this testing guide is a great starting point toward achieving WCAG compliance. It is a solid starting point for Android too, although you will have to translate the assistive technology names.

Instead of testing every screen and every feature in your app, Apple suggests a "common task" approach, narrowing your testing down to the following: First launch experience, login (including sign-up), purchase, settings, and your app's primary functionality.

Once you have applied your labels in the App Store, ensure you retest whenever a change is made to any of your common tasks. If your accessibility assertions become out of date, the App Store review may block your release.

[12] https://developer.apple.com/help/app-store-connect/manage-app-accessibility/overview-of-accessibility-nutrition-labels

Audits

If you work in a medium-to-large company and have ever had an accessibility initiative of any kind, you'll likely have seen an accessibility audit. This is where an expert, or group of experts, often external to your organization, reviews your app and reports on any issues they find that do not meet WCAG requirements.

Such reports are essential from a reporting perspective, as they provide a document detailing exactly where failures lie and what needs to change to resolve them. I offer this as someone who has both received and authored such reports: the power of audits to make meaningful improvements in your application is limited.

Such a report is necessarily negative. It is a list of everywhere your team has made mistakes, sometimes providing code-level suggestions. Understandably, developers can bristle at such a report. Audits are also a snapshot in time, and by the time you receive it, your software has likely already changed; this model rarely fits with modern agile software practice.

That said, if you disagree with a finding in one of these reports, it's always possible to query a finding and provide more context. If your aim is to get a baseline against the WCAG standard or receive an objective report from someone who knows the standard inside-out, these reports do have value.

A much more valuable and meaningful approach is to build a relationship with your accessibility team or contractor and bring them into the design and planning stages of building a feature. By doing this, they can flag potential issues before they arise, show code you need to add to provide support for assistive technologies, and give you details on how to test with those assistive technologies. By reducing the possibility of accessibility issues occurring in the first instance, this not only reduces the likelihood of issues reaching users but also significantly cuts the cost of remediation.

One final note on working with an external accessibility expert - if possible, find someone with expertise in mobile. The expectations for assistive experiences in native apps are different from those on the Web, and domain-specific knowledge is needed to avoid creating some very confusing experiences.

User Feedback

Consider adding an option to your app for your customers to contact you with feedback. AppleVis,[13] an online community of blind and low-vision Apple users, recommends its members contact app developers when they have experienced accessibility issues to outline the problem.[14] Many people who discover accessibility concerns do just that. The reality is that many developers don't know enough about accessibility to realize there may be an issue and are happy to resolve problems when they are flagged. As a result, users who send feedback often find they get good results. But even if you're following everything in this book, you still won't have the experience your customers do when using your app. A feedback option is a low-cost, low-effort, but effective way of doing user testing.

One benefit we have as mobile developers, although it's perhaps not always seen as a benefit, is that we receive feedback from our customers in the form of app reviews. These can also be a source of accessibility feedback.

User Testing

Earlier in this book, I emphasized the importance of having empathy in software engineering. Empathy is an incredibly valuable skill for any software craftsperson. But empathy can sometimes lead us down the wrong path – the path toward thinking something must be done without thinking about whether what we chose to do is having the right effect. One reason for improving accessibility in your app is indeed because helping others makes you feel good, but that shouldn't be the main reason. Design strategist Liz Jackson asks us to rethink the strategy of empathy.

> *[Empathy] reifies class and power structures. You always have the empathizer and then you always have the empathizee, right? The empathizer is cast as the savior, and the empathizee is always the recipient, and those roles never change.*

[13] https://www.applevis.com/

[14] https://applevis.com/apps

> *[Empathy] silences the recipient. You are expected to be grateful for that which has been done for you.*
>
> —Liz Jackson, Empathy Reifies Disability Stigmas[15]

My point here is that if you're not user testing your app with users with disabilities, you're not doing accessibility - you may simply be boosting your ego.

Listening to, and acting on, feedback is important. Do not dismiss accessibility-based feedback because you disagree, or even because it goes against something you read in this book. Use it as a reason to dig deeper into how you can create a better experience. However, like any users, users of assistive technologies are all different with different needs and expectations, so one piece of feedback should not necessarily be a reason to make a major change if it goes against established accessibility guidance.

User testing methodologies are well covered elsewhere, and many vendors will provide this as a service for you, so I won't cover how to set up user testing sessions or labs here. But I do wish to express how important it is to make your participants in user testing sessions varied. Be sure to include people with disabilities, along with people from different backgrounds and a range of technical abilities. Most importantly, listen to their feedback. It may be the case that a change you made thinking it would improve accessibility has made it worse. Disabled people don't have an obligation to be grateful to you for considering them. Instead, your duty as a developer is to work with their feedback.

Summary

- As with any other aspect of software, if you don't test it, how do you know it worked?
- The most accurate and useful insights come from user testing with people with a range of abilities. Be sure to listen to and trust their experiences.
- Regular manual testing as part of your development flow will mean accessibility testing will soon become second nature.

---

[15] Liz Jackson, "Empathy Reifies Disability Stigmas", 2nd June, 2019, `http://opentranscripts.org/transcript/empathy-reifies-disability-stigmas/`

- Augment manual testing with automated testing and other tools where possible – this can catch issues earlier in the process, reducing time, cost, and the likelihood of shipping bugs. But automated testing is limited in scope and must never be a replacement for human testing.
- Prioritization is important. Fix issues that block users from completing core flows before moving to quality-of-life improvements and rarely used features – but don't forget these entirely.
- Accessibility is a process, not an end state.

CHAPTER 12

Making Your App Inclusive

By now, I'm hoping I've convinced you of the argument for why accessibility and inclusion are essential. We've covered what each platform is capable of in the form of technologies and features provided for people with disabilities, and when and how you may use them. We also covered why you may use them when discussing the purpose of accessibility and the Web Content Accessibility Guidelines (WCAG). In this final chapter, I want to try to tie together accessibility and digital inclusion and highlight some ways we may be able to make more explicit considerations that allow us to build software that is more inclusive.

Trade-Offs

Software engineering is all about constraints and trade-offs. We must balance those trade-offs in order to build solutions that fulfill the needs of our users and customers, and our business. These limitations could be server costs, battery life, or data consistency across multiple threads. Equally, constraints apply when considering how our users perceive and interact with our software, and we should consider these alongside any other engineering decisions.

Ultimately, we'd all love to make our apps into truly inclusive experiences that work for everyone. But much like having infinite compute power or network connectivity that never drops, this desire is unrealistic. Some of the engineering decisions we must make will exclude people from being able to use the resulting software or will have a negative impact on some of our users. This is not ok, but it is inevitable, and it is important that we recognize this. What we can do, however, is be explicit about what these decisions are, recognize when a decision we make may affect some of our users, and understand how we can do better.

R. Whitaker, *Developing Inclusive Mobile Apps*, https://doi.org/10.1007/979-8-8688-2809-6_12

In the UK, a government computer system, Horizon, built by Fujitsu for the Post Office had such poor engineering practices that hundreds of innocent people were jailed; people lost their life savings, businesses, reputations, and health.[1] The stories of the effects of this system on its users are so deeply upsetting I will not repeat them here. However, the story of how this system was created is a cautionary tale for exactly how to not build software: designs were not created and decisions not documented, code was not tested, defensive coding was not implemented, engineers and managers were inexperienced and had little professionalism,[2] bugs weren't fixed, no coherent release strategy was followed, and anyone within Fujitsu was able to manually edit data with no logging enabled.

The effects of the Horizon system may be at the extreme end but are a stark example of the effects our engineering decisions can have on our users. Through accountability, craft, and pragmatic decision-making, we can do better.

You ≠ Your Users

> *In the past 25 years we have been designing [software] mostly for people who design [software].*
>
> —Vasilis van Gemert, Exclusive Design[3]

As people who make a living, one way or another, from computers, it's easy for us to forget that we are in a privileged position when it comes to knowing how to use the products we create. In reality, our customers are not like us; they're not even that likely to be like our friends.

I'm sure we can all think of a family member who doesn't use technology. If they needed to pick up a device today to do a task, would they know that the frying pan icon means they can search? Will they care about the cutesy names you've given to things,

[1] Nick Wallis, The Great Post Office Scandal (Bath: Bath Publishing, 2021).

[2] One internal Fujitsu report included the phrase "Whoever wrote this code clearly has no understanding of elementary mathematics or the most basic rules of programming."Nick Wallis, "Inquiry Phase 2: Star Witness – Dave Gives It Both Barrels," Post Office Scandal, November 17, 2022, `https://www.postofficescandal.uk/post/inquiry-phase-2-star-witness-dave-gives-it-both-barrels/`.

[3] Vasilis van Gemert, "Exclusive Design," accessed October 19, 2025, `https://exclusive-design.vasilis.nl/`.

like "the cloud" when you mean storage? I remember a time from working in an Apple reseller. A customer believed AirPort, Apple's brand name for Wi-Fi, meant they could only use Wi-Fi on flights.

We can't be there to hold our customers' hands. And I don't think either we or our customers would want that either. There's a fine line between thinking about what our customers are capable of and being patronizing. Avoiding jargon, both written and visual, is an excellent first step. To be successful at the rest, we need to know more about our users. This is where well-designed user testing, using people with mixed abilities and experiences, as covered in chapter 11, can be really valuable.

Digital Literacy

As a regular, long-time digital citizen, it's easy to forget about or even look down on, the many people who don't use the Internet, or maybe even fear the Internet. But worries about the security of our personal data online, for example, are genuine and one that 60% of us share. The UK Government, in partnership with Lloyds Bank, produced a list of Essential Digital Skills – A skills benchmark for any person to be able to use the Internet competently.[4]

As you're reading this book, it's likely that you can do all these essential digital skills. Indeed, many of them may seem so basic they're barely worth mentioning. The reality for many people in the United Kingdom, however, is that they can't do these things we'd consider obvious – 15% of the UK adult population don't have these skills.

The 10 least possessed essential digital skills include tasks such as "I can post messages, photographs, videos, or blogs on social media platforms," "I can recognize what information or content online may, or may not, be trustworthy," and "I can use software to create, write, or edit documents." 23% of respondents could not access content in the cloud.

The great news is that these skill gaps are reducing, with the proportion of people with all eight foundation skills increasing by five percentage points since 2022.

[4] Lloyds Bank, Essential Digital Skills 2025 (November 2025), `https://www.lloydsbankinggroup.com/assets/pdfs/who-we-are/what-we-do/financial-wellbeing/lloyd-essential-digital-skills-2025.pdf`.

Avoiding jargon, using clear and consistent layouts, and relying on recognizable patterns and iconography can go a long way here. Where possible, guide and signpost users through your interface, provide help and reassurance when needed, and guard against errors or irreversible actions.

Age

Technology has a generational gap. Ninety-nine percent of 18- to 24-year-olds use the Internet, compared to 90% of those aged 65 or over.[5] Many of us grew up with the ubiquity of computing. Others had likely never heard of computers or knew them as an obscure industrial tool they would never use. Who among us, having not grown up on a farm, would feel confident, or even enjoy, learning the intricate details of sophisticated farming machinery in our thirties if this were suddenly to become part of our everyday lives?

While this skills gap is gradually closing, we can't escape that the world has an aging population, and with aging comes changes to our bodies. As life expectancy grows, it's a truism that most of us will live to see our body begin to fail us. So, although you might not use assistive technology now, in the future as your eyes, cognition, motor abilities, or any other physical facet begins to fail, you will begin to appreciate their presence. This is the same for your customers.

The "gateway" accessibility feature for age is the ability to change text sizes. Supporting Dynamic Type on iOS and using scalable point sizes on Android is a must-have first step for accessibility in any app. Adjustable text sizes are commonly the first accessibility feature a customer may use, often without considering it an accessibility feature.

Financial Status

A computer, tablet, or smartphone, along with an Internet connection, is not an insignificant financial outlay – and a recurring one too. Almost a fifth of adults who are online have access to the internet only via a smartphone.[6] Smartphone-only internet use is a pattern that is more common among lower socio-economic groups who are more likely to face affordability barriers to more traditional broadband or device access.

---

[5] Pew Research Center, "Internet, Broadband Fact Sheet," November 20, 2025, `https://www.pewresearch.org/internet/fact-sheet/internet-broadband/`.

[6] Ofcom, Adults' Media Use and Attitudes Report 2024 (April 2024), `https://www.ofcom.org.uk/siteassets/resources/documents/research-and-data/media-literacy-research/adults/adults-media-use-and-attitudes-2024/adults-media-use-and-attitudes-report-2024.pdf`.

Therefore, as mobile developers, we have a responsibility to offer experiences that are as complete as possible when compared with desktop. At the same time, we must choose which devices and operating systems to support. Dropping older platforms can reduce complexity and enable new features, but it can also exclude users who are less able to upgrade — often those who are already disadvantaged.

Consider too that people with disabilities often have a more substantial cost burden than those without. UK Disability charity Scope estimates this to be over US$1,460 extra per month.[7] People with disabilities are also 2.3 times more likely to be out of employment.[8] As a result, people with disabilities are more likely to fall into the financially disadvantaged category.

In addition to considering your device support policy, being a good platform citizen can have a significant impact for users in this category. Using system resources mindfully and supporting low-data and low-power modes when possible can reduce ongoing costs and make your app more compatible on constrained devices.

Anxiety and Mental Health

Many headlines cover the health effects of smartphones, such as "Putting Down Your Phone May Help You Live Longer,"[9] endless opinion pieces, such as "How I Ditched My Phone and Unbroke My Brain,"[10] and a wealth of health guides, such as "5 ways your phone is affecting your anxiety."[11] Seeing these headlines, it may be tempting to believe we mobile developers have created a monster.

[7] Scope, The Disability Price Tag 2025 (June 2025), `https://www.scope.org.uk/campaigns/disability-price-tag`.

[8] OECD, Disability, Work and Inclusion (October 2022), `https://www.oecd.org/en/publications/disability-work-and-inclusion_1eaa5e9c-en.html`

[9] Catherine Price, "Putting Down Your Phone May Help You Live Longer," New York Times, April 24, 2019, `https://www.nytimes.com/2019/04/24/well/mind/putting-down-your-phone-may-help-you-live-longer.html`

[10] Kevin Roose, "Do Not Disturb: How I Ditched My Phone and Unbroke My Brain," New York Times, February 23, 2019, `https://www.nytimes.com/2019/02/23/business/cell-phone-addiction.html`

[11] Eleanor Jones, "5 Ways Your Phone Is Affecting Your Anxiety," Cosmopolitan UK, February 14, 2018, `https://www.cosmopolitan.com/uk/body/health/a17851630/mobile-phone-affecting-anxiety-mental-health/`

Panics about information overload and innovative technologies are older than technology itself. In around 360 BC, Socrates warned that the written word would "create forgetfulness" and that readers would struggle to differentiate fantasy from reality.[12] It is true that Internet or mobile phone addiction exists and that it can be as damaging as any other addiction. It is also true that overuse of smartphones can cause stress, depression, sleeping problems, anxiety, and loneliness.[13]

While overuse of technology is an indicator of poor mental health, so too is technology underuse. Bélanger and colleagues found, in a 2011 study, a "U-shaped association" between Internet use and mental health.[14] Their oft-cited research discovered that those with little or no Internet use had increased levels of depression resulting from feeling isolated. So, while our chosen platform may cause the effects listed above for some, for the majority, it has the exact opposite effect. By creating immersive experiences, we allow people to enrich their lives and find belonging. This is something we should celebrate.

Finding what areas of smartphone use are risk factors for mental health is all but impossible. The wide range of tasks that we can perform on smartphones, combined with the fact that heavy smartphone use is a societal norm, makes it difficult to identify patterns.[15] But we can apply more general research into mental health risk factors to create practical guidelines.

Deceptive Patterns

User experience specialist Harry Brignull coined the phrase Deceptive Patterns (sometimes Dark Patterns) to describe hostile design patterns intended to make users do things they hadn't intended. Brignull defined some common dark patterns on his web

[12] Plato, Phaedrus, trans. Benjamin Jowett (c. 360 BCE), `http://classics.mit.edu/Plato/phaedrus.html`.

[13] Beryl Noë et al., "Identifying Indicators of Smartphone Addiction Through User-App Interaction," Computers in Human Behavior 99 (October 2019): 56–65, `https://www.sciencedirect.com/science/article/pii/S0747563219301712`.

[14] Richard E. Bélanger et al., "A U-Shaped Association Between Intensity of Internet Use and Adolescent Health," Pediatrics 127, no. 2 (February 2011): e330–e335, `https://publications.aap.org/pediatrics/article-abstract/127/2/e330/65234/A-U-Shaped-Association-Between-Intensity-of`

[15] Noë et al., "Identifying Indicators of Smartphone Addiction," 56–65.

site, www.deceptive.design.[16] These include, but are not limited to, fake urgency, confirm shaming, and trick wording. The International Consumer Protection and Enforcement Network found in 2024 that over 75% of websites and apps examined used at least one deceptive pattern, with over 66% employing more than one.[17]

The intentional use of deceptive patterns to manipulate users into behavior that benefits your business shows contempt for your users and is unethical. For your customers with cognitive impairments, these traps can be even more upsetting and confusing.

Self-Control

Many people with anxiety, mental conditions, or learning difficulties often find the ability to add restrictions for themselves to be a positive action. A 2019 study from Noë et al. found that apps that don't provide a defined endpoint to content, for example, infinite scrolling, can lead to smartphone addiction.[18] Forcing a stop to our smartphone use allows us to take a break and refocus. Implementing these controls in your app will vary greatly depending on your app's purpose. While adding pauses or explicit end states may not fit with your product's aims, opt-in limits give users the ability to introduce friction where it matters to them.

A great example of allowing customers to manage themselves comes from UK challenger bank, Monzo. Monzo introduced blocks on certain transactions in their app, providing a setting for customers to disallow any transactions related to online gambling. This became so successful that the feature was adopted into UK regulation, requiring all banks to implement similar blocks.

Gamification

Gamification is the practice of using game-like mechanics such as streaks, XP, and achievements in non-game contexts. In apps, these can be used to nudge users towards positive behaviors and to make otherwise mundane experiences more enjoyable.

---

[16] Deceptive Patterns, "Types of Deceptive Pattern," accessed January 17, 2026, `https://www.deceptive.design/types`.

[17] International Consumer Protection and Enforcement Network, Dark Patterns in Subscription Services Sweep (July 2024), `https://www.icpen.org/sites/default/files/2024-07/Public%20Report%20ICPEN%20Dark%20Patterns%20Sweep.pdf`.

[18] Noë et al., "Identifying Indicators of Smartphone Addiction," 56–65

Duolingo (Figure 12-1), the language learning app, uses gamification to stand out. It employs a combination of small, achievable, progressive goals, visualizing progress, and prompts to return and stay engaged.[19]

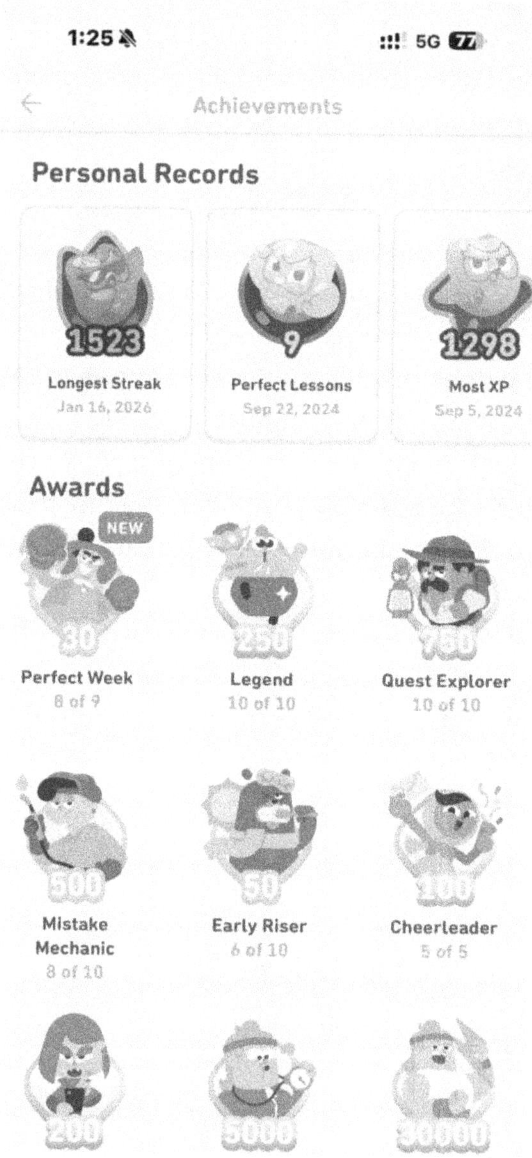

Figure 12-1. *Achievements in Duolingo*

[19] Richard Draycott, "Gamification Is the Key to Duolingo Success, Says Product Manager Gilani at Canvas Conference," The Drum, October 26, 2017, `https://www.thedrum.com/news/2017/10/26/gamification-the-key-duolingo-success-says-product-manager-gilani-canvas-conference`.

While the use of gamification can be positive for both users and app developers, it can be easy to overstep into either appearing or being manipulative. Aim to use this as a tool to add enjoyment, rather than a way to hide deceptive patterns.

It's a subtle but important line between engaging your customers with gamification and seeding bad habits. Noë and colleagues suggest that gamification in the form of competing against friends online can contribute to smartphone addiction.[20] Noë's team uses the example of Snapchat's Snapstreak feature. Snapstreak rewards regular posting with a fire emoji and the number of days the streak has been maintained. Users are encouraged to keep this streak alive, which can lead some users to feel pressured into posting, resulting in stress and anxiety.

Guide

The feeling of being lost or trapped can be a catalyst for anxiety. A common occurrence of this in mobile is forcing customers to perform actions at a time chosen by us, for example, showing an interstitial, rather than allowing our customer to make the decision when they're ready - we've all experienced a "Not now" button.

You can combat feelings of disorientation by guiding and signposting. Show users their progress when they are performing a task to reiterate what they have achieved and how much remains.[21] Allow your customers to progress at their own pace, and, if possible, allow them to advance in their order, skipping, or returning to steps, as necessary.

When your customer has completed a task, before they commit, offer the opportunity to review what they've done. Allow the chance to change their responses, as necessary. If any action is going to make a noticeable change in service, such as a destructive action, clearly explain the consequences in an easy-to-follow way before allowing them to continue. We often aim to speed up interactions in our apps but consider employing positive friction where a flow could result in a significant or negative outcome. Positive friction provides a pause, giving users time to think and double-check their intent.[22]

---

[20] Noë et al., "Identifying Indicators of Smartphone Addiction," 56–65.

[21] Design Patterns for Mental Health, "Provide a Visible Record of Progress," accessed January 17, 2026, `https://designpatternsformentalhealth.org/patterns/provide-a-visible-record-of-progress`.

[22] Design Council, "Monzo: Designing Good Mental Health into the Way We Bank," October 17, 2018, `https://www.designcouncil.org.uk/news-opinion/monzo-designing-good-mental-health-way-we-bank`.

Make sure your app's look and feel are consistent, sticking with system controls where possible to aid consistency with the platform. Changes in the way something works, especially unexpected ones, can cause feelings of discomfort and increase anxiety.

Design Simplicity

Sticking to sound design principles and keeping interfaces simple, consistent, and predictable has a significant impact on reducing cognitive load for all. Great design is rarely about "more" and instead about clarity and subtle guidance. A clear and logical information architecture goes a long way.

Avoid overcrowding your interface with too many fonts, text sizes, colors, animations, stylistic variations, or transparency. This can make an app feel messy and inconsistent. Using well-understood system patterns helps make your app feel familiar and at home on the platform.

Where possible, provide redundancy of information. Instead of relying only on text, the addition of an image, graph, or video can aid understanding. Providing captions on video or audio content helps more people than only those with hearing impairments. For larger groups of text, such as an article, offering an audio recording is a good addition.

Redundancy also applies with color use - don't rely on color alone to convey meaning, as people experience color differently, both physically and culturally. Wherever color is used to indicate status, it should be paired with another cue such as text, icons, or shape.

Animation should be used to guide attention and add meaning, not to carry meaning on its own. Motion can help to show relationships, but overuse can massively increase cognitive load, distract from content, or exclude those who have motion disabled.

Clear Copy

Written content should be clear, direct, and predictable. Avoid idioms, acronyms, abbreviations, and unnecessary technical language. If using any of these is necessary, provide a definition, either inline at first use or by providing definitions elsewhere in your app. Be explicit about what actions to do and what will happen next. This applies just as much to button labels and error messages as it does to longer explanatory text.

If something matters, say it plainly and surface it clearly, without overwhelming your user. Any action with consequences - destructive actions, purchases, or changes in features or functionality - benefits from extra consideration when communicating to your user.

Investing in a good copywriter will provide a significant benefit to the clarity of your app. Communicating clearly and efficiently is a true art.

Identity

I remember learning about basic data types in high school. The exercise was to create a data capture form for people to register for a party. Although anyone who required registration for a party in an Excel spreadsheet would be unlikely to have very many guests. We stored age as an integer, name as a string, and gender as a Boolean. From an engineering perspective, storing gender as a Boolean is brittle, and many other engineering assumptions around gender have caused similar tech debt.

Representing any real-world value as a Boolean is usually a decision that will cause future refactoring, as real life is rarely binary. Secondly, allowing only two options for anything involving identity means making assumptions about the people who are using your app, which may be incorrect.

With anything identity-related, the first decision should be "Is this information actually required?"

Preferred Names

A common requirement for software is to store a legal or birth name. We expect the requirement for "real" names in software for HR, banking, or government services, for example. But it is not unusual for us to want to be known differently. My preference is to be called Rob, but my passport says Robert. This can cause me problems booking international travel through work, where the systems automatically book everything in the name Rob.

The ability to have my given name separate from my preferred name, for me, is just a convenience. I would neither have to ask colleagues to call me Rob nor correct travel bookings to match my passport. But for many, this is a crucial part of their identity. For anyone who has or is changing identity, being known by a name they no longer identify with can be hugely upsetting.

Human rights groups have criticized "real name" policies as being dangerous for victims of domestic abuse, political activists, and members of the LGBTQ+ community, while also being problematic for people with non-western names.[23]

Allow your customers to be known by the name that they feel comfortable with and allow them to change this as they need to. There may be apps where a birth or legal name is needed, but they should only collect this and use it if this is essential.

Pronouns and Titles

As with names and gender, pronouns and titles can have similarly brittle engineering decisions surrounding them when we make assumptions. The best course of action is to treat them as entirely separate, ideally optional, user preferences, using neutral copy where needed. If a user does provide a pronoun or title, allow them to change this in the future if needed.

Titles pose a similar problem. Some people dislike being addressed by a title at all, while others expect one in formal or professional contexts or have legitimately earned titles such as "Dr." or "Captain" and not allowing these options can feel disrespectful. The most essential advice here is never to assume a gender based on a title.

Harassment and Abuse

The reality is stark but simple. If your app gives any way for your users to interact with one another, your app can, and will, be used for harassment, regardless of your app's primary purpose. There are examples of finance apps like Square[24] being used to harass people by sending tiny amounts of money along with a short note. A blocking mechanism is essential anywhere personal interaction is possible. You may also need moderation and reporting systems. All of this means we need to thoroughly consider the decision to add user interaction and its consequences into our apps.

[23] K. G. Orphanides, "Facebook's Real Name Policy Is 'Dangerous to Users,'" Wired, October 6, 2015, `https://www.wired.com/story/facebook-real-name-policy-dangerous/`

[24] Anna Marie Clifton, Twitter post, October 22, 2016, `https://twitter.com/TweetAnnaMarie/status/789957313649967104`.

Some of the starkest examples of such abuse come from gay dating app Grindr, which has been used by repressive regimes to identify and persecute members of the LGBTQ+ community.[25] In the United Kingdom, Grindr and other apps were used by serial killer Stephen Port to lure his victims.[26]

The model I find most powerful to consider when adding social interaction features into an app is what I call the "abusive ex-partner scenario." How would an abusive ex-partner use your interactivity features to harass, intimidate, abuse, or control someone, and what controls can be added to prevent this or at least reduce the harm?

Race and Nationality

Race is a perfect example of why it's essential to involve people with a range of backgrounds throughout our development process. Ensure that your team includes talented engineers from different countries and cultures. This way, you'll learn much more about your unconscious assumptions around the people who use your app.

Machine learning and AI, unfortunately, provides us with some stark examples of where a lack of diverse thinking can backfire. Machine learning reflects and amplifies the data it is provided, meaning any subtle unconscious biases in training data become hugely unsubtle in the system's output. New model releases are predictably followed by reports of output relating to racist, sexist, and ableist biases.[27,28]

---

[25] Joseph McCormick, "Egyptian Police Use Grindr to Lure Gay Men to Hotel Rooms," PinkNews, October 29, 2017, `https://www.pinknews.co.uk/2017/10/29/egyptian-police-use-grindr-to-lure-gay-men-to-hotel-rooms/`

[26] BBC News, "Stephen Port: Serial Killer Guilty of Murdering Four Men," November 23, 2016, `https://www.bbc.co.uk/news/uk-england-38077859`.

[27] Reece Rogers, "OpenAI's Sora Is Plagued by Sexist, Racist, and Ableist Biases", Wired, March 23, 2025, `https://www.wired.com/story/openai-sora-video-generator-bias/`

[28] Aisha Down, "Google's AI Nano Banana Pro accused of generating racialised 'white saviour' visuals", The Guardian, December 4, 2025, `https://www.theguardian.com/technology/2025/dec/04/google-ai-nano-banana-pro-racialised-white-saviour-images`.

This isn't always as simple as generating potentially hurtful text or images. AI used in law enforcement is repeatedly found to misidentify black people[29] and rate black defendants as higher risk than white.[30]

Localization

Localization is a vast topic. We covered the basics of localizing an app for languages in earlier chapters. But localization is a topic that could comfortably fill a new book. As well as translating text, remember that right-to-left languages require consideration of your app's layout, both in UX design and in the implementation.

Date, time, number, and currency formats are different across locales. Rely on the system to format these for you, as this will handle output as your user expects it. Living in the United Kingdom, I am regularly confused when booking trips to the United States and must double-check I have entered the correct month and day order for dates. If booking apps respected my locale setting by default, this would reduce the stress and friction of my booking experience.

Even if your app is only available in a single market, we live in a global society. In 2017 the US Census Bureau found that nearly 22% of Americans spoke a language other than English when at home.[31] That's around 70 million people in the United States who would likely find your app more approachable if another language were available to them.

Analytics

Analytics is an important part of any modern app – if you don't know how your app is used, how can you know what is working for your users? Balancing user privacy with the need to gain necessary insights is important. I don't intend to go into detail here, aside from saying that if you are considering tracking any of the characteristics mentioned in this chapter, you should reconsider.

[29] Alyxaundria Sanford, "Artificial Intelligence Is Putting Innocent People at Risk of Being Incarcerated", Innocence Project, February 14, 2024, `https://innocenceproject.org/news/artificial-intelligence-is-putting-innocent-people-at-risk-of-being-incarcerated/`

[30] Julia Angwin, Jeff Larson, Surya Mattu and Lauren Kirchner, "Machine Bias", ProPublica, May 23, 2016, `https://www.propublica.org/article/machine-bias-risk-assessments-in-criminal-sentencing`

[31] United States Census Bureau, "New American Community Survey Statistics for Income, Poverty and Health Insurance Available for States and Local Areas," September 14, 2017, `https://www.census.gov/newsroom/press-releases/2017/acs-single-year.html`

In earlier chapters, we have discussed techniques for detecting whether a given assistive technology is enabled. Disability status is often classified as a protected status under law. Tracking it also carries significant reputational risk, not to mention the ethical concerns.

Treating users differently based on their disability status, or tracking it, should be avoided. Additionally, tracking the state of an assistive technology tells you about the user's computing environment, not about the user themselves. You cannot reliably infer a person's disability status from their assistive technology settings.

Let the System Help

Google and Apple have provided a wealth of tools to help you make accessible experiences. Neither vendor gets it right every time, but they do have large teams with deep experience in accessibility. Using system-provided APIs, following common system patterns, and using system-provided tools for things such as localization and appearance switching will get you moving further and faster than building custom controls and tools from scratch and will be more robust in the long term.

In addition to creating elements with accessibility considerations built-in, both mobile platforms provide various accessibility settings for your users to enable, such as text scaling, captions, and appearance preferences. Listen to these settings and adjust your app's behavior where appropriate. Not doing so is ignoring explicit instructions given to you by your users.

Integrate

But it's not just APIs and patterns the systems provide that help you create an accessible experience. Both platforms offer various options for your apps to integrate with system services and share content externally. Both disability and assistive technology can cause interactions with technology to take longer, require extra steps, and demand more effort. Integrating with system services allows your app to meet users where they are.

On Android, Google provides App Shortcuts, allowing you to expose app actions to the system. Similarly, iOS provides App Intents, allowing integration with Shortcuts, Siri, and other areas of the system. These integrations unlock the ability to trigger actions based on external events such as NFC tags, voice commands, and time or location-based cues. Both platforms also provide widget systems allowing small amounts of data from your app to be shown without the user needing to open the application.

Accessible Design Makes Boring Apps?

A common objection to making accessible and inclusive experiences is that it adds constraints to our creativity and results in bland and boring experiences. As we covered at the start of this chapter, engineering is all about constraints and engineering around trade-offs. Objecting only to the constraints that relate to human needs is highly telling. Personally, solving constraints is what makes software engineering interesting.

iOS puzzle game The Art of Fauna is beautifully crafted by developer Klemens Strasser. It has won an App Store Award an Apple Design Award and has been featured multiple times by Apple, who have praised it for its beauty.

The app is also highly accessible and inclusive - something Klemens takes very seriously. The app uses the accessibility APIs thoughtfully, but the more interesting challenge is that jigsaw puzzles are inherently visual. To resolve this, each puzzle can be flipped to reveal a text description of the object pictured (Figure 12-2). This provides all users with alternative options for solving the puzzle - resulting in an accessible experience for people with visual or cognitive impairments while also extending gameplay mechanics for everyone.

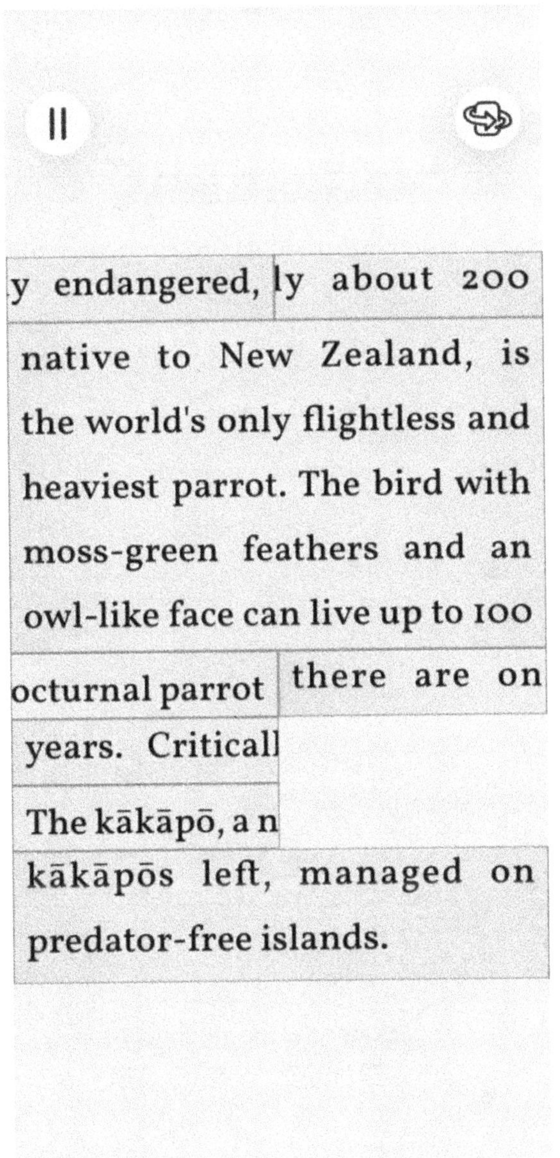

Figure 12-2. *An Art of Fauna puzzle in text mode*

This is not the only clever consideration in the game. Puzzle text can be configured to remove scientific language, puzzle difficulty is adjustable, custom fonts can be replaced with highly legible alternatives, and categories of images that could cause phobia or distress can be hidden, among other considerations (Figure 12-3). Plus, the screen shown when launching the game for the first time is the accessibility settings, letting everyone know right from the start that the game can be made to work for them.

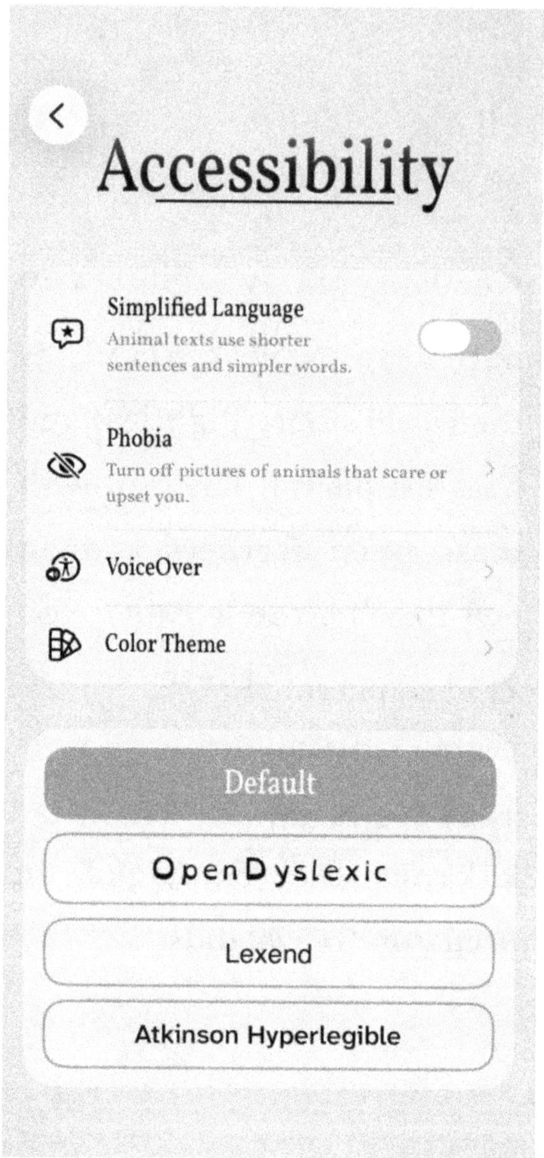

Figure 12-3. *Art of Fauna accessibility settings*

The Art of Fauna is an excellent example of how accessibility and inclusive design can result in a beautiful, richer experience for everyone. It inspires me to do better, and I hope it does the same for you.

Developing Accessibility and Inclusion

I am genuinely grateful you've chosen to pick up my book, not just because this book means a lot to me personally but because I'm always excited when people want to know more about mobile accessibility and inclusion. We have a privileged position as people who are shaping how the modern world works and progresses. And we have opportunities that colleagues in other fields don't have. If a building with step-only access is found to be inaccessible, replacing the steps is a major undertaking. In software, we can find and fix parallel issues rapidly and have the improved experience in the hands of our customers within the time it takes for an app review.

Hopefully, with this new knowledge, you'll begin to identify potential accessibility issues in your app. As you gain knowledge and confidence, please pass on this information. Arrange workshops or speak at a lunch-and-learn session. For larger teams, consider starting an accessibility community of practice program. Sharing potential issues and fixes will only result in a better outcome for your customers.

From my experience, most of our fellow developers are interested in accessibility and want to do the right thing; they are often just lacking the knowledge or confidence to get started.

I want to leave you with some wisdom I picked up from my good friend and hugely knowledgeable accessibility colleague Dani Devesa Derksen-Staats: "Progress over perfection." Accessibility is a huge topic. These nearly 300 pages are only an introduction, and I am learning new things and reconsidering what I thought I knew daily. It's ok to feel a little overwhelmed, and it's ok to get things wrong sometimes. The most important thing is to listen to people's experiences and be open to learning from them. Accessibility is a journey, not a destination.

Index

R. Whitaker, *Developing Inclusive Mobile Apps*, https://doi.org/10.1007/979-8-8688-2809-6

E

F

J

K

L

M

N, O

P, Q

R

S

T

W

X, Y, Z

www.ingramcontent.com/pod-product-compliance
Lightning Source LLC
Chambersburg PA
CBHW081435100826
49614CB00018B/499

9798868828089